always up to date

The law changes, but Nolo is on top of it! We offer several ways to make sure you and your Nolo products are up to date:

 Nolo's Legal Updater

We'll send you an email whenever a new edition of this book is published! Sign up at **www.nolo.com/legalupdater**.

 Updates @ Nolo.com

Check www.nolo.com/update to find recent changes in the law that affect the current edition of your book.

 Nolo Customer Service

To make sure that this edition of the book is the most recent one, call us at **800-728-3555** and ask one of our friendly customer service representatives. Or find out at **www.nolo.com**.

please note

We believe accurate, plain-English legal information should help you solve many of your own legal problems. But this text is not a substitute for personalized advice from a knowledgeable lawyer. If you want the help of a trained professional—and we'll always point out situations in which we think that's a good idea—consult an attorney licensed to practice in your state.

NOLO

5th edition

Form Your Own
Limited
Liability
Company

By Attorney Anthony Mancuso

FIFTH EDITION   SEPTEMBER 2007

Editor   ALAYNA SCHROEDER

Book and Cover Design SUSAN PUTNEY

Proofreader   SUSAN CARLSON GREENE

CD-ROM Preparation   ELLEN BITTER

Index   BAYSIDE INDEXING SERVICE

Printing   DELTA PRINTING SOLUTIONS, INC.

Mancuso, Anthony.

   Form your own limited liability company / by Anthony Mancuso ; edited by Alayna
Schroeder. -- 5th ed.

     p. cm.

   ISBN-13: 978-1-4133-0708-5 (pbk.)

   ISBN-10: 1-4133-0708-6 (pbk.)

   1. Limited partnership--United States--Popular works. 2. Private companies--
United States--Popular works. I. Schroeder, Alayna, 1975- II. Title.

KF1380.Z9M36 2007

346.73'0668--dc22

                   2007013023

Quantity sales: For information on bulk purchases or corporate premium sales, please contact the Special Sales
Department. For academic sales or textbook adoptions, ask for Academic Sales. Call 800-955-4775 or write to
Nolo, 950 Parker Street, Berkeley, CA 94710.

Acknowledgments

The author thanks Alayna Schroeder for a superb job of editing and organizing the material for this edition. A special thanks to the entire Nolo crew for producing and publishing this book.

About the Author

Anthony Mancuso is a corporations and limited liability company expert. He graduated from Hastings College of Law in San Francisco, is an active member of the California State Bar, performs research, writes books, and programs software in the fields of corporate and LLC law, and studies advanced business taxation at Golden Gate University in San Francisco. He also has been a consultant for Silicon Valley EDA (Electronic Design Automation) companies, working on software development project teams.

He is the author of some of Nolo's bestselling titles on forming and operating corporations (both profit and nonprofit) and limited liability companies. His titles include *Incorporate Your Business, How to Form a Nonprofit Corporation* (national and California editions), *The Corporate Records Handbook*, and *LLC or Corporation?* He researched, wrote, and programmed *LLCMaker*, published by Nolo, which generates state-by-state articles of organization and other forms for setting up an LLC in every state. His books and software have shown over a quarter of a million businesses and organizations how to form an LLC or corporation. He also is a licensed helicopter pilot and has performed as a guitarist in various musical idioms, including jazz and blues.

Table of Contents

Appendix C: How to Use the CD-ROM

Index

Your LLC Companion

Running a business is an exciting experience. It may mean pursuing a lifelong passion, investing in a creative opportunity, or just formalizing an already flourishing venture. But along with the excitement come new responsibilities: choosing the type of business entity that best suits your needs, understanding how to follow the legal and tax requirements for forming that entity, and working with business partners and associates to make decisions that everyone can agree on, to name a few. At the same time, you're probably trying to do it all without breaking the bank. And if you're considering forming a limited liability company, or LLC, you doubtlessly have another important consideration: limiting your personal liability for business debts or claims.

This book gives you all the information you need to make an informed choice on whether to form an LLC, either from scratch or by converting an existing partnership. It also provides helpful information and forms for existing LLCs, such as information about ongoing legal formalities and instructions for preparing minutes of LLC meetings.

Readers who decide to set up business as an LLC will find step-by-step information on how to form one in their states. Using the state sheets in Appendix A, you'll learn:

- which state administrative offices to contact
- how to prepare standard organizational and operational documents to get your LLC started, including LLC articles of organization and an LLC operating agreement, and
- how to comply with legal rules for your state.

The typical candidates for forming an LLC are business associates, friends, or family members who decide to pool energies and resources to own and operate a business. With few exceptions, all types of businesses may form an LLC. You may even form one LLC to engage in several businesses—for example, furniture sales, trucking, and redecorating all under one legal, if not physical, roof.

There are many advantages to forming an LLC, as explained in "Top Ten Questions" in Chapter 1. Are there any disadvantages to forming an LLC? Not many. True, LLCs are a relatively new legal entity and, as a result, you might run into some minor hassles with some state and local bureaucracies and commercial institutions. Fortunately, the passage of LLC-enabling legislation has received reams of favorable publicity, so by and large you shouldn't expect any major red tape.

In general, we recommend checking with a small business tax or legal adviser before taking the plunge and filing your papers with the state. Expert advice will ensure that an LLC is your best choice, that you have up-to-date state-specific information, and that you have considered all legal and tax angles that apply to your business. Although you'll have to pay for an initial consultation with a tax or legal adviser, you'll save quite a bit by not handing over all your paperwork to a professional. We believe it is well worth the price in terms of the peace of mind you'll get knowing you've reached the right business conclusions. In Chapter 8, we discuss how to find a legal "coach"—a helpful legal professional who will work with you, review your papers, and augment (not redo) your self-help legal efforts in organizing and operating your LLC.

We are confident that a careful reading of this book can help make you an informed LLC organizer, manager, and member. We wish you all the best on the road to forming and running a successful LLC. ●

Overview of the LLC

In this chapter, we'll cover the nuts and bolts of the limited liability company, or "LLC": the most common questions, the primary benefits, which businesses should choose LLC status, and what other types of business entities there are. We'll delve into the specific legal and tax characteristics of LLCs in the next two chapters.

SKIP AHEAD

If you are familiar with LLCs. If you have followed the development of the LLC over the last few years and know its general legal and tax characteristics (or you simply want to look at the specifics of forming an LLC right now), you can skip the introductory material in this and the following two chapters. Move right ahead to Chapter 4, where you'll learn how to prepare LLC articles of organization.

Top Ten Questions About LLCs

1. What is an LLC?

An LLC is a business structure that gives its owners corporate-style limited liability, while at the same time allowing partnership-style taxation.

- Like owners of a corporation, LLC owners are protected from personal liability for business debts and claims—a feature known as "limited liability." This means that if the business owes money or faces a lawsuit, the assets of the business itself are at risk but usually not the personal assets of the LLC owners, such as their houses or cars.

- Like owners of partnerships or sole proprie-torships, LLC owners report their share of the business profits or losses on their personal income tax returns. The LLC itself is not a separate taxable entity.

Because of these attributes, the LLC fits somewhere between the partnership and the corporation (or, for one-owner businesses, the sole proprietorship and the one-person corporation).

2. How many people do I need to form an LLC?

You can form an LLC with just one owner. For reasons we'll explain later, LLCs are appropriate for businesses with no more than 35 owners and investors.

3. Who should form an LLC?

Consider forming an LLC if you are concerned about personal exposure to lawsuits arising from your business. For example, an LLC will shield your personal assets from:

- suppliers' claims for unpaid bills, and

- for businesses that deal directly with the public, slip-and-fall lawsuits that your commercial liability insurance policy may not adequately cover.

Not all businesses can operate as LLCs, however. Those in the banking, trust, and insurance industries, for example, are typically prohibited from forming LLCs. Some states (including California) prohibit licensed pro-fessionals such as architects, accountants, doctors, health care workers, lawyers, and other state-licensed practitioners from forming LLCs. Many of these professionals may benefit from forming a limited liability *partnership*.

4. How do I form an LLC?

In most states, the only legal requirement to form an LLC is that you file "articles of organi-zation" with your state's LLC filing office, which is usually part of the Secretary of State's office. (Several states refer to this organizational document as a "certificate of organization" or a "certificate of formation.") A few states require an additional step: Prior to or immediately after filing your articles of organization, you must publish your intention to form an LLC, or a notice that you have formed an LLC, in a local newspaper. We'll explain how to prepare and file articles of organization in Chapter 4.

5. Do I need a lawyer to form an LLC?

You don't need a lawyer. In most states, the information required for the articles of organization is simple—it typically includes the name of the LLC, the location of its principal office, the names and addresses of the LLC's owners and/or managers, and the name and address of the LLC's registered agent (a person or company that agrees to accept legal papers on behalf of the LLC).

The process itself is simple, too. Most states have fill-in-the-blank forms and instructions that can be downloaded. Some states even let you prepare and file articles online at the state filing website, which means you can create your LLC in a matter of minutes. LLC filing offices increasingly allow owners to send them email questions, too.

6. Does my LLC need an operating agreement?

Although most states' LLC laws don't require a written operating agreement, don't even consider starting an LLC without one. An operating agreement is necessary because it:

- sets out rules that govern how profits and losses will be split up, how major business decisions will be made, and the procedures for handling the departure and addition of members

- keeps your LLC from being governed by the default rules in your state's LLC laws, which might not be to your benefit, and

- helps ensure that courts will respect your personal liability protection, because it shows that you have been conscientious about organizing your LLC.

In Chapters 5 and 6, you'll learn how to create an operating agreement.

7. How do LLCs pay taxes?

Like partnerships and sole proprietorships, an LLC is not a separate entity from its owners for income tax purposes. This means that the LLC itself does not pay income taxes. Instead, the LLC owners use their personal tax returns to pay tax on their allocated share of profits (or deduct their share of business losses).

LLC owners can elect to have their LLC taxed like a corporation. This may reduce taxes for established LLC owners who will regularly need to keep a significant amount of profit in the company.

These tax consequences will be discussed in detail in Chapter 3.

8. What are the differences between a limited liability company and a partnership?

The main difference between an LLC and a partnership is that LLC owners are not personally liable for the company's debts and liabilities. Partners, on the other hand, do not have this limited liability protection. Also, owners of limited liability companies must file formal articles of organization with their state's LLC filing office, pay a filing fee, and comply with other state filing requirements before they open for business. Partners don't need to file any formal paperwork and don't have to pay special fees.

LLCs and partnerships are almost identical when it comes to taxation, however. In both types of businesses, the owners report business income or losses on their personal tax returns. In fact, co-owned LLCs and partnerships file the same informational tax return with the IRS (Form 1065) and distribute the same schedules to the business's owners (Schedule K-1, which lists each owner's share of income).

9. Can I convert my existing business to an LLC?

Converting a partnership or a sole proprietorship to an LLC is an easy way for partners and sole proprietors to protect their personal assets without changing the way their business income is taxed. Some states have a simple form for converting a partnership to an LLC (often called a "certificate of conversion"). Partners and sole proprietors in states that don't use a conversion form must file regular articles of organization to create an LLC.

10. Do I need to know about securities laws to set up an LLC?

If you'll be the sole owner of your LLC, which you will manage and operate, and you don't plan to take investments from outsiders, your ownership interest in the LLC is not a "security" and you don't have to concern yourself with these laws. For co-owned LLCs, however, the answer to this question is a bit more involved.

If all of the owners of your LLC will actively manage the LLC, their ownership interests in the company will usually not be treated as securities. However, when someone invests in your business expecting to make money from the efforts of others, that person's investment is generally considered a security under federal and state law.

If your LLC's ownership interests are considered securities, you must get an exemption from the state and federal securities laws before the

initial owners of your LLC invest their money. Fortunately, smaller LLCs, even those that plan to sell memberships to passive investors, usually qualify for securities law exemptions.

We'll explain this further in Chapter 2.

The Benefits of LLCs

The LLC stands as a unique alternative to five traditional legal and tax ways of doing business: sole proprietorships, general partnerships, limited partnerships, C corporations (also called "regular" corporations), and S corporations. While these business entities offer *some* of the same benefits as LLCs, none offer *all* of the same benefits. The combination of structural and tax benefits unique to LLCs include:

- limited liability status
- taxation of business profits and losses at individual rates
- flexible management structure, and
- flexible distribution of profits and losses.

Limited Liability Status

The legal characteristic most interesting to business owners is undoubtedly the limited liability status of LLC owners. With the exception of corporate entities, the LLC is the only form of legal entity that lets *all* of its owners off the hook for business debts and other legal liabilities, such as court judgments and legal settlements obtained against the business. Another way of saying this is that an investor in an LLC normally has at risk only his or her share of capital paid into the business.

There's Never Limited Liability for Personally Guaranteed Debts

No matter how a small business is organized (LLC, corporation, partnership, or sole proprietorship), its owners must normally cosign business loans made by banks—at least until the business establishes its own positive credit history.

When you cosign a loan, you promise to voluntarily assume personal liability if your business fails to pay back the loan. In some cases, the bank may ask you to pledge all your personal assets as security; in others, it may only require you to pledge specific personal assets—for example, the equity in your home.

EXAMPLE:

A married couple owns and operates Books & Bagels, a coffee shop and bookstore. In need of funds (dough, really) to expand into a larger location, the owners go to the bank to get a small loan for their corporation. The bank grants the loan on the condition that the two owners personally pledge their equity in their house as security for the loan. Because the owners personally guaranteed the loan, the bank can seek repayment from the owners personally by foreclosing on their home if Books & Bagels defaults. No form of business ownership can insulate them from the personal liability they agreed to.

For more information about pledging personal assets to secure business loans, see *Legal Guide for Starting and Running a Small Business*, by Fred Steingold (Nolo).

Business Profits and Losses Taxed at Individuals' Income Tax Rates

The LLC is recognized by the IRS as a "pass-through" tax entity. That is, the profits or losses of the LLC pass through the business and are reflected and taxed on the individual tax returns of the owners, rather than being reported and taxed at a separate business level. (Other pass-through entities include general and limited partnerships, sole proprietorships, and S corporations—those that have elected S corporation tax status with the IRS.) We'll discuss pass-through taxation further below.

Flexible Management Structure

LLC owners are referred to as members. A member may be an individual or a separate legal entity, such as a partnership or corporation. Members invest in the LLC and receive percentage ownership interests in return. These ownership interests are used to divide up the assets of the LLC when it is sold or liquidated and are typically used for other purposes as well—for example, to split up profits and losses of the LLC or to divide up its voting rights.

LLCs are run by their members unless they elect to be managed by a management group, which may consist of some members and/or nonmembers. Small LLCs are normally member-managed—after all, most small business owners want and need to have an active hand in the management of the business. However, this isn't always true. Especially with a growing business or one that makes fairly passive investments, such as in real estate, investors may not want a day-to-day role. Fortunately, an LLC can easily adopt a management-run structure in situations such as these:

- the members want the LLC to be managed by some, but not all, members

- the members decide to employ outside management help, or

- the members choose to cater to an outsider who wishes to invest in or loan capital to the LLC on condition that he or she be given a vote in management.

Uniform LLC Laws

For many years, legal scholars and state legislators have worked hard to have all states adopt the same (or very similar) laws affecting key areas of American business and life. A bit belatedly, efforts are being made to adopt a national model LLC act that can be used by individual state legislatures to pass future LLC legislation. One model is the Prototype Limited Liability Company Act, sponsored by the American Bar Association's Section of Business Law. Another is the Uniform Limited Liability Company Act, developed by the National Conference of Commissioners on Uniform State Laws.

Both of these acts are still in development, and there is justified skepticism as to whether states will replace current LLC laws with either model act. More likely, states probably will adopt portions of the model acts to supplement their current LLC statutes. In short, while LLC laws are fairly similar (they generally try to conform to IRS regulations and to LLC statutory schemes in other states), state-by-state differences are likely to remain.

Flexible Distribution of Profits and Losses

An LLC allows business owners to split profits and losses any way they wish (this flexibility is afforded partnerships as well). You are not restricted to dividing up profits proportionate to the members' capital contributions (this is the standard legal rule for corporations).

EXAMPLE:

Steve and Frankie form an educational seminar business. Steve puts up all the cash necessary to purchase a computer with graphics and multimedia presentation capabilities, rent out initial seminar sites, send out mass mailings, and purchase advertising. As the traveling lecturer, cash-poor Frankie will contribute services to the LLC. Although the two owners could agree to split profits and losses equally, they decide that Steve will get 65% of the business's profits and losses for the first three years as a way of paying him back for taking the risk of putting up cash.

By contrast, rules governing the distribution of corporate profits and losses are fairly restrictive. A C corporation cannot allocate profits and losses to shareholders at all—shareholders get a financial return from the corporation by receiving dividends or a share of the corporation's assets when it is sold or liquidated. In an S corporation (covered in detail below), profits and losses generally must follow shareholdings. For example, an S corporation shareholder holding 10% of the shares ordinarily must be allocated a 10% share of yearly profits and losses.

There are a few wrinkles in the flexibility afforded to LLCs. Because LLCs are treated like partnerships for tax purposes, LLCs must comply with technical partnership tax rules:

- **Tax laws require special (disproportionate) allocations of LLC profits or losses to have "substantial economic effect."** In Chapter 3, we'll discuss exactly what that means and how to make sure your LLC complies with the requirement. For now, simply understand that the purpose of the rule is to ensure that the members bear the economic responsibility for profits and losses allocated to them.

- **Members contributing future services to the LLC may be subject to income taxes on the value of their services.** Again, we'll discuss the tax effects of a member's future personal services to the LLC in Chapter 3.

Which Businesses Benefit as LLCs?

Here is an overview of the types of persons and businesses for which the LLC form makes the most and least sense. These guidelines aren't set in stone—certainly you may find that your business breaks the mold.

Businesses That Benefit From the LLC Structure

LLCs generally work best for:

- **Actively run businesses with a limited number of owners.** The logistics of making collective business decisions are manageable with a maximum of around 35 owners.

- **Small new businesses.** New businesses generally wish to pass early-year losses along to owners to deduct against their other income (usually salary earned working for another company or income earned from investments).

- **Anyone thinking of forming an S corporation.** Like LLCs, S corporations provide limited liability protection to all owners and allow profits and losses to be taxed at individual shareholder rates. However, as we'll discuss in "S corporations," below, these benefits

come at a pretty high price: S corporations are significantly restrictive and a business can inadvertently lose its eligibility—for example, when a disqualified shareholder inherits or buys stock or the number of shareholders exceeds the maximum allowed—resulting in a big tax bill.

- **Existing partnerships.** Only the LLC provides partnership-style pass-through tax treatment of business income while insulating *all* owners (not just limited partners as in a limited partnership) from personal liability for business debts.

- **Businesses planning to hold property that will appreciate, such as real property.** C corporations and their shareholders are subject to a double tax on appreciation when assets are sold or liquidated—taxation occurs at both the corporate and individual level. S corporations that were originally organized as C corporations may also be subject to double tax on gains from appreciated assets, as well as a penalty tax on passive income (money from rents, royalties, interest, or dividends) if it gets too high. Because the LLC is a true pass-through tax entity, it allows a business that will hold appreciating assets to avoid double taxation. When the business is sold, generally just the owners, not the entity itself, pay taxes on the profits from the sale.

Businesses That Should Normally Not Form an LLC Using This Book

The LLC is not normally suitable for:

- **Existing S or C corporations.** While it may be possible to convert an existing corporation to an LLC without hefty tax or legal costs, you'll need the help of a lawyer and a tax adviser to make sure you don't get stung.

• **Highly profitable LLCs in certain states.** Some states have a graduated LLC license fee schedule, meaning the more profitable the LLC, the higher the tax. In California, for example, LLCs with reportable income over $5 million must pay an annual fee of more than $11,000. Such a stiff tax is unusual; check your state sheet in Appendix A or ask your tax adviser to find out whether you face this unpleasant prospect. Of course, in states with a high LLC fee or tax, chances are good that the state also has enacted fees that apply to other pass-through tax entities (limited partnerships and S corporations). In these states, you may decide that forming a general partnership, which isn't taxed separately, is the least expensive way to go—but you won't qualify for limited liability for business debts.

Comparing LLCs and Other Business Forms

Anyone considering an LLC will want to compare this business form to the three traditional ways of doing business:

- sole proprietorships
- partnerships, and
- C corporations.

In addition, to fully understand the pros and cons of LLC status, you'll need to compare the LLC to two variants on these traditional business forms that come closest to resembling the legal and tax characteristics of the LLC:

- limited partnerships, and
- S corporations.

This section provides general information on the characteristics of each type of legal entity, focusing on the main reasons why business-people adopt one form over another. Our aim is to explain most of the information you'll need to decide whether the LLC is right for you. However, please realize that we can't cover every nuance of tax and business organization law as it applies to your business. Furthermore, the area of pass-through taxation is no piece of cake, even to tax specialists. You may need to check with a tax adviser to make sure the LLC makes sense to you from a tax standpoint, and to learn about any of the special tax areas (some of which are covered in Chapter 3) that may have special relevance to your business.

Other Ways of Doing Business: More Information from Nolo

For further examination of the legal and tax characteristics of the various ways of doing business, see the following Nolo titles:

- *LLC or Corporation?* by Anthony Mancuso. This book explains in depth the legal and tax differences between LLCs and corporations, as well as the legal and tax effects of different forms of doing business as a company grows.

- *The Partnership Book*, by Denis Clifford and Ralph Warner. This book discusses general partnerships and shows you step by step how to prepare a general partnership agreement.

- *Incorporate Your Business: A Legal Guide to Forming a Corporation in Your State* and *How to Form Your Own California Corporation*, by Anthony Mancuso. These books provide an in-depth treatment of the corporate structure and show you how to incorporate in each state. Incorporation forms are included as tear-outs and on CD-ROMs.

Sole Proprietorship

The simplest way of being in business for yourself is as a sole proprietor. This is just a fancy way of saying that you are the owner of a one-person business. There's little red tape and cost—other than the usual business licenses, sales tax permits, and local and state regulations that any business must face. As a practical matter, most one-person businesses start out as sole proprietorships just to keep things simple.

Sole Proprietorship Is Limited to One Person

If your sole proprietorship grows, you'll need to move to a more complicated type of business structure. Once you decide to own and split profits with another person (other than your spouse), by definition, you have at least a partnership on your hands.

Sole Proprietor Is Personally Liable for Business Debts

Unfortunately, although a sole proprietorship is simple, it can also be a dangerous way to operate, especially if the work you do might result in large debts or liabilities from lawsuits. The sole proprietor is personally liable for all debts and claims against a business. For example, if someone slips and falls in a sole proprietor's business and sues, the owner is on the line for paying any court award (if commercial liability insurance doesn't cover it). Similarly, if the business fails to pay suppliers, banks, or other businesses' bills, the owner is personally liable for the unpaid debts. The owner's personal assets, such as a home, car, and bank accounts, are fair game for repayment of these amounts.

Sole Proprietor's Taxes

Sole proprietors report business profits or losses on IRS Schedule C, *Profit and Loss From*

Spousal Business

Generally, if a husband and wife carry on a business together and share in the profits and losses, they are considered the co-owners of a partnership, not a sole proprietorship. But there's an exception: IRS rules say that an unincorporated business that is the owned solely by a husband and wife as community property in the community property states of Arizona, California, Idaho, Louisiana, Nevada, New Mexico, Texas, Washington, and Wisconsin, can treat itself as a sole proprietorship by filing an IRS Form 1040 Schedule C for the business, listing one of the spouses as the owner. Only the listed spouse pays income and self-employment taxes on the reported Schedule C net profits. Note that the IRS may treat the filing of a Schedule C for a jointly owned spousal business as the conversion of a partnership to a sole proprietorship, which can have significant tax consequences. For more information, see "Forming a Partnership" in IRS Publication 541, and be sure to check with your tax adviser before deciding on the best way to own, operate, and file tax returns for a spousal business.

Business (Sole Proprietorship), included with a Form 1040 individual federal tax return. Profits are taxed at the owner's individual income tax rates.

Because the owner is self-employed, he or she must pay an increased amount of self-employment (FICA) tax based upon these profits—about twice as much as an incorporated business or corporate employee would personally pay. This increased FICA tax doesn't necessarily mean that sole proprietorships are more expensive tax-wise than other business forms. For instance, if you are both a corporate shareholder and employee, as is the case for the owner/employees of most small corporations, you end up paying close to the same total FICA taxes.

Sole Proprietorships Compared to LLCs

The LLC requires more paperwork to get started and is more complicated than a sole proprietorship from a legal and tax perspective. Although LLC owners, like sole proprietors, report business profits on their individual tax returns, the co-owned LLC itself is treated as a partnership and must prepare its own annual informational tax return. The payoff of the LLC for this added complexity is that owners are not personally liable for business claims or debts (unless personally guaranteed, as with a personally guaranteed bank loan).

General Partnerships

A partnership is a business in which two or more owners agree to share profits. If you go into business with at least one other person and you don't file formal papers with the state to set up an LLC, corporation, or limited partnership, the law says you have formed a general partnership. A general partnership can be started with a handshake (a simple verbal agreement or understanding) or a formal partnership agreement.

> ⚠ **CAUTION**
>
> **Partners should always create a written partnership agreement.** Without an agreement, the default rules of each state's general partnership law apply to the business. These provisions usually say that profits and losses of the business should be split up equally among the partners, regardless of the amount of capital contributed to the business by each partner. Rather than relying on state laws, general partners should prepare an agreement that

covers issues such as the division of profits and losses, the payment of salaries and draws to partners, and the procedure for selling partnership interests back to the partnership or to outsiders.

Number of Partners in a General Partnership

General partnerships may be formed by two or more people; there is no such thing as a one-person partnership. Legally, there is no upper limit on the number of partners who may be admitted into a partnership, but general partnerships with many owners may have problems reaching a consensus on business decisions and may be subject to divisive disputes between contending management factions.

General Partnership Liability

Each owner of a general partnership is individually liable for the debts and claims of the business. In other words, if the partnership owes money, a creditor may go after any member of the partnership for the entire debt, regardless of his or her ownership percentage (although one partner can sue other partners to force them to repay their shares of the debt).

In addition, each partner may bind the partnership to contracts or enter a business deal that binds the partnership, as long as the contract or deal is within the scope of business undertaken by the partnership. In legal jargon, this authority is expressed by saying that each partner is an agent of the partnership.

The personal liability for partnership debts, coupled with the agency authority of each partner, makes the general partnership riskier than limited liability businesses (corporations, LLCs, and limited partnerships).

General Partnership Taxes

A general partnership is not a separate taxable entity. Profits (and losses) pass through the business to the partners, who pay taxes on profits at their individual tax rates. Although the partnership does not pay its own taxes, it must file an information return each year, IRS Form 1065, *U.S. Partnership Return of Income.* The partnership must give each partner a filled-in IRS Schedule K-1 (1065), *Partner's Share of Income, Credits, Deductions,* which shows the proportionate share of profits or losses each person carries over to his or her individual 1040 tax return at the end of the year.

General Partnerships Compared to LLCs

General partnerships are less costly to start than LLCs because most states do not require a state filing (and fees) to form them. The major downside to running a general partnership over an LLC is the exposure to personal liability by each of the general partners. Although a general business insurance package (possibly supplemented by more specialized coverage for unusual risks) can mitigate possible effects, each partner is still personally responsible for all business debts and for any liabilities not covered by the business's insurance policy. LLC owners, on the other hand, avoid this personal liability problem altogether.

General partnerships and LLCs come out about even on a couple of important issues:

- **Partnership agreement or operating agreement.** Even small partnerships and LLCs should start off with a good written partnership agreement or operating agreement. This, of course, takes time and if you don't do the work yourself, is likely to cost $1,000 to $5,000 in legal fees, depending on the complexity of your business and the thickness of your lawyer's

rug. (We help you prepare an operating agreement in Chapters 5 and 6 of this book.)

- **Taxes.** General partnerships and LLCs can count on about the same amount of tax complexity, preparation time, and paperwork. Even though you'll probably turn over most year-end tax work to a tax adviser (for either a co-owned LLC or partnership), understanding and following basic partnership tax procedures takes a fair amount of time and effort.

C Corporations

To establish a C corporation, you prepare and file formal articles of incorporation papers with a state agency (usually the secretary of state) and pay corporate filing fees and initial taxes. A corporation assumes an independent legal and tax life separate from its owners, with the result that it pays taxes at its own corporate tax rates and files its own income tax returns each year (IRS Form 1120).

Corporations are owned by shareholders and managed by a board of directors. Most management decisions are left to the directors, although a few must be ratified by the shareholders as well, such as the amendment of corporate articles of incorporation, sale of substantially all of the corporation's assets, or the merger or dissolution of the corporation. Corporate officers are normally appointed by the board of directors to handle the day-to-day supervision of corporate business, and usually consist of a corporate president, vice president, secretary, and treasurer.

TIP

A C corporation is nothing more than a regular corporation. The letter "C" simply distinguishes the regular corporation (one taxed under normal corporate income tax rules) from a more specialized type of corporation regulated under Subchapter S of the Internal Revenue Code, discussed in "S Corporations," below.

Number of Corporate Shareholders and Directors

In most states, one or more persons can form and operate a corporation. In a few states, the number of directors necessary for a multi-owner corporation is related to the number of shareholders. For example, if there are two shareholders, two or more directors must be named; if three shareholders, then three or more directors are necessary.

Corporate Limited Liability

As we have mentioned, a corporation provided all its owners (shareholders) with the benefits of limited liability—before other limited liability options were available, a major reason many businesses organized as corporations.

Corporation's Separate Legal and Tax Existence

The corporation has a legal and tax existence separate from its owners. This leads to the following corporate characteristics:

- **Separate taxes.** A corporation files its own income tax return and pays its own income taxes.

- **Tax benefits of employee fringe benefits.** The corporate form allows owner-employees (shareholders who also work in the business) to deduct a number of corporate fringes paid to employees (including themselves) from corporate income, such as the direct reimbursement of medical expenses. Also, corporations can provide tax-favored stock bonus and stock option plans for employees.

- **Legal formalities.** Because a corporation has a separate legal existence, you must pay more attention to its legal care. This means owners must don directors' and shareholders' hats and hold and document annual meetings required under state law. Owners must keep minutes of meetings, prepare other formal documentation of important decisions made during the life of the corporation, and keep a paper trail of all financial dealings between the corporation and its shareholders. Owners also need to tend to other formalities, such as appointing officers required under corporate statutes. A corporation should issue stock to its shareholders and keep adequate capital on hand to handle foreseeable business debts and liabilities.

CAUTION

Shoddy corporate procedures can cost you. It can be dangerous to set up a thinly capitalized corporation, treat corporate coffers as an incorporated pocketbook for your personal finances, fail to issue stock, neglect to hold meetings, or overlook other formalities required under your state's corporation code. If you do (or don't do) these things, a court or the IRS may "pierce the corporate veil" (a metaphor carried over from a long line of court cases) and decide that the corporation is simply an "alter ego" of the shareholders of a small corporation. If this happens, the business owners (shareholders) can be held personally liable for any money awarded by a court against the corporation.

Corporations Compared to LLCs

Corporations are similar to LLCs in the types of paperwork and fees necessary to get them started with the state. Both must prepare and file organizational papers with the secretary of state and pay filing fees. Both should adopt a set of operating rules that sets out the basic requirements for operating the business— corporations adopt bylaws; LLCs adopt operating agreements.

What sets the corporate form apart from LLCs is how they are taxed. Corporations are taxed separately from their owners at corporate income tax rates. This can result in tax savings if money is left in a business for expansion or for other business needs. That's because initial tax rates applied to corporate income are normally lower than the individual tax rates of business owners.

EXAMPLE:

Justine and Janine own and operate Just Jams & Jellies, a specialty store selling gourmet canned preserves. Business has boomed and their net taxable income, split equally by the partners, has reached a level where it is taxed at an individual tax rate of over 30%. If the owners incorporate, or if they form an LLC and elect corporate tax treatment, they can keep money in their business, which is taxed at the lower corporate tax rates of 15% and 25%, saving overall tax dollars on business income.

This corporate tax distinction can be eliminated if the LLC members wish. That is, LLC members can elect to have their LLC taxed as a corporation. We'll discuss this option, and why some LLCs take it, in Chapter 3.

What About the Double Taxation of Corporate Profits?

You've probably read about the awful consequence of double taxation when a corporation makes money. Specifically, corporate profits are first taxed at the corporate level, then any profits paid out as dividends to shareholders are taxed at each shareholder's dividend tax rate. Doesn't this result in a big comparative benefit to LLCs that are taxed as partnerships, where the owners just pay taxes once on business income at their personal rates?

For small, actively run corporations, we say no. Here's why. To avoid the penalty of double taxation, smaller corporations rarely pay dividends to the owners. Instead, the owner-employees are paid salaries and fringe benefits that are tax deductible to the corporation. As a result, only employee-shareholders pay income taxes on this business income.

So cast a critical eye on any article decrying the double taxation of corporate profits for small businesses. Unless you are forming a corporation with passive investors who expect to receive regular dividends as a return on their investment in your corporation, double taxation will generally not be a big deal.

Exception: When (and if) appreciated assets of a corporation are sold, both the corporation and its owners may have to pay income taxes on profits from the sale. If you are thinking of incorporating, it's important to plan for this possibility of double taxation of sales proceeds received from the sale of appreciated assets (such as real estate that has risen in value).

Even though an LLC may now elect corporate tax treatment, there may be other reasons to favor the corporate form over the LLC, such as the availability of corporate equity sharing plans. Also, a number of people—perhaps including persons you may wish to do business with—associate the corporate form with an added degree of formality and solidity. And, of course, the ability to go public (make a public offering of corporate shares) is a traditional feature of the corporate form that more successful small businesses may be able to capitalize on. (Forget about going public with an LLC; the practical and tax restrictions on transferring membership interests rule out this possibility.)

There are several downsides to corporate life. We've already mentioned the complexity of complying with state law corporate procedures by preparing annual and special director and shareholder meetings. (Some states have tried to lessen the impact of these state-mandated formalities with the creation of the close corporation form—see the sidebar on the following page, "A Look at Close Corporations.")

Limited Partnerships

A limited partnership is similar to a general partnership (discussed above), except that instead of only being composed of general partners, it has two types:

- **Limited partners.** One or more partners contribute capital to the business, but neither participate in its day-to-day operations nor have personal liability for business debts and claims.
- **General partners.** One or more partners manage business operations and have personal liability for business debts and claims.

To get this special type of partnership started, you must file papers (certificate of limited partnership) with the state and pay an initial filing fee.

Number of Partners

Limited partnerships may be formed by two or more people, with:

- at least one person acting as the general partner, who has management authority and personal liability, and
- at least one person in the role of limited partner.

Limited Liability Only for Limited Partners

Limited partners enjoy the same kind of limited liability for the debts and liabilities of the business as do the shareholders of a corporation and the members of an LLC. General partners of limited partnerships, on the other hand, have the same personal liability described above for general partnerships.

Limited Partnership Taxes

For tax purposes, limited partnerships normally are treated like general partnerships, with all owners having to report and pay taxes personally on their share of the profits each year. The limited partnership files an informational tax return only, and is not subject to an entity level federal income tax.

Limited Partnerships Compared to LLCs

There are two major differences between limited partnerships and LLCs. First, a limited partnership must have at least one general partner, who is personally liable for the debts and other liabilities of the business. This differs from LLCs, where all members are covered by the cloak of limited liability.

A Look at Close Corporations

Several states have enacted special corporate statutes that allow small corporations to dispense with normal operating rules. These corporations, called "close" or "statutory close" corporations, usually must meet a number of legal requirements:

- The corporation must have a limited number of shareholders, usually no more than 35.
- Shares of stock must not be sold or transferred to outsiders unless approved by all shareholders.
- The corporation must elect close corporation status in its formation documents or in an amendment to these papers.
- The corporation must operate under partnership-type rules specified in a shareholders' agreement. (The drafting of this agreement is time-consuming and can involve fairly high attorney fees.)

Ten to 15 years ago, legislators in corporately active states, including California, Delaware, Illinois, and Texas, expected business organizers to line up to form close corporations under the newly enacted state laws, but few were formed. The close corporation's failure to spark the interest of business organizers was due to the following reasons:

- Few corporations want to forego the customary formality of appointing a board of directors, electing officers, and assuming the other traditional accoutrements of corporate life.
- Management of a corporation by its shareholders is normally seen as novel and potentially chaotic.
- Preparation and adoption of a custom-tailored shareholders' agreement is a time-consuming incorporation step most organizers want to avoid.
- Shareholders do not want restrictions on their right to sell or transfer shares, which are mandatory under typical close corporation statutes.

In many ways, the close corporation resembles the LLC by giving owners the protection of limited liability while allowing them to operate under partnership-type legal rules. The big difference is that unlike LLCs, the IRS never bestowed the general mantle of pass-through tax treatment on close corporations. Had close corporations successfully obtained pass-through tax treatment with the IRS and been able to operate informally without having to prepare a special shareholders' agreement, perhaps they would be vying today for the popular attention currently enjoyed by LLCs.

Second, limited partners are generally prohibited from managing the business. If a limited partner is active in the business of the limited partnership, he or she typically loses the limited partner status with its attendant limited liability protection. (There are exceptions to this ban under the newer Revised Uniform Limited Partnership Act, which has made the rounds through state legislatures and has been adopted, at least in part, in most states.) In contrast, LLC members are given a free hand in managing and running the business, either by themselves or in conjunction with outside managers.

This second restriction of the limited partnership makes it more of a gamble for investors, who must turn over management of the business to a general partner. Such an arrangement may work well for outsiders who want to invest cash or property in a business run by others, but it won't work well for businesses that are funded and run primarily by their owners. Investors in actively run businesses who want limited liability status for all owners generally benefit by forming an LLC or a corporation; both of these entities permit investors to help run the business while enjoying the personal protection of limited liability.

S Corporations

Now we come to our last comparison, and the one with the pickiest technical distinctions: the S corporation versus the LLC. Below, we address the main similarities and differences, but you may need to ask your tax adviser for further particulars if you want to understand the ins and outs of comparing these two business forms.

For starters, an S corporation follows the same state incorporation formalities as a C corporation. Typically, this means filing articles of incorporation and paying a state filing fee. An S corporation also must make a special one-page tax election under Subchapter S of the Internal Revenue Code to have the corporation taxed as a partnership (by filing IRS Form 2553, the *S Corporation Tax Election* form, with the IRS).

Number of S Corporation Owners

Generally, an S corporation may have no more than 100 shareholders (who must be individuals or certain types of trusts or estates). But spouses and other members of a shareholder's family who own shares in an S corporation are counted as one shareholder.

Limited Liability of S Corporation Shareholders

All S corporation shareholders are granted personal protection from the debts and other liabilities of the business, just like C corporation shareholders and LLC members.

Tax Election of S Corporation

S corporations benefit from the same basic pass-through treatment afforded partnerships and LLCs, so profits and losses are reported on the individual tax returns of the S corporation's shareholders. However, the S corporation must still prepare and file an S corporation annual income tax return each year, similar (from a time and energy standpoint) to the co-owned LLC preparing its own partnership informational tax return.

S Corporations Compared to LLCs

Like any other type of corporation, an S corporation requires some legal care and maintenance—more than is typically needed for an LLC. Regular and special meetings of directors and shareholders are held and recorded to transact important corporate business or decide key legal or tax formalities.

The main difference between S corporations and LLCs has to do with the requirements for electing S corporation tax treatment and some of the unique tax effects that result from this election. To be eligible to make an S corporation tax election with the IRS, the corporation and its shareholders must meet a number of special requirements. Here are a few of the S corporation tax requirements that can present a problem:

- **Individual shareholders of an S corporation must be U.S. citizens or have U.S. residency status**. If shares are sold, passed to (by will, divorce, or other means), or otherwise fall into the hands of a foreign national, the corporation loses its S corporation tax status.

- **Shareholders must be individuals or certain types of qualified trusts or estates.** Generally, S corporations can't have partnerships or other corporations as shareholders. Under typical state statutes, LLCs may have both natural (individual) and artificial (corporate, LLC, partnership, trust, and estate) members.

- **There can be no more than 100 shareholders in an S corporation.**

- **S corporations must have only one class of stock.** Different voting rights are permitted, meaning that S corporations may have one class of voting shares and another consisting of nonvoting shares. But all shares must have the same rights to participate in dividends and the assets of the corporation when the business is sold or liquidated. Having only one class of stock limits the usefulness of the S corporation as an investment vehicle. Investors typically like to receive special classes of shares that have preferences regarding corporate dividends and participation in the liquidation assets of the corporation when it is sold or dissolved.

- **An S corporation that loses its status cannot reelect it for five years.** An S corporation can lose its S corporation tax status—perhaps inadvertently, for example, if some shares fall into the hands of a disqualified shareholder. Even if the corporation again becomes qualified, it must wait until five years have elapsed from the year of the disqualification.

Two special tax effects not suffered by other pass-through tax entities, such as LLCs and limited partnerships, often present problems for S corporation shareholders:

- **S corporation shareholders can't receive special allocations of profits and losses.** Corporate profits and losses must be split up proportionately to the percentage of shares owned by each shareholder. This point may sound technical or theoretical, but even for smaller businesses it has practical—and sometimes negative— significance.

EXAMPLE:

Ted and Natalie want to go into business designing solar-powered hot tubs. Ted is the "money" person and agrees to pitch in 80% of the first-year funds necessary to get the business going. Natalie is the hot tub and solar specialist and will contribute her skills as a solar systems and hot tub designer in overseeing the design and manufacture of the tubs. Ted and Natalie want a portion of Natalie's first-year salary to go toward paying for her initial shares in the enterprise. They also want Ted to get a disproportionate number of shares in recognition of the extra risk associated with putting cash into the business up front. Instead of getting two shares for every one of Natalie's shares, which reflects the ratio of Ted's cash to the value of Natalie's services, they want him to receive four shares for every share that she gets. Unfortunately, while this disproportionate doling out of shares may make a lot of practical sense, it is not permitted under S corporation rules.

- **S corporation entity-level debt can't be passed along to shareholders.** An S corporation generally can't pass the potential tax benefits of borrowing money along to its shareholders. In other pass-through entities, such as partnerships and LLCs, business debt (money borrowed by the business) increases the tax basis of the owners (we're simplifying here, but this is the effect of these special rules). This is good for a couple of reasons. First, the owners can deduct more losses from the business on their tax returns. Second, the higher the basis, the less gain—and the lower the taxes due—when owners sell their interests or the business itself is sold. This technical tax point is illustrated in the following example.

EXAMPLE:

Mitch's Barbecue Pit Corp., organized as an S corporation, is a promising business in search of outside capital for expansion. A special blend of seasonings in Mitch's secret rib sauce consistently brings in overflow crowds to his two downtown locations. A number of people have expressed interest in investing in Mitch's expansion into other cities. It's expected that the venture will generate business losses in its first years immediately following the capital infusion. Mitch's will borrow funds from banks to supplement cash reserves and working capital. At first, interested investors plan to simply use the early S corporation losses to offset other income on their personal tax returns. However, the investors' tax advisers warn that because S corporation debt cannot be used to increase the tax basis of the shares held by the investors (as it could in a partnership or LLC) investors won't get to write off all the expected business losses on their individual tax returns. This technical tax disadvantage of the S corporation ultimately results in Mitch's having difficulty finding investors to fund its planned business expansion.

We won't go into this technical point further. Just realize that an S corporation has less flexibility than other pass-through entities to use borrowed money of the business to increase the tax deductions of the owners on their annual individual tax returns and lower the tax bite when the business or their interests in it are ultimately sold. Your tax adviser can fill you in on the details if you want more information.

Electing S Corporation Tax Status May Cut Your Self-Employment Tax Bill

There is still a potential advantage of the S corporation over the LLC under current self-employment tax rules. Specifically, profits of the S corporation, which automatically pass through to the shareholders, are not subject to the self-employment (Social Security and Medicare) taxes. In an LLC taxed as a pass-through entity whose members are active in the business, the members pay self-employment taxes on all LLC profits allocated to them each year. And, presumably, if an LLC elects corporate tax treatment, the LLC pays its share (½) of the self-employment tax on profits paid to members as salaries, with the members picking up the tab on the other half. For further information on the current Social Security tax rules that apply to LLCs, see Chapter 3.

To summarize, even if S corporation status makes sense to gain the benefits of limited liability for the owners but keep the pass-through tax status for business income and losses (and maybe save on self-employment taxes as mentioned above), it is often inconvenient or uncertain because of the requirements for adopting and keeping

S corporation tax eligibility. By comparison, the tax status of an LLC is sustained and certain throughout the life of the business. Further, the above technical tax considerations make the S corporation less attractive to investors seeking to maximize the deductions and losses they can pass through the business and claim on their individual tax returns.

Business Entity Comparison Tables

In the tables below, we highlight and compare general and specific legal and tax traits of each type of business entity. We include a few technical issues in our chart (partially covered above). Should any of the additional points of comparison seem relevant to your particular business operation, we encourage you to talk them over with a legal or tax professional.

Business Entity Comparison Chart – Legal Characteristics

	Sole Proprietorship	General Partnership	Limited Partnership	C Corporation	S Corporation	LLC
Who owns business?	sole proprietor	general partners	general and limited partners	shareholders	same as C corporation	members
Personal liability for business debts	sole proprietor personally liable	general partners personally liable	only general partner(s) personally liable	no personal liability of shareholders	same as C corporation	no personal liability of members
Restrictions on kind of business	may engage in any lawful business	may engage in any lawful business	same as general partnership	some states prohibit formation of banking, insurance, and other special businesses	same as C corporation—but excessive passive income (such as from rents, royalties, interest) can jeopardize tax status if corporation converted from C to S corporation	same as C corporation, and some states may prohibit the performance of professional services
Restrictions on number of owners	only one sole proprietor	minimum two general partners	minimum one general partner and one limited partner	most states allow one-person corporations; some require two individuals to serve as officers	same as C corporation, but no more than 100 shareholders permitted	one member allowed in all states
Who makes management decisions?	sole proprietor	general partners	general partner(s) only (not limited partners)	board of directors	same as C corporation	ordinarily members; or managers if manager-managed LLC
Who may legally obligate business?	sole proprietor	any general partner	any general partner (not limited partners)	directors and officers	same as C corporation	ordinarily any member; or any manager if manager-managed LLC
Effect on business if an owner dies or departs	dissolves automatically	dissolves automatically unless otherwise stated in partnership agreement	same as general partnership	no effect, unless corporation is solely owned	same as C corporation	in a small number of states, dissolves unless remaining members vote to continue business
Limits on transfer of ownership interests	free transferability	consent of all general partners usually required under partnership agreement	same as general partnership	transfer of stock may be limited under securities laws or restrictions in articles of incorporation or bylaws	same as C corporation—but transfers limited to persons and entities that qualify as S corporation shareholders	unanimous consent of nontransferring members may be required under state law or operating agreement
Amount of organizational paperwork and ongoing legal formalities	minimal	minimal; partnership agreement recommended	start-up filing required; partnership agreement recommended	start-up filing required; bylaws recommended; annual meetings required	same as C corporation	start-up filing required; operating agreement recommended; meetings not normally required

Business Entity Comparison Chart – Legal Characteristics (cont'd.)

	Sole Proprietorship	General Partnership	Limited Partnership	C Corporation	S Corporation	LLC
Source of start-up funds	sole proprietor	general partners	general and limited partners	initial shareholders (in some states, cannot buy shares with a promise to perform services or contribute cash in the future)	same as C corporation—but cannot issue different classes of stock with different financial provisions	members (may usually invest with promise to perform services or contribute cash in the future)
How business usually obtains capital, if needed	sole proprietor's contributions; working capital loans backed by personal assets of sole proprietor	capital contributions from general partners; business loans from banks backed by partnership and personal assets	investment capital from limited partners; bank loans backed by general partners' personal assets	flexible; outside investors may buy various classes of shares; bank loans backed by shareholders' personal assets (if corporation has insufficient credit history); may go public if need substantial infusion of cash	generally same as C corportion—but can't have foreign, partnership, or corporate shareholders; must limit number of shareholders to 100; can't offer different classes of stock to investors except for shares with different voting rights	capital contributions from members; bank loans backed by members; personal assets (if LLC has insufficient credit history)
Ease of conversion to another business form	may change form at will; legal paperwork involved	may change to limited partnership, corporation, or LLC; legal paperwork involved	may change to corporation or LLC; legal paperwork involved	may change to S corporation by filing simple tax election; change to LLC can involve tax cost and legal complexity	generally same as C corporation—may terminate S tax status to become C corporation but cannot reelect S status for five years after	may change to general or limited partnership or corporation; legal paperwork involved
Is establishment or sale of ownership interests subject to federal and states securities laws?	generally not	generally not	yes, issuance or sale of limited partnership interests must qualify for securities laws exemption, otherwise must register with federal and state securities laws offices	yes, issuance or transfer of stock subject to state and federal securities laws or must qualify for securities laws exemptions	same as C corporation	probably not, if all members are active in business
Who generally finds this the best way to do business?	owner who wants legal and managerial autonomy and minimal organizational red tape	joint owners who are not concerned with personal liability for business debts	joint owners who want partnership tax treatment and some nonmanaging investors; general partners must be willing to assume personal liability for business debts	owners who want limited liability and ability to split income between themselves and a separately taxed business	owners who want limited liability and individual tax rates to apply to business income; must be willing to meet initial and ongoing S corporation requirements	generally, owners who want imited liability and pass-through taxation; particularly beneficial for smaller, privately held businesses

Business Entity Comparison Chart – Tax Characteristics

	Sole Proprietorship	General Partnership	Limited Partnership	C Corporation	S Corporation	LLC
How business profits are taxed	individual tax rates of sole proprietor	individual tax rates of general partners, unless business elects corporate treatment	individual tax rates of general and limited partners, unless business elects corporate tax treatment	split up and taxed at corporate rates and individual tax rates of shareholders	individual tax rates of shareholders	individual tax rates of members
Tax-deductible fringe benefits available to owners who work in business	sole proprietor may set up IRA or Keogh retirement plan	general partners and other employees may set up IRA or Keogh plans	same as general partnership	tax-deductible fringe benefits for employee-shareholders; can reimburse employees' medical expenses and provide tax-free term life insurance; can set up stock equity plans for employees	same as general partnership, but employee-shareholders owning 2% or more of stock are restricted from receiving deductible corporate fringe benefits; equity-sharing plans generally not available	owners get tax benefits associated with sole proprietorship (one-member LLCs) or partnership (multi-member LLCs)
Automatic tax status	yes	yes	yes, upon filing certificate of limited partnership with state corporate filing office	yes, upon filing Articles of Incorporation with state corporate filing office	no; must meet requirement and file tax election form with IRS (and sometimes state); revoked or terminated tax status cannot be re-elected for five years	yes, one-member LLC treated as sole proprietorship; multi-member LLC treated as partnership
Are taxes due when business is formed?	generally tax free to set up	generally tax free to set up; individual income taxes may be due if a general partner contributes services as capital contribution	usually same as general partnership	generally not taxable if under IRC Section 351	same as C corporation	generally tax free to set up; individual income taxes may be due if a member contributes services as capital contribution
Deductibility of business losses	owner may use losses to deduct against other income on individual tax returns (subject to passive loss rules that apply to all businesses)	partners may use losses to deduct on individual tax returns if "at risk" for loss or debt and subject to active-passive loss rules	same as general partnership, but limited partners may only deduct "nonrecourse debts" (for which general partners are not specifically liable)	corporation may deduct business losses (shareholders may not deduct losses)	shareholders may deduct share of corporate losses on individual tax returns, but must comply with passive loss limitation; shareholders normally do not get the tax benefit of entity-level debt	follows sole proprietorship or partnership rules depending on tax status of LLC
Tax level when business is sold	personal tax level of owner	personal tax level of individual general partners	personal tax level of individual general and limited partners	two levels: shareholders and corporation may be taxed on sale of business	normally taxed at personal tax levels of individual shareholders, but corporate level tax sometimes due if S corporation was formerly a C corporation	follows sole proprietorship or partnership rules depending on tax status of LLC

Basic LLC Legalities

This chapter examines basic legal issues and procedures involved in setting up and running an LLC. We'll explain the paperwork, operating structure, and liability rules for new LLCs. With this information, you can decide how you want your LLC to be set up and managed. In later chapters, we'll help you draft and file your articles of incorporation and create an operating agreement.

Number of Members

You can have as many LLC members as you want, although we think that more than 35 is unwieldy. You can have only one member if you want. You indicate the ownership percentage of each member in your operating agreement, discussed in Chapters 5 and 6.

Paperwork Required to Set Up an LLC

Let's look at the basic legal documents and procedures involved with starting your own LLC. Fortunately, it's a simple process, meaning that it should take you relatively little time to turn your idea of forming an LLC into a legal reality.

> **TIP**
>
> **One person may prepare and file the paperwork.** Generally, one person may prepare, sign, and file the basic documents to set up an LLC. This person need not be a member of the LLC, but must turn the reins of management over to LLC members or a management team after the LLC is formed. The purpose of this law is to allow a lawyer to do the filing for you—which is fine if that's what you want. Normally, you can just as well prepare the paperwork yourself and drop it in the nearest mailbox.

Form Your LLC Using Nolo's *LLC Maker*™ Software

LLC Maker is an interactive software program for Windows® that prepares the articles of organization, operating agreement, and other essential legal forms for you. Just fill in the information for your LLC according to the state-specific instructions on the screen, and *LLC Maker* will assemble the forms required in your state. It contains information you need to make an informed choice on whether to form an LLC, online legal and program help, tables of state-by-state LLC rules and information, and information and forms for existing LLCs, such as information on ongoing legal formalities and instructions for preparing minutes of LLC meetings. You can purchase and download *LLC Maker* from www.nolo.com.

LLC Articles of Organization

The only formal legal step normally required to create an LLC is to prepare and file LLC articles of organization with your state's LLC filing office. A few states require an additional step: the publication in a local newspaper of a simple notice of intention to form an LLC prior to filing your articles. (See your state sheet in Appendix A for particulars.)

The LLC filing office is usually the same one that handles your state's corporate filings, typically the Department or Secretary of State's office, located in the state capital. Larger states usually have branch filing offices in secondary cities as well.

LLC articles of organization don't have to be lengthy or complex. In fact, you can usually prepare your own in just a few minutes by filling in the blanks and checking the boxes on a relatively simple form provided by your state's

LLC filing office. Typically, you need only specify a few basic details about your LLC, such as its name, principal office address, agent and office for receiving legal papers, and the names of its initial members (or managers, if you're designating a special management team to run the LLC).

RESOURCE
Instructions for completing articles of organization. We provide a sample LLC articles of organization form with instructions and show you how to get your state's form to fill in and file in Chapter 4.

LLC Operating Agreement

An LLC should always create a written operating agreement to define the basic rights and responsibilities of LLC members (and managers, if you decide to form a manager-run LLC—more on this option later). Without a written agreement to refer to, you may get stuck in a crisis trying to answer such questions as:

- When members are faced with an important management decision, does each get one vote, or do they vote according to their percentage interests in the LLC?

- Are owners expected to make additional capital contributions (meaning invest more money) if the LLC needs additional operating capital?

- Are owners entitled to periodic draws from the profits of the business?

- Will interest be paid to the owners on their capital contributions?

- May members leave the LLC any time they wish and expect an immediate payout of their capital contributions?

- How much should an owner be paid when he or she decides to leave the business?

- Is a departing owner allowed to sell an interest to an outsider?

Please believe us when we say that these kinds of unanswered questions can, and frequently do, come back to haunt small businesses. They are far better addressed in a written operating agreement, signed around the time your new LLC entity is created.

RESOURCE
Instructions for completing LLC operating agreements. Chapters 5 and 6 provide instructions for completing the two different types of operating agreements included in Appendix B.

Responsibility for Managing an LLC

At least one person needs to be responsible for overall management of a business, and the LLC is no exception. Under most states' default legal rules, all members (owners) are automatically responsible for managing the business (this arrangement is called "member-management"), unless they specifically appoint one or more members and/or nonmembers to manage the LLC (this option is called "manager-management").

Member-Managed or Manager-Managed LLC?

Most LLC owners will choose member-management, not manager-management. That's because most smaller LLCs won't want an extra level of bureaucracy; they'll want to let the LLC members run the business they own. Unless you are planning to bring in outside investors who want a management role in your business, it's likely that you'll naturally decide to be member-managed.

Nonvoting vs. Nonmanaging Members

LLC members have special voting rights under state law, which include voting to amend the articles or operating agreement, to merge or dissolve the LLC, to approve the admission of new members, and to approve the transfer of a membership by an existing member to an outsider. In addition, in manager-managed LLCs, members have a right to vote to elect or reelect the managers (even though some members may also be managers and can vote to reelect themselves).

Many of these voting rights can be eliminated or restricted in LLC articles or an operating agreement by giving the member no voting power in the LLC operating agreement. Even here, though, some states require the vote, and sometimes approval, of all or a majority of members to certain major structural changes to the LLC, such as amending the articles or operating agreement or dissolving the LLC, no matter what your operating agreement says. This issue of membership voting power leads to the following question: Is eliminating the voting power of a member the same thing as making the member a nonmanaging member? The answer, in our view, is no. State LLC statutes, for the most part, treat members' voting rights as separate from members' management responsibilities and make all LLC members of a member-managed LLC responsible for managing the LLC without reference to specific voting rights of the member. For example, state law typically says that all members of a member-managed LLC are charged with managing it in good faith and can act as "agents" of the LLC by binding it to a contract or business deal with outsiders.

Another way to look at this issue is to think of members as you would the shareholders (owners) of a corporation. Shareholders can be given voting or nonvoting shares in a corporation, but the people responsible for management of a corporation are the board of directors, regardless of the types of shares (voting or nonvoting) held by the owners. Unless you select a separate management team for your LLC—by choosing a manager-management structure—state law pretty much treats your members as the "board of directors" of your LLC, each of whom is responsible for its management (without considering whether these LLC members also have specific voting rights under state law or your operating agreement). In fact, in some states like North Dakota, this corporate analogy is embodied in the state LLC law, with the managers of the LLC (whether the LLC is member- or manager-managed) called the "Board of Governors." Finally, one of the primary voting rights of a member in a manager-managed LLC is the right to vote for the election or reelection of the managers—clearly, state law intends to make membership voting rights separate from management power, just as in the corporate context where voting shareholders get to vote for the election of the board of directors.

Manager Options

If you wish to elect a special management team for your LLC, you'll have to select a group of managers. These are the options when selecting managers in a manager-managed LLC:

- **Select members as managers.** Some larger LLCs—for example, those with passive investors who will not work in the business—may decide to name only active members as managers.
- **Select only nonmembers.** Some LLCs decide that management should consist exclusively of nonmembers with particular expertise in the business of the LLC (by hiring an outside consultant or an LLC officer as manager).
- **Select some or all LLC members, plus nonmembers as managers.** Still other LLCs may settle for a combination of members, investors, and nonmember managers.

Tax Consequences

The non-managing members of a manager-managed LLC may be able to avoid paying self-employment tax on their share of LLC profits. We'll discuss this further in Chapter 3.

Securities Law Consequences

We cover the securities law implications of LLC management choices later in this chapter. For now, just realize if one or more of your members does not participate in management, membership interests in your LLC may be considered securities, and you may need to comply with extra federal and state securities procedures when setting up your LLC.

LLC Lacking Operating Agreement Is Controlled By State LLC Statutes

If you run your LLC without an operating agreement, your state's LLC statutes will control basic elements of how your LLC is run and terminated. These statutes may not reflect the choices you want to make for your LLC. For example, typical state statutes specify that an LLC is managed by the members (owners). In addition, some states establish that profits and losses are to be divided up among the members equally (per capita), regardless of each member's capital contribution.

EXAMPLE:

Yvonne and Joe form an LLC with Yvonne contributing 30% of the capital to get started and Joe contributing 70%. Under their state's default rule, Yvonne and Joe each would be entitled to receive one-half the profits of the LLC each year, even though they pay disproportionate amounts to get the LLC up and running. If Yvonne and Joe prepare their own operating agreement, however, they can divide profits according to their capital contributions, if they wish.

Selection and Removal of Members and Managers

Initial members or managers of the LLC are usually named in the articles of organization filed with the state LLC filing office. According to the default rule in most states, which operates unless your operating agreement says something else, new members can be admitted only by the vote of all members of the LLC. If your LLC has chosen manager-management, the default rule is that anyone selected to replace an initial manager must be voted in by a majority of the members. But you can vary this latter rule in your operating agreement to let the managers (by a majority or greater vote), rather than the members, vote to fill a manager vacancy.

State law is usually silent on the issue of how and why members or managers of an LLC may be removed. Under typical provisions found in LLC operating agreements, members cannot be removed from the LLC member roster except for specific reasons, such as bankruptcy, incapacity, or another listed reason, and then only with the vote of all other members.

Manager removal is usually easier under most operating agreements and often is allowed "without cause" (for any or no particular reason) upon a vote of the membership. Managers are also typically elected by the members to specific terms of office—in other words, they can be voted out of office at the expiration of their management term if the members elect someone else in their place.

Legal Authority of LLC Members and Managers

Generally, the members (if member-managed) or managers (if manager-managed), or other duly appointed representative (such as an officer) of the LLC can legally bind the LLC to a contract, business transaction, or course of action, as long as the transaction is within the LLC's normal scope of business. A common legal exception states that a contract with an outsider who knows, or should have known, that the LLC agent does not have specific authority for a transaction is not binding on the LLC. Unfortunately, this type of knowledge is hard to prove.

EXAMPLE:

Gary is a member and VP of Fish and Fritters Fast Foods, LLC ("4F")—a member-managed LLC. He orders $500 in stationery from Joe's Stationery Supply Company, a local merchant, consisting of $400 of 4F stationery and $100 of personal letterhead. When he places the order, he does so on behalf of 4F, and charges the bill to 4F's account. Joe gets a check from 4F for $400, with a note from the accounts payable officer advising Joe to collect the $100 balance from Gary because the order for personal letterhead was not approved by 4F. Would a small claims court let Joe recover the $100 balance from 4F? Probably. Joe would normally be justified in believing that an officer of 4F had authority to place the full order on its behalf, unless Gary specifically told Joe that the extra stationery should be billed to him alone.

It's safest to assume that any contract or transaction signed on behalf of your LLC by anyone in management will be legally binding. This legal authority should not present a problem if you choose the right people to be members or managers of your LLC.

> **CAUTION**
>
> **If you're uncomfortable with others obligating your business, an LLC is probably not the right business entity for you.** You may want to stick to a sole proprietorship, where you have the only say, or to a limited partnership, where you can get full management authority if you are the only general partner.

Member and Manager Voting Rules

The default laws of many states (those that apply unless your operating agreement says otherwise) specify that members' voting rights are allocated according to the capital contributions made by each member. In other words, a member contributing 50% of the capital usually gets 50% of the voting power. But in some states, the default voting right rule is that members are given voting rights on a per capita basis (one vote per member) if the LLC operating agreement doesn't set a different standard. And other states use members' interests in LLC *profits*, which may be different from capital interests, as the default measure of member voting rights.

Under state default rules, most LLC matters brought to a vote of the members must be approved by at least a majority of the LLC's voting power—that is, by more than 50% of the full voting interests of the members.

EXAMPLE:

Sit-u-ational Awareness, LLC, a three-member computer furniture ergonomics consulting firm, has parceled out its voting interests to the three owners as follows: Kathlyn—30%, Evan—25%, and Alyson—45%. The vote of at least two of the three members is necessary to obtain a majority and decide an issue brought to the membership for resolution.

If the LLC is manager-managed, states typically give managers one vote each, with a majority-manager vote required to approve a decision.

EXAMPLE:

Dollars to Donuts, LLC, is owned by four entrepreneurs but managed by a team of five persons consisting of the four members and a nonmember pastry chef, Pierre (who brings the recipe for a delectable French twist pastry—the hallmark of the enterprise—to the business, plus his formidable baking skills). When an important management vote needs to be made, each manager gets one vote, and the vote of at least three of

the five managers is required to resolve the matter. Pierre doesn't function as a fifth wheel on the management team—he becomes the all-important deadlock-breaking vote whenever the four owners don't see eye to eye and split their votes two-to-two.

Remember, as with most state law rules mentioned in this chapter, these are default member and manager voting rules. You can override them by defining voting rights any way you wish in your operating agreement.

CAUTION

Different default rules may apply when admitting new members. State LLC statutes contain special voting rules concerning the membership vote required to admit new members into the LLC and the vote necessary to continue the LLC after a member dies, resigns, or is expelled. Most states, however, now allow you to override the state's default rules on these matters by stating different rules in your operating agreement.

CAUTION

Nonvoting members may sometimes get a vote. You can have one or more nonvoting members—just specify in your operating agreement that the nonvoting member has zero votes. Just realize that even if you give a member zero votes, the nonvoting member may be given some voting power in special situations under your state's LLC laws. For example, it is common for state law to require the votes, if not approval, of all LLC members to amend the LLC articles of organization or operating agreement, to dissolve the LLC, or in other significant legal matters involving changes to the structure of the LLC.

Membership and Management Meetings

Most states do not give mandatory rules for when and how membership meetings should take place. It's ordinarily up to you to come up with your own rules for the frequency, notification procedures, and conduct of membership meetings.

Regular LLC meetings are not required in the operating agreements in this book (although you can require meetings if you're so inclined), because you don't need to hold formal meetings to make many of the important decisions that keep your business operating smoothly. Requiring these meetings can be time-consuming, and if they aren't necessary, time may be better spent on the business itself.

Ordinarily, you should need to meet for formal LLC meetings (which are recorded in written minutes) only in situations such as these:

- An important legal or tax formality needs to be approved and recorded (the LLC is undertaking a legal or tax election that should be documented in your LLC records, such as approving the buy-back of a departing member's interest in the LLC).

- You need to meet face-to-face with your full membership and formally approve an out-of-the-ordinary or disputed business decision (sell important LLC assets or dissolve the LLC contrary to the wishes of some of the members).

- You have elected a management team (set up a manager-managed LLC) and need to reelect them to another term (more on this just below).

TIP

You may be required to hold a membership meeting to elect managers if your LLC is manager-managed. States typically say that members must elect the managers at a membership meeting, without specifying terms of office for managers or how often members should meet to elect or reelect managers. However, some states do limit the term for managers to one year unless you override it in your operating agreement. If your LLC is manager-managed and you adopt a one-year term for your managers, you will want to hold annual membership meetings to reelect your managers. The appointment of managers is a routine task for most LLCs unless a manager is withdrawing or is not performing satisfactorily.

RESOURCE

For forms and instructions, plus state-by-state legal requirements, for holding LLC meetings and taking care of ongoing LLC business, see *Your Limited Liability Company: An Operating Manual,* by Anthony Mancuso (Nolo).

Member and Manager Liability to Insiders and Outsiders

One of the nicest parts of forming an LLC is the general immunity from personal liability the members and managers enjoy. But it's important to realize that this immunity has its limits; there are some situations in which a person acting as an LLC member or manager may end up liable to the LLC, other members or managers, or outsiders. There are also situations when "outside" liability of an LLC member can impact the LLC and the other members. We discuss these exceptions below.

LLC Members and Managers Must Act in Good Faith Towards Each Other

Members of a member-managed LLC and managers of a manager-managed LLC have a legal obligation in managing the LLC to act in good faith, in the best interests of the LLC and its members. In legal jargon, this duty is known as their "duty of care." It is similar to the obligation corporate directors have to a corporation.

Courts have interpreted this duty in the corporate context by promulgating the "business judgment rule." This says that in making management decisions, honest business mistakes will not subject managers and members to personal liability. Another way of saying this is that decisions that have some rational basis—based upon facts known to managers and members or presented to them in a report from someone else with superior knowledge—should not give rise to personal liability if they turn out to be wrong-headed and result in financial loss to other members or to the LLC.

EXAMPLE:

Bob and Juliet are two of three owners of the Lucky Lock Company LLC—a member-managed LLC. They vote at a management meeting to use one-quarter of the company's accumulated earnings to market and sell Bob's Big-Lock, a unique lock plate with a neon clock display that Bob invented. Greg, the third owner at the meeting, is against the idea of committing company funds to promote a device with such an uncertain future. The uncertainty of the profitability of Bob's Big-Lock is fully discussed at the membership meeting, but Greg is outvoted two-to-one by his co-owners. The clock-lock idea doesn't catch on, and the project loses money big time.

Can Greg sue the other owners personally for their bad business judgment? As long as Bob and Juliet made a bad business decision without underhandedness, concealment, or misrepresentation of facts or other fraud or illegality, the answer should be "no" under the business judgment rule. But let's say Bob and Juliet knew that certain features of the purported master timepiece would be difficult to produce, yet kept this knowledge from Greg when they pitched Bob's Big-Lock idea. Greg may be able to recover some or all of the clock-loss money personally from Bob and Juliet for failing to disclose all material facts at the management meeting.

The above example points out a basic LLC legal rule: Full and fair disclosure of facts is part and parcel of an LLC member/manager's duty to the LLC—a duty that isn't mitigated or otherwise lessened by the business judgment rule.

Liability to Other Members for Unjustifiable Loss

Most states have provisions in their LLC laws that permit members to sue other members or managers on behalf of (in the name of) the LLC. Often called "derivative actions" in legal lingo, these lawsuits can occur if a member feels that other members or managers caused unjustifiable financial loss to the LLC.

EXAMPLE:

Let's use the same Lucky Lock Company, LLC described above. This time, members Bob and Juliet siphon off some of the funds for themselves, personally, rather than using them to prototype and sell Bob's Big-Lock. Bob and Juliet can expect to be sued by and be held personally liable to the LLC and/or to Greg for the amount of the diverted funds.

Many states have "indemnification" provisions in their LLC laws. This fancy legal word means that the LLC will pay the legal expenses, settlements, court judgment awards, fines, fees, and other liabilities personally assessed or awarded against an LLC member or manager for ill-advised management decisions or other liability-causing events. Generally, state rules say that the person to be indemnified must have acted in good faith, in the best interests of the LLC, before he or she can be reimbursed or advanced legal expenses or receive other indemnification. And, as you might guess, intentional misconduct, fraud, and illegal acts normally can't be covered under these statutes. Indemnification provisions vary and are technical, so check with an LLC legal adviser or take a closer look at your state's LLC indemnification statute if this area of LLC law interests you.

Liability to Outsiders

No matter how an LLC is managed—whether by LLC members or a management team—one basic limited liability rule applies. LLC members and managers are not normally personally responsible to outsiders for any mistakes in management that they make.

EXAMPLE:

A customer of Jen & Len's Computers LLC sues the company, as well as each owner personally, for not fixing a problem with his two-gigabyte hard drive, resulting in 40 hours of extra work for her to get the data back online. Are Jen and Len personally liable to the customer? No. Limited liability should protect them.

What about torts? (Here we're talking about the legal, not edible, kind.) Basically, a tort is an act that harms another person and causes monetary loss—for example, running a red light, which causes an accident and damages another automobile. Members of an LLC, like corporate directors, partners, and all other business managers, can be personally liable for financial loss caused by their negligent tortious behavior. Whether working for an LLC as an employee or acting in the capacity of a member, if a member does something negligently that causes harm to another person or that person's property, the member can be held personally liable for the damage.

EXAMPLE:

Otto, one of the two employee/members of Otto's Oughto Order Auto Parts Supply LLC, gets in his Mazda Miata to pick up a throwout bearing for a customer's Mercedes station wagon. On the way, he sideswipes a slow-moving Geo, a stunt that results in a $5,000 repair bill to the Geo owner and a $25,000 medical claim for whiplash to George, the Geo driver. Otto can be held personally liable for $30,000.

Of course, insurance—commercial, automotive, workers' compensation, or even the employee's individual homeowner policy—may cover some or all damage caused by LLC manager or worker torts. Check LLC and personal insurance policies to see what protection may be available to you in the event of an accident.

LLC Exposure to Personal Claims— The Flip Side of Limited Liability

The discussions above cover several exceptions to the standard rule that the LLC protects the members from creditor claims against the LLC. Let's turn the tables: Can a creditor of an LLC owner seize the owner's membership interest in an LLC? The answer is "yes" under the laws of most states. Since an interest in an LLC is the personal property of each LLC owner, state law

LLCs Should Have Liability Insurance Coverage

Our advice is to get reliable liability insurance to cover potential personal and business liabilities arising from the LLC's operations. Typically, a commercial general liability insurance policy will cover:

- tort liability (bodily injury and property damage, so-called "slip-and-fall" coverage) caused by business owners and employees in the course of business or on the business premises, and

- fire, theft, catastrophe, and the like.

Most smaller LLCs, at least to begin with, rely primarily on their commercial liability insurance to protect them in the event of lawsuits brought by outsiders. They may go beyond this basic coverage later if they can afford to supplement it with personal liability policies for members or other managers. Such policies can protect members and managers from personal liability for torts to outsiders as well as inside liability to the LLC for losses caused by members' or managers' faulty decisions.

Make sure you look for newer policies that recognize the legal status of your LLC and its members. Because LLCs are relatively new, insurance companies may need to adapt their current corporate director and officer "errors and omissions" policies for use by LLC members and managers.

EXAMPLE:
Sam defaults on a personal bank loan, and the bank obtains a charging order against Sam's LLC membership interest. This order allows the bank to be paid any profits distributed to Sam under the terms of the LLC's operating agreement.

A charging order may not do a creditor much good if an LLC does not regularly distribute profits to members. In that case, a creditor may ask a state court to foreclose on the LLC's member's interest. If state law allows this foreclosure, and if the court agrees, a personal creditor of an LLC member can become a new legal owner of the LLC.

However, under most state laws, the creditor who forecloses on an LLC interest does not become a full owner. Instead, the law says that the foreclosing creditor becomes a "transferee" or "assignee" who is entitled to all economic rights associated with the interest, including the value of the interest when the business is sold or liquidated. Typically, an assignee or transferee is not allowed to manage or vote in the LLC nor assume other membership rights granted to full members under the LLC operating agreement.

If the LLC does not pay out profits regularly and if there is little likelihood of the business being sold or liquidated, these economic rights may mean very little to a creditor. However, if a creditor can step in as a full voting member when foreclosing on a member's interest, this can have a crippling effect on the operation of the LLC. After all, the creditor's primary interest is liquidating the value of the member's interest to obtain repayment on the delinquent debt or claim, not on signing on as part of a continuing enterprise.

One final downside associated with creditor claims against LLC membership interests is that some state laws allow transferees or assignees of

normally allows a creditor of an individual to obtain a charging order against that individual's interest in a business, such as a partnership or LLC interest or a person's stockholdings in a corporation. Essentially, a charging order acts as a lien against the business interest, allowing the creditor to receive the payments of profits that would otherwise go to the owner of the interest.

LLC memberships to petition a court to force a dissolution of the LLC. This is an extreme remedy that may be available to creditors who can foreclose on an LLC membership interest in some states.

To determine whether a personal creditor of an LLC member can obtain a charging order, foreclose, or force a dissolution of an LLC, consult an experienced lawyer in your state.

Are LLC Membership Interests Considered Securities?

When someone buys into or invests in an LLC, they are being sold an interest in the business. Is this sale of an LLC interest the sale of a "security" within the meaning of state or federal law? If it is, it must either be registered at the federal level—with the Securities and Exchange Commission—and with the state securities office, or it must be eligible for an exemption from these federal and state securities registration requirements.

The question of whether and under what circumstances LLC memberships may be a security interest isn't black-and-white but we'll mention a few basic expectations of the securities law treatment of LLCs. A helpful generalization is that when the owner of an interest in a business relies on his or her own efforts to make a profit, the interest normally is not a security interest. Conversely, if a person invests in a business with the expectation of making money from others' efforts, federal and state statutes as well as the courts usually treat the interest purchased with the investment as a security.

Securities laws are meant to protect investors from unscrupulous operators, not active business owners from the results of their own business decisions.

Member-Managed LLCs and Securities Laws

If you and your co-owners plan to set up a member-managed LLC— where, by definition, all members are legally responsible for its management—it is likely that your membership interests will not be treated as securities. Why? Because all members plan to make a profit in the business from their own efforts, not the efforts of others.

Manager-Managed LLCs and Securities Laws

If you set up a manager-managed LLC, it is likely that the interests of at least the nonmanaging members will be treated as securities under state and federal law. It's even possible that the feds and the state will treat all membership interests in such an LLC as securities (securities agencies have been known to take an "all or none" position—either all LLC memberships are exempted from the definition of securities or none are).

Don't give up if your LLC membership interests fall within the definition of "securities." There are other exemptions from securities that your LLC may qualify for if it is a one-state operation or if it has a limited number of members. Below is a summary of the most commonly relied upon federal securities law exemptions that may apply. Many states either defer to or adopt one or more of these federal exemptions in their securities statutes and regulations. Note that the first two exemptions do not require the filing of any paperwork—you informally rely on them without notification to any securities agency.

- **Private placements.** Under federal statutes and case (court-developed) law, the selling of securities privately—without advertising or promotion—to a limited number of people may be eligible for the private placement exemption contained in Section 4(2) of the federal Securities Act of 1933. You stand a better chance of being eligible for this exemption if transfers of the securities—memberships—are restricted (for example, language restricting transfer of the stock is placed on all membership certificates and a conspicuous notation is made in the LLC membership book that memberships are nontransferable), and if persons buying memberships are doing so for themselves (that is, not for resale to other investors). Many smaller LLCs will neatly fit within this traditional securities law exemption because memberships are issued to a limited number of people (the number 35 is often used, but not written into this section of law), memberships are a personal investment, and transfer of memberships to outsiders is restricted to satisfy tax requirements (for more on this point, see Chapter 3).

- **Inside-the-state sales.** Another federal exemption, the intrastate offering exemption contained in Section 3(a)(11) of the Securities Act, exempts from registration the offer and sale of securities made within one state only. If you privately offer and sell memberships within one state to residents of that state only, you may qualify for this exemption from federal registration of your memberships.

- **Regulation D.** Getting a Regulation D exemption is a formal process requiring you to follow the Regulation D statutes and file Form D with the Securities and Exchange Commission (SEC). We won't cover the requirements in detail, but offer the following gloss: You stand a good chance of qualifying under Regulation D rules if you privately offer and sell small membership interests to 35 or fewer people (measured in dollar value; the limits vary from $1 million

to $5 million, but one exemption does not have a monetary limit) each of whom is a close personal friend, family member, or business associate or has the capability to protect his or her own interests (because of past investment history or current and anticipated net worth and income earning capacity). In addition, you must place restrictions on the transfer of your LLC memberships (language on membership certificates and in LLC membership records that limits transfers), as explained in the discussion above of the Section 4(2) private placement exemption.

Again, state law securities exemptions tend to parallel one or more of the federal exemptions. For example, a state may exempt from registration the private sale of securities solely within the state or to a limited number of persons, such as 10 or 35. In some states, you may need to file an exemption form, sometimes along with a filing fee.

How Should You Handle Securities Law Issues?

Your decision on how to approach securities law issues will be a personal decision, based upon the particular facts of your LLC formation and your own personal comfort level in this unsettled area of law. For example, if you're setting up a small LLC with your spouse and you plan to actively run the business yourself (say a car repair service, retail outlet, or consulting business), you will very likely decide that you are exempt from securities laws and need not file paperwork. Similarly, if you are setting up your LLC with a handful of owners who know one another and have worked together in the past and who will actively run the LLC, you may likely conclude that you are also on safe legal ground if you do not treat your memberships as securities.

If, however, you bring in outside LLC members who are not active in the day-to-day business of the LLC, or if you bring in outside managers, we strongly recommend making sure your LLC qualifies from exemptions from both federal and state securities laws. You can do your own research in this area, but the securities laws are murky, and the newness of the LLC throws a little extra mud in the water.

RESOURCE

Consider hiring a lawyer. To get the latest LLC securities rules in your state, call the state securities board (or similar agency) and ask for a copy of state laws and regulations dealing with the issuance and sale of LLC membership interests. If you don't want to deal with this admittedly complex analysis, *call a small business lawyer.* Brainstorming with an LLC legal coach to learn the latest legal rules and come up with a safe securities law approach should be well worth the estimated one to three hours' worth of legal fees necessary to put this technical issue to rest. (See "How to Find the Right Lawyer" in Chapter 8 for more information on finding an LLC legal coach.)

The Most Important Securities Law Rule of All: Disclose, Disclose, Disclose!

One important securities law rule always applies to any business venture: Always fully disclose all pertinent facts to potential investors. Let everyone know all known and foreseeable risks of investing in your enterprise, and make all financial records available to prospective purchasers. If you go out of your way to disclose all possible risks of investment, you'll stand a much better chance of fending off securities law problems later if a member or investor starts feeling surly about lower-than-expected profits or returns from the LLC.

Tax Aspects of Forming an LLC

This chapter covers the tax treatment of LLCs. It explains how LLCs are taxed by federal and state governments, as well as special tax considerations when forming an LLC.

Pass-Through Taxation

As explained in Chapter 1, one of the main benefits of forming an LLC is "pass-through" taxation, which allows LLC owners to enjoy the tax advantages of a partnership (or sole proprietorship, for a one-person LLC). Business income is taxed just once when it is allocated to each member's LLC account (whether or not the income is actually distributed to them). The LLC members pay individual income taxes on these profits. This is different than a corporation: Usually, the corporation pays taxes, and then individual shareholders pay taxes a second time when profits are distributed in the form of dividends. For this reason, LLC owners usually decide that pass-through tax treatment is the best way to go.

But that isn't always the case. Sometimes, it's more advantageous for an LLC to be taxed like a corporation. That's because corporate tax rates are low on relatively low taxable income—15% to 25% on profits (roughly below $75,000) left in an LLC that elects corporate tax treatment (compared to individual tax rates of up to 35%). Because some LLCs want to keep profits in the business anyway—for example, to expand or because the profits are tied up in inventory—electing corporate tax treatment can sometimes save money. However, this benefit starts to decrease as profits rise. Profits are taxed at rates of up to 34% on taxable incomes up to $10 million (with a 39% rate "bubble" on taxable incomes from $100,001 to $335,000). Higher corporate tax rates of 35% and 38% apply to net taxable incomes of $10 million or more.

EXAMPLE:

Sally and Randolph run their own lumber supply LLC (S & R Wood, LLC). Because they know that they'll need to keep profits in the business to buy new equipment and increase inventory, they elect corporate tax treatment for S & R Wood. Sales for the year are $1.2 million, and after paying business expenses, including salaries and bonuses to the working members, S & R shows a $70,000 net taxable profit. This is taxed at the corporate rates of 15% on the first $50,000 and 25% on the next $20,000. If Sally and Randy had not elected corporate tax treatment for their LLC, these profits would be passed along to them and taxed at their higher individual income tax rates.

If you decide that being taxed like a corporation is what you want—with separate corporate tax rates applied to net income left in the business (not paid out as salaries and other deductible expenses)—you must file IRS Form 8832, as explained below. But remember—this only affects tax status, not legal status, and the company will still be treated as an LLC under state law.

A Flat Corporate Tax Rate Applies to Certain Professional Service LLCs That Elect Corporate Tax Treatment

If your LLC elects corporate tax treatment and provides professional services in the fields of health, law, engineering, architecture, accounting, actuarial science, performing arts, or consulting, a flat federal corporate income tax rate of 35% applies to all its net taxable income, not the lower graduated corporate income tax rates of 15% and 25% that apply to most corporations.

How LLCs Report and Pay Federal Income Taxes

In this section, we look at what, if anything, your LLC needs to do to qualify for the type of tax status it prefers.

- **If an LLC wants pass-through tax status:** An LLC with more than one owner (member) is automatically treated as a partnership for federal tax purposes, unless it elects to be taxed as a corporation by filing IRS Form 8832. Each tax year, your LLC must prepare and file the same tax forms used by a partnership—IRS Form 1065, *U.S. Partnership Return of Income,* which includes a Schedule K showing the allocation of profits, losses, credits, and deductions passed through to your members. Your LLC also must prepare and distribute to each member a Schedule K-1 form, which shows each member's allocation of LLC profits, losses, credits, and deductions. The members, in turn, use this Schedule K-1 information to complete their annual 1040 income tax returns.

    If an LLC has one member and it has not elected to be taxed as a corporation using IRS Form 8832, the IRS treats the LLC as a sole proprietorship. This means business profits (and losses, credits, and deductions) are reported on Schedule C, *Profit or Loss From a Business,* of the sole member's individual income tax return.

- **If an LLC wants corporate tax status:** If an LLC wants corporate tax treatment, it must check the "corporation" box on IRS Form 8832 (the line next to this box reads: "A domestic eligible entity electing to be classified as an association taxable as a corporation"). The election takes effect on the date you specify on the form, but this date cannot be more than 75 days before

or more than 12 months after the date the form is filed. So a new LLC that wishes to start out being taxed as a corporation should file this election within 75 days of the date its articles of organization are filed with the state LLC filing office. An election to be taxed as a corporation cannot normally be changed for 60 months (five years), but there are exceptions to this rule—for example, the LLC can ask to change its tax status within the five years of its election if there has been a fifty percent or greater change in LLC ownership.

An LLC that has elected to be taxed as a corporation must file a corporate tax return, IRS Form 1120, for each year the corporate tax election is in effect. The LLC pays income taxes on profits left in the business at corporate income tax rates, at the rates discussed in the last section.

LLCs and Self-Employment Taxes

Whether LLC members must pay federal self-employment taxes on profits is unsettled. Basically, the rule (with some exceptions—see below) is that all income a member of an LLC receives is subject to self-employment tax if the member is "active in the business." This is a major issue for some LLC organizers who feel that the current self-employment tax rate of 15.3% is far too high.

Some disgruntled business organizers choose to form an S corporation instead of an LLC because S corporation shareholders are required to pay self-employment taxes only on money paid to them as compensation for services, not on profits that automatically pass through the S corporation to them. Some even decide to form an LLC, elect corporate tax treatment for their LLC, and then make an S corporation tax election for their LLC. This is a lot of work to avoid self-employment taxes on allocated LLC income, but some business owners don't mind if it reduces taxes.

What does "active in the business" mean? Some tax practitioners look to the rules that the IRS tried to pass on the issue. These proposed regulations were withdrawn by the IRS, but they still provide guidance on how the IRS is likely to view things. According to the proposed regulations (proposed Treasury Regulation Section 1.402(a)-2(h)(2) and following), an LLC member must pay self-employment taxes on his or her share of LLC profits if the member:

- participates in the trade or business for more than 500 hours during the LLC's tax year, or

- works in the LLC and the LLC renders professional services in the fields of health, law, engineering, architecture, accounting, actuarial science, or consulting.

The above regulations were not adopted, but they can be useful in helping you or your tax adviser decide if you are active enough in your LLC to worry about paying self-employment tax on your share of LLC profits.

State Law and the Tax Treatment of LLCs

As you know, LLCs are regulated by state law. This means you must organize and operate your LLC under the provisions of your state's LLC laws, in addition to following the federal tax rules. The main sources of state regulation that impact an LLCs tax treatment can be found in the state's LLC Act and in its tax statutes and regulations.

Outdated State LLC Laws Related to IRS LLC Tax Status

In past years, many states included provisions in their LLC acts designed to help you achieve favorable tax status with the IRS (the IRS used to require that LLCs be organized substantially different from corporations). These state laws are no longer necessary—as we've explained, the IRS now lets you choose how your LLC will be taxed—but the result is that the existing state statutes no longer serve a useful purpose and have become a nuisance. We are not going to make a big deal of these rules, except to summarize them below, because: 1) the states that haven't already done so are expected to quickly repeal these outdated tax-related provisions, and 2) in Chapters 5 and 6, we show you how to deal with them without compromising the efficient operation of your LLC.

To help you understand what is involved if you bump into any of these outdated requirements, here are two types of laws you may encounter:

- **Limited duration of the LLC:** Some states ask you to limit the legal life of your LLC in your articles of organization to a specific date in the future, or to a set number of years from the date your articles are filed. (The articles of organization section of your state sheet in Appendix A alerts you to any duration requirements in effect in your state and shows you how to fill in this item if required in your state's articles.) But here's why this isn't a big worry: Even if you must follow your state's requirement to limit the duration of your LLC in your articles now, when your state deletes this requirement, you can file amended articles which do not limit your LLC's duration. Or in the unlikely event that this requirement is still in effect when the duration of your LLC is up (30 or more years from now), you can then simply file amended articles to extend the duration for another thirty or more years.

- **Membership voting rules when a member sells or loses a membership interest.** Many states require the approval of all or a majority of members in two circumstances: 1) when an existing member wishes to transfer his or her membership to a new person (a nonmember), the members must vote to approve it; and 2) when a member is dissociated—when he or she loses his or her membership interest due to withdrawal from the LLC, death, incapacity, expulsion, or for another reason—the remaining members must vote to continue the business of the LLC. Even if these approvals are required under your state's law (see the Operating Rules section of your state sheet in Appendix A), all you need to do is have the nontransferring or remaining members agree to the transfer of membership or continuance of the LLC business. In Chapters 5 and 6, we show you how to adopt provisions in your operating agreement to establish membership voting procedures that comply with these state requirements.

State Tax Statutes and Regulations

Don't confuse the outdated state LLC laws just discussed with how your state classifies your LLC for state income tax purposes (assuming your state has an income tax). Remember, the above state rules were enacted to help LLCs get favorable tax treatment with the IRS at a time when the IRS was fussy about qualifying LLCs as pass-through entities for federal tax purposes.

So how will your state classify your LLC for state income tax purposes? Probably, exactly the same as the IRS. Rather than get bogged down in all of this technical material, just call your state tax department (better yet, go online to the state tax office website listed on your state sheet) and ask if your state follows the current federal tax classification system for business entities. One easy way to ask is: "If my LLC is classified as a partnership, sole proprietorship, or corporation under the IRS rules, will the state tax department do the same?" If they say "No," ask them exactly how your LLC will be treated or ask your tax adviser to fill you in.

RESOURCE

See your state sheet in Appendix A to get started. In the Tax Status section, we list the expected tax treatment by your state. This treatment may change, so call the state tax office (or ask your tax adviser) to double check.

Other LLC Formation Tax Considerations

Let's turn to two other tax issues that may arise when you're forming your LLC:

- tax liability for members who contribute services or property to start the LLC, and
- the division of LLC profits and losses among LLC members.

The types of questions raised here relate to partnership tax law (the LLC inherits the complexities and benefits of this branch of tax law). Specifically, we will focus on questions that are likely to arise as you fill in your LLC operating agreement (as part of Chapters 5 or 6).

This field is a specialty all to itself, so if your questions are important enough, it makes sense to buy yourself some specialized tax advice to find an answer. (See Chapter 8 and think about asking your regular LLC legal or tax adviser for a referral to a partnership tax specialist.)

Capital Contributions of Services or Property

Let's start with some background on how start-up LLCs are usually funded. The initial members, like partners in a partnership, ordinarily make financial contributions to the business. In return, each member normally gets a percentage (capital) interest in the LLC. This capital interest reflects how much of the business's assets a member is entitled to if and when the business is liquidated and establishes a relative value for the membership interest when it is sold prior to a sale of the LLC itself. For example, a member with a 50% capital interest in an LLC receives $25,000 when the business sells for $50,000 (an oversimplified example, but makes the basic point).

In addition to receiving a stake in the LLC's assets upon liquidation, LLC members are also entitled to share in its profits and losses during the life of the LLC. Typically, divisions of profits and losses parallel LLC members' capital interests, although they may be distributed disproportionately. Disproportionate splits of profits and losses are called "special allocations" under the tax law and are subject to special rules, discussed below.

EXAMPLE 1:

Tony and Lisa set up Elk-n-Stuff LLC. Both members contribute equal amounts of start-up capital. In their operating agreement, Tony and Lisa agree that each member has a 50% capital interest and will receive 50% of the business's profits (or losses).

EXAMPLE 2:

Tony and Lisa set up the same Elk-n-Stuff LLC, but this time Tony puts up the cash, while Lisa signs over her interest in an equal amount of property that can be used by the LLC (an interest in a lease and some retail store counters and equipment). Tony will work full time in the LLC, but Lisa only part time (and neither will be paid a guaranteed salary). They agree that Tony will have a 50% capital interest and will receive 75% of the business's profits (or losses) for the first two years. Lisa will have a 50% capital interest and will get 25% of the business's profits (or losses) during the business's initial two years—after that, both members will split LLC profits and losses 50-50. Tony gets the extra share in recognition of his full-time commitment to the LLC. Note: For technical reasons, the LLC operating agreement makes it clear that Lisa's capital interest is given in return for her contribution of property, not for her agreement to work in the LLC (see "Contributions of Services," below, for information on contributing services to the LLC).

Under most state statutes, members may make capital contributions of cash, property, or services—or the promise to provide any of these in the future. As we discuss in the remainder of this section, any member who contributes property or services should take into account several important tax considerations.

CROSS REFERENCE

Your state sheet in Appendix A alerts you to any special contribution rules or restrictions in your state. For example, a few states prohibit or restrict capitalizing (issuing memberships in return for) an LLC with a promise to pay cash, property, or services. If your state has such a rule, we list it under the item "Special Statutory Rules" in the "Operating Rules" section of your state sheet. You should also check your state LCC act to make sure your state does not prohibit or restrict the issuance of LLC interests for services or promissory notes—we list the web address for each state's LLC act in the state sheets in Appendix A.

Cash Contributions

When all members contribute cash, there are no special tax consequences. Skip below to "Special Allocations of Profits and Losses" to read about special profit and loss rules that may affect your LLC.

Contribution of Services

If a person is given a capital interest in an LLC in return for performing services, the IRS views this as payment for personal services rendered. So if the operating agreement allocates capital contributions in exchange for a member's (often unpaid, future) services, that person will have to pay personal income tax on the value of the services.

EXAMPLE:

Five Austin computer programmers start Future Tex LLC. Four put up $20,000 each as 20% capital contributions. Cash-strapped Sharon is allotted her 20% membership in exchange for a promise to work for the company for six months without pay. The IRS considers this $20,000 capital interest as Sharon's personal income. She will be liable for personal income taxes on the entire $20,000 (to be estimated and paid by her during the year).

Reporting and paying personal service income on the value of the capital interest in an LLC can be painful for the service-member, who may have to wait to receive income from the LLC before he or she can afford to pay the taxes that result from joining the LLC. Fortunately, the following options may get around this income tax liability problem:

- **A profits interest only.** A member who's contributing services can be given an interest in the profits of the LLC, but not a capital (percentage) interest in LLC assets.

In this situation, as long as the amount of profits to be paid to the members is not clearly discernible or predictable (see IRS Revenue Procedure 93-27), income taxes normally are not due until profits are actually paid to the member. This may be easier for the member, who should at least receive some cash closer to the time when taxes must be paid.

EXAMPLE:

Hubert Allis Overalls, Ltd. Co. (HAO), a supplier of denim fabric to clothes manufacturers, brings Hank Allis (son of founding member Hubert) to help run the LLC. Business is busting at the rivets, with HAO supplying fabric to all leading domestic brand-name jeans manufacturers. In return for signing a ten-year employment contract, Hank is given a 25% stake in LLC profits, plus a guaranteed annual salary. Because Hank does not receive a capital interest in the LLC, he will not be taxed up front on his promise to perform services for HAO.

But note the following additional points:

- Even if a profits-only interest is issued to a member, the member may owe taxes if the interest is sold or transferred within two years of its issuance grant.

- Under proposed Treasury Regulation 105346-03, dated May 24, 2005, LLCs and their members must follow special rules, adopt special agreements, and make sure that special tax elections are filed by persons receiving LLC interests in return for the performance of services within 30 days of the issuance of the interests to obtain favorable tax treatment of that interest.

Ask your tax adviser how to comply with these and the other special rules and requirements before you decide to issue profits or other

LLC interests in return for the performance of services. For more information, see Notice 2005-43, "Proposed Revenue Procedure Regarding Partnership Interests Transferred in Connection With the Performance of Services," available at www.irs.gov (although the notice speaks in terms of partnership interests, it also applies to LLC interests).

- **A loan to buy a capital interest for cash.** A member can get a loan from the LLC, another member, or an outside source to buy a capital interest. To help define and secure repayment of the loan, the member may be asked by the lender to sign a promissory note specifying repayment terms, including interest. He or she may also be required to pledge property as security for repayment.

EXAMPLE:

Bella and Xavier form Happy Hoofs Equestrian Academy and Stables LLC, with the idea of operating a horse-riding and boarding facility in Riverside, California. Bella can contribute $50,000 in cash and property as her stake in the new business—enough to finance a down payment on a barn with surrounding acreage that can be converted to a stable with riding trails. Xavier is low on funds, but champing at the bit with energy that he'll use to fix up and convert the farm. Bella agrees to loan Xavier the money to become a cash member of the LLC at the start. Xavier will receive a capital interest without having to pay taxes on the value of the future services he promises to perform for the LLC. Instead, as Xavier gets paid for his services, he can pay Bella back (of course, he'll also pay individual income taxes on the salary the LLC pays him).

- **Buy into membership later.** Yet another approach is for a member wannabe to hold off joining the LLC until he or she has the cash to buy in. For example, a person can enter the LLC ranks as an employee and buy a capital interest in the LLC (assuming the members agree) with savings the employee socks away out of earned LLC salary.

EXAMPLE:

Let's return to the Happy Hoofs Equestrian Academy and Stables LLC. Bella and her husband, Clyde, form the LLC as the two initial members. Xavier bides his time to buy into the LLC. He does not become a member right away, but simply works for the ranch as a regular employee and saves his money. When Xavier has sufficient cash, he buys out Clyde's capital interest in the LLC.

Capital Contribution of Property to an LLC

Tax technicalities also arise when a member wants to contribute property to the LLC that has appreciated (increased in value) since the time he or she purchased, inherited, or otherwise received title to the property. Ordinarily, this will involve "real" property—a fancy way of saying an interest in land or a building—although this discussion applies to personal property (collectibles, airplanes, and so on), too.

First the good news. Contributions of property to an LLC are generally tax free at the time they occur. The tax consequences are generally realized later when the LLC or a member's interest in it is sold. (By the way, this is one benefit of forming a pass-through tax business, such as an LLC or partnership: Corporations are not so kindly treated and transfers must pass muster under technical "control tests" to be tax free.)

The not-so-good news is that the member who transferred the property must pay taxes on the appreciation (increase in value) that occurred prior to the transfer, either when the LLC is sold or when the member sells his or her LLC interest. This member's income tax basis (known simply as "basis") in the property carries over to his or her basis in the LLC. The result is that taxes due from appreciation on the property transferred to the LLC are paid later by the member when he or she sells an LLC membership, not when the property is contributed to the LLC. The following example illustrates how this works.

EXAMPLE:

Jim buys a building for $20,000. It is worth $120,000 when he transfers it to his newly formed LLC (it has appreciated $100,000). For the transfer of this property, he receives a $120,000 capital stake in his LLC. Jim's basis in the property is $20,000 (his cost—for simplicity, we assume there have been no adjustments to the basis; in real life, it increases with capital improvements and decreases as depreciation is taken on property). Jim pays no taxes at the time of transfer, but his basis in his LLC membership becomes $20,000 (his basis in the real property at the time of transfer).

Assuming no further adjustments to Jim's basis in his LLC (another unrealistic but convenient assumption), when the LLC is liquidated or sold, or when Jim sells his interest in the LLC, his gain—the amount he will have to pay taxes on—will equal the amount he receives for the sale of his LLC interest minus his basis. In other words, if Jim sells his interest back to the other members for $120,000 (assuming his interest is worth the same amount when he sells as when he bought it), then he will have to report a gain of $100,000 and pay taxes on that amount at the time of sale.

There are additional complexities when real property is contributed to an LLC. For example, separate tax issues arise when real property is encumbered (subject to a mortgage or other debt). This liability needs to be reflected on the LLC books, and also has bearing on gains or losses realized by LLC members during the life of the LLC and when the business or membership interests are later sold. The bottom line: Before transferring property to your LLC, ask your tax adviser about any immediate and deferred tax consequences.

Special Allocations of Profits and Losses

Like partnerships, LLCs are subject to special IRS rules if members decide not to follow the standard practice of splitting up profits and losses proportionately with each member's capital contribution. A disproportionate split of profits and losses is known as a "special allocation"—for example, if a member who contributes 10% of the initial LLC cash is allocated a 20% share of profits and losses.

Although special allocations are perfectly legal, the IRS has pages upon pages of regulations designed to handle them. Basically, these regulations say that for special allocations of profits and losses to be valid (recognized and accepted by the IRS), they must have "substantial economic effect." In other words, special allocations should not be made simply to lessen the tax burden of the owners. For instance, the IRS might object if, without placing a real economic burden on a member, an LLC allocated all its losses to a member with significant income from non-LLC sources, simply so that member can fully deduct these losses and scale down on his or her personal income taxes.

EXAMPLE:

Up Up and Away Ventures, LLC, is a passive investment company that puts investors' money into business operations run by others. Its prime moneymakers are multitiered parking garages located in inner city business districts, plus a widely dispersed network of vending machines installed at suburban shopping malls. Joe and Kenneth have invested equally, and each holds a 50% capital interest in the business. Joe wants to be allocated most of the LLC deductions for the first two years when he will be in the 35% income tax bracket, and Kenneth wants to be allocated most of the income since he is in a low tax bracket. Will the IRS object? Probably, unless the LLC makes sure that Joe's capital account is decreased by his allocated deductions and, conversely, that Ken's capital account is increased by his allocated share of LLC income.

If the IRS audits an LLC's tax returns—or the returns of its members—and does not approve special allocations, it will reallocate income and losses of the LLC according to each member's interest in the LLC. This usually means that the IRS will reallocate income and losses to members according to each member's capital interests.

IRS Safe Harbor Rules for Special Allocations

The IRS has adopted complex regulations that show LLC owners (their tax advisers really) how to make adjustments to their capital accounts so that special allocations made to them will be approved by the IRS as having substantial economic effect to the owners. Generally, these "safe harbor" rules require an LLC to make adjustments to members' capital accounts for special allocations. Since capital accounts define each member's economic interest in the LLC, and since members normally must look to the

capital account to determine how much (or little) each would receive on the liquidation of the LLC, making the capital accounts track special allocations ensures that special allocations of income or loss will have real economic consequences for each member.

So as long as your operating agreement requires your LLC to maintain its capital accounts and make other adjustments according to the safe harbor rules, all of your special allocations shall have "substantial economic effect" under IRS regulations. As a practical matter, that means including special language, from Internal Revenue Code Section 704(b) ("704(b) language"), in your operating agreement.

EXAMPLE:

Cuneiform Widgets Works Ltd. Liability Co. is founded by Sol Shimmaker. The business makes wedge-shaped objects of all descriptions, including a unique form-fitting doorstop named the Toe-Hold 2000. Expanding orders spur Sol on to seek additional capital to retool and expand CWW's fabrication facilities. Sol's friends Arnie and Lillian have the bucks and agree to contribute an amount of cash equal to half of the existing capital of the enterprise. They insist, however, on receiving a five-year 65% profits interest in the Toe-Hold 2000, plus a 50% share of net profits derived from other CWW product sales. The LLC asks its tax adviser to prepare and add 704(b) language to its operating agreement, which requires it to maintain its capital accounts under the safe harbor rules and requires members to restore any deficits in their capital accounts when the LLC liquidates or in other specified circumstances, to make sure its special allocations will be respected by the IRS.

Effect of Safe Harbor Rules

There are some real financial and tax consequences associated with adopting 704(b) language in your LLC operating agreement—after all, that's the purpose of these rules. Generally, the lengthy series of provisions that you must adopt in your operating agreement to satisfy the IRS safe harbor special allocations rules come down to these basic points:

- The business's capital accounts must be set up and maintained on the financial books under special rules based on Section 704(b).

- Distributions of cash or property to owners upon liquidation of the business must be made in accordance with capital account balances maintained under Section 704(b), as mentioned just above.

- When an owner leaves, or the business is sold or liquidated, any partners or members with negative capital account balances (capital accounts go negative if members are allocated losses in excess of their capital account balance) must restore their accounts to zero balances. They do this by contributing cash or property equal to their negative capital account balances before their interests, or the LLC itself, is sold or liquidated.

- Rule #3 can result in an LLC member's being personally liable for LLC losses—since he or she has to pay back money to the LLC if his or her capital account falls below zero as a result of the allocation of losses to the member. Fortunately, the safe harbor regulations provide an alternative rule that tax advisers can add to an LLC operating agreement (called a qualified income offset provision) that can help an LLC member avoid personal liability for a negative capital account balance.

If you want to make special allocations of profits or losses in your LLC, do what a big business would—hand your operating agreement over to a partnership or LLC tax specialist to insert the various technical provisions you'll need to rely on the IRS safe harbor rules. These rules are lengthy and complex. For all these reasons, plus the fact that most smaller LLC owners will not wish to make special allocations of profits and losses, we don't include them in the operating agreements provided in this book.

How to Prepare LLC Articles of Incorporation

In this chapter, we explain how to prepare articles of organization for your LLC and file them with your state LLC filing office. Once you perform this important task, your LLC will be a legal entity recognized by your state, as well as other states.

TIP

Don't be concerned if your state uses different LLC terminology. Different states use different legalese in their LLC statutes, regulations, and bureaucracies. We have tried to use the most common terms to describe LLC documents and offices, but your state may use other language. For example, although we refer to the charter document used to form an LLC as the articles of organization, some states use a different name such as a "certificate of formation" or a "certificate of organization."

LLC Maker™ — Nolo's National LLC Software

Nolo produces *LLC Maker*, an interactive software program for Windows® that prepares the articles of organization, operating agreement, and other essential legal forms for you. Just fill in the information for your LLC according to the state-specific instructions on the screen, and *LLC Maker* will assemble the forms required in your state. It contains online legal and program help, plus tables of state-by-state LLC rules and information for your reference. Use the program to cut through the legal red tape and form your LLC in minutes!

Read State Sheets and Order LLC Materials

Each state has its own requirements for preparing and filing LLC articles of organization, so follow the steps below to learn about your state's LLC rules. As you'll see, you'll need to contact your state's LLC filing office to obtain forms and state-specific information (usually by simply going online to your state's LLC website).

TIP

Get forms quickly over the Internet. All Secretary of State offices have Web addresses, listed in the state sheets in Appendix A. From most sites, you can download the latest version of the state's LLC articles form.

Read Your State Sheet

Your first step is to carefully read your state sheet in Appendix A. Among other valuable pieces of information, your state sheet provides the title, Web address, physical address, and phone number of your state's LLC filing office. Most state LLC filing offices are part of the Secretary of State's Division of Corporations office, but some are a division of the Department of State or a different state office. Many of the more populous states maintain LLC filing branch offices in several cities.

Most states provide their own fill-in-the-blank LLC articles of organization form. Some states give a sample form that is completed for a fictional or sample company; you retype the form and provide information that applies to your LLC. State forms are updated regularly, and their accompanying instructions contain the latest information on state filing procedures and fees.

Materials Available From LLC Filing Offices

Each state's LLC filing office and website operates a little differently, but most states are likely to supply a number of helpful materials, including:

- fill-in-the-blank or sample LLC articles of organization with instructions

- a fee schedule showing current charges for filing, copying, and certifying various LLC documents

- forms and instructions to check LLC name availability and reserve an LLC name for your use

- forms and instructions for post-formation procedures—these may include materials to amend LLC articles, change the LLC's registered office or registered agent, or register an assumed or fictitious LLC name (one that is different from the official LLC name shown in the articles of organization), and

- a summary or complete collection of the state's LLC act (sometimes available for a small fee). Some states don't supply the statutes, but tell you how to obtain them from a commercial publisher. However, all states except Pennsylvania currently post their LLC acts online, so you normally don't need to order a printout or book. We give you the online link to your state's LLC act in your state sheet in Appendix A—see "Forms and Statutes."

We don't include copies of each state's articles of organization form. If your state provides fill-in-the-blank forms, you are better off getting the latest version from your state's LLC filing office or its website when you decide to form an LLC. If your state does not provide its own fill-in-the-blank form, we give information about how to use the sample articles of organization form in Appendix B to meet the requirements in your state.

Order LLC Materials

Going to your state's website is the quickest way to get available LLC information. If you can't find what you need there, call your state's LLC filing office and ask for its LLC materials. Your state's LLC filing office phone number is listed on your state sheet in Appendix A. The LLC materials you need are listed in the sample LLC contact letter shown below.

Sometimes a letter can be used as a last resort (if you don't use a computer). In Appendix B, we provide a tear-out LLC contact letter you can use to request specific information on forming an LLC in your state. A sample letter with instructions follows below.

 CD-ROM

The LLC contact letter is included on the CD-ROM at the back of this book.

Sample LLC Filing Office Contact Letter

[date]

[name and address of your state's LLC filing office]

LLC Filings Office:

I am in the process of forming a domestic limited liability company (LLC). Please note: ❶

☐ I am or ☐ I am not converting an existing _[if applicable, specify "general" or "limited"]_ partnership to an LLC.

☐ I am or ☐ I am not forming an LLC to perform the professional services of _[if applicable, specify name of profession]_ , which are licensed by the state.

Please send me the following forms, material, and other information:

1. printed, sample, or specimen LLC articles of organization, with instructions. If your office reviews articles of organization for correctness prior to filing, please advise me of the procedure I should follow to obtain this pre-filing review;

2. the telephone number or address I can contact to determine if a proposed limited liability company name is available for my use, plus any forms necessary to reserve an LLC name;

3. a current schedule of fees for LLC filings;

4. other LLC forms and publications provided by your office (or a list of these) for forming, operating, and dissolving an LLC in this state; and

5. the name and price of a publication that contains the limited liability company statutes of this state. Please indicate whether it may be ordered from your office or, if applicable, another office or supplier.

If there is a fee for any of the above materials, please advise. Enclosed is a self-addressed, stamped envelope for your reply.

Thank you for your assistance,

[your signature]   ❷

[your name, address, and phone number]

Enclosure: Self-addressed, stamped envelope

Special Instructions

❶ In the first paragraph, you may need to check one of the boxes to indicate whether or not you are converting an existing partnership to an LLC and whether or not your LLC is being set up to perform state-licensed professional services. The state office will use this information to supply you with the proper form for articles of organization. Some states have a special form for forming an LLC that is converting from a general or limited partnership form; some have a separate form for forming a professional LLC.

Here's how to complete the blanks:

- If converting a partnership, insert whether you are converting a "general" or "limited" partnership in the first blank.

- If forming an LLC to practice a state licensed profession, insert the name of the profession in the blank in the second sentence, such as "law," "accounting," "medicine," "engineering," or "architecture."

❷ Sign the letter and fill in your name, address, and telephone number in the space provided at the bottom. Enclose a self-addressed, stamped envelope and mail the letter to your LLC filing office, keeping a copy for your own files.

Review and Organize Your State's LLC Information

Once your state LLC materials are in hand or available for viewing on your computer, take a little time to read them over.

Then, get an accordion file or large file folder (or if you are an extra tidy sort, a number of folders) and place all forms, statutes, and other legal material you received or downloaded from the filing office in it. You may want to organize this material with index tabs or dividers, separating out forms for articles of organization, name reservation, fee information, and the like.

In any case, save the forms and instructions in a file folder or on your computer. You will need to refer to this information throughout your LLC formation process and don't want to lose any of it.

Choose a Name for Your LLC

When you prepare your LLC articles of organization, you'll need to supply the name of your LLC. If the name, or one similar to it, is already in use by another LLC on file with the LLC filing office, your articles of organization will be returned unfiled to you. It pays, therefore, to plan ahead and check whether your proposed LLC name is available before you complete your articles. Take a little time to read through the material in this section and to choose a good name for your LLC.

Choosing a Unique LLC Name

Our primary task is to show you how to choose a name that is not already in use—one that is acceptable to your state's LLC office when you file your articles.

Name Cannot Resemble Another Business's Name

Make sure your proposed name is not very similar to any famous business name (McDonald's, Procter & Gamble, The Quaker Oats Company, Honda, and the like). If so, you shouldn't use the name, even if it is available for use by an LLC in your state. Companies with famous names and marks are fanatical about protecting them.

Name Cannot Infringe on Trademarks or Service Marks

If the name you choose is the same or similar to one already registered by another business (LLC or otherwise) as a federal or state trademark or service mark, the other business may be able to sue you for trademark or service mark infringement. The infringed business may also stop you from continuing to use your name to market your goods or services, and may seek money damages from your LLC.

What Are Trademarks and Service Marks?

A trademark generally consists of a distinctive word, phrase, or graphic symbol that is used to identify a product and distinguish it from anyone else's. Well-known trademarked products include Ford cars and trucks, IBM computers, and Kellogg's cereals.

A service mark promotes services in the same way that a trademark promotes products. Some common service marks are Blue Cross (sells health insurance) and Greyhound (transports people by bus).

We show you several things you can do to help satisfy yourself that your proposed LLC name is not in use by others as a federal trademark or service mark, in "Performing Your Own Name Search," below.

RESOURCE

How to learn more about trademark law. Get a copy of *Trademark: Legal Care for Your Business & Product Name*, by Stephen Elias (Nolo), which you can purchase online at www.nolo.com. In addition to educating you about trademark law, the book will help you choose a strong marketing name, search for possibly conflicting trademarks and service marks, and, if the circumstances warrant, register your LLC name as a mark with state and federal trademark agencies. For a general overview of trademark law and other intellectual property law, you may be interested in *Patent, Copyright and Trademark: An Intellectual Property Desk Reference*, by Stephen Elias and Richard Stim (Nolo).

If Your LLC Name Will Identify Products or Services

Businesses often market goods or services using a name that is different from their company name—for example, Bausch & Lomb manufactures Renu® contact lens cleaner. Companies do, however, frequently use (and register) their business names as trademarks or service marks: The Rug Doctor (company) puts out The Rug Doctor® Steam Cleaner (product) and McDonald's Corp. uses "McDonald's" as a service mark. And of course, many companies use their business name together with additional words and symbols to make up trademarks and service marks for their products and services—for example, Apple Computer Corporation uses the name Apple® Macintosh for its personal computer line.

If your LLC decides to use its business name as, or as part of, a trademark or service mark to identify products or services, you will face a number of issues:

- **Is the name identical or similar to any trademark or service mark being used on goods or services that are similar or related enough to yours to likely cause marketplace confusion?** To answer this you will need to conduct what's called a trademark search.

- **Assuming your name doesn't conflict with an existing mark, do the circumstances justify the time and expense involved in placing the name on the federal trademark register and/or your state's trademark register?** If you do the work yourself, you can easily keep costs to a minimum.

Don't overlook these important additional legal chores now if you anticipate marketing goods or services later under your proposed LLC name. If you hastily choose a name for your LLC and later use it to promote product sales in a competitive market, you may face a legal conflict just when business is humming, and your LLC and its product or service names are beginning to become known.

State LLC Name Requirements

Your LLC name must conform to your state's legal requirements. Your state sheet in Appendix A summarizes these LLC name requirements, but it's a good idea to double check this information against the name requirements posted on your state's filing office website. Most states' LLC name requirements incorporate the basic rules that follow.

LLC Designator Is Required in LLC Name

Your LLC name must normally include an LLC designator, such as "Limited Liability Company" or "Limited Company." Capitalization is normally not specified under state statutes—upper or lower case may generally be used for these words.

You must, however, follow your state's specific rules for abbreviations. Some states allow both "LLC" and "L.L.C." as acceptable abbreviations; others stick with one of these two forms. Further, the words "limited" and "company" can usually be abbreviated as "Ltd." and "Co.," but you normally can't abbreviate the word "liability"—for example, "Liab." is normally not a valid abbreviated form. The result is usually that the words "Limited Liability Company" can be abbreviated in most states to "Ltd. Liability Co."

EXAMPLE:

Valid names for the ABC limited liability company would typically include one or more of the following:

- ABC Limited Liability Company
- ABC Limited Liability Co.
- ABC Ltd. Liability Co.
- ABC Limited Company
- ABC Ltd. Co.
- ABC L.C.
- ABC L.L.C., or
- ABC LLC.

Finally, realize that in a minority of states, you may be required to place the LLC designator—the words "Limited Liability Company" or one of the other approved LLC designators—at the end of your LLC name. For example, you'd have to settle on "Maladroit Ventures LLC," not "Maladroit LLC Ventures." So be on the lookout for this requirement as you read your state sheet and the instructions to your state's articles form (where LLC name requirements are usually listed).

Certain Words Are Prohibited or Restricted in LLC Name

An LLC name usually cannot include words reserved for use by special businesses. In many states, prohibited words include references to banking, insurance, trust companies, or similar financial service businesses.

Many states either prohibit regular (non-professional) LLCs from practicing certain state-licensed professions, such as law, accounting, medicine, engineering, and architecture, just to name a few, or require that they set up professional LLCs and operate under special rules. If professional LLCs are allowed in your state, it normally requires the LLC name to include special designators, such as "Professional LLC" or "P.L.L.C." If you are forming a professional LLC, check your state's professional LLC name requirements online to be sure.

LLC Name Must Not Conflict With a Name Already On File

Another state LLC name requirement is that your LLC name must not be the same as, or too closely similar to, the name of an LLC already on file with the state LLC filing office. Names on file that are not available for your LLC may include the names of:

- domestic LLCs (those formed in the state)
- foreign LLCs (registered out-of-state LLCs that have qualified to do business in the state), and
- names on reserve for LLCs in the process of formation (names being held for 30 to 120 days for businesses planning to form LLCs soon; see "Reserve Your LLC Name," below).

If your proposed LLC name is similar to another name already on file with the state LLC office, some states allow you to use it anyway if you can get the other business's written approval to use your similar name. But there are problems with this approach. For starters, the other business is likely to refuse to let you use the similar name unless you carefully limit or distinguish it in some way from its own name. Even if the other business does agree, it probably will ask you to pay big bucks to use any version of the name. In addition, it's messy to use a name already in use by others—even if you get their permission.

TIP
Some states also check proposed LLC names against names of other business structures. In some states, if your proposed LLC name is the same or similar to one in use by a corporation or limited partnership, you will not be able to use it.

So, if you find that your proposed LLC name resembles one already on file with your state LLC office (or generally conflicts with a name discovered in your search efforts explained in "Performing Your Own Name Search," below), we recommend you come up with another name.

Important Business Name Facts

There's a lot of misinformation and confusion about choosing names for LLCs and other businesses. Here are a few points of clarification:

- **Filing your LLC name with the LLC filing office does not guarantee your right to use it.** We've said this already, but it bears repeating: Another business may be able to prevent you from using the name if the other business is already using your LLC name (or one close to it) in a trademark or service mark to identify goods or services.

- **You are allowed to use a name that's different from the official name shown in your articles of organization.** If you do, this alternate name is known as an assumed or fictitious business name, and you may need to register it at the state and/or county level. (See "Filing a Fictitious or Assumed Business Name Statement" in Chapter 7.)

- **You can change your official LLC name later by amending your articles.** You may later decide to change the name of your LLC to a new name (again, which must be available for your use with the LLC filing office) by amending your articles of organization. Naturally, most LLC owners choose not to change their LLC name after they have been in business for a while, but this option is available if absolutely necessary.

Check Availability of LLC Name With the State

Let's say you've come up with a name or two that you'd like to use for your LLC. How can you find out if the name is available for your use? Simple. Often you can check the availability of your name online from the state filing office website. Many states provide a name search link while others simply let you search the state filing office database of registered names. Either way, you should be able to find any obvious name conflicts using the online links.

Alternatively, call your state LLC filing office at the telephone number listed in your state sheet in Appendix A, and ask. The state LLC office will normally tell you over the phone, at no charge, whether one or two proposed names are available for your use. A few offices will ask you to send a written name availability request. If this happens, we suggest you use a written letter to request that your proposed LLC name be reserved for your use if it is available. (We show you how in "Reserve Your LLC Name," below.)

> ! **CAUTION**
>
> **Don't count on using a name that you haven't reserved or filed.** An online telephone or written name check is just a preliminary indication of the availability of your proposed LLC name. Unless you formally reserve your name, you do not secure your right to use your name with the state LLC office until you file your articles of organization. So don't order your business stationery, cards, signs, or anything else until your name has been secured for your use (after your articles have been filed with the LLC filing office, or after reserving your name, if you are absolutely certain that you will file your articles within the reservation period).

Performing Your Own Name Search

There are a few simple name searching procedures you can use, in addition to checking the availability of your name with the state LLC office, to find out if your proposed LLC name is in use by other businesses. Why is this important to know? For one thing, most business owners would like their names to be unique.

Another reason, mentioned earlier, is that you'd like to stay clear from names already being used by other businesses to market their goods and services. This not only helps you avoid names that others will lay legal claim to as trademarks and service marks, but can help you if you wish to use your LLC name yourself as a registered state or federal trademark or service mark (to identify and market your LLC's goods and services).

Below are several self-help search techniques you can employ to see if others are using a name similar to your proposed LLC name. If you decide to perform any of these steps, it makes sense to do so before filing your LLC articles, to avoid having to amend your articles to change your name if you find your proposed name is already in use by another business.

- **Check state and county assumed business name files.** Your state LLC information should indicate whether assumed (or fictitious) business names are registered with your Secretary of State's office, at the county level, or both. If they are registered at the state level, call the assumed or fictitious business name section of the Secretary of State's office and ask if your proposed LLC name is the same or similar to a registered assumed or fictitious name. (Assumed or fictitious names normally do not appear in the searchable online name databases maintained by the state.) Or, call your local county clerk's office to ask how you can check assumed business name filings; in most states, assumed or fictitious business name statements, or "doing business as" (dba) statements, are filed with the county clerk's office. Generally, you must go in and check the assumed business name files in person—it takes just a few minutes to do this.

- **Check business directories.** Check such sources as major metropolitan phone book listings, business directories, and trade directories to see if another company or group is using a name similar to your proposed LLC name. These directories often can be searched online. Also, larger public libraries keep phone directories for many major cities throughout the country, as well as trade directories.

- **Check state trademarks and service marks.** Call the trademark section of your Secretary of State's office and ask if your proposed LLC name is the same or similar to trademarks and service marks registered with the state. Some offices may ask for a written request and a small fee before performing this search. Also, some states may let you search your state's trademark database online. If so, you should see a link to the trademark database on your state's filing office website.

- **Check the federal *Trademark Register*.** Another logical step is to check federal trademarks and service marks. The federal *Trademark Register* consists of a listing of trademark and service mark names broken into categories of goods and services. The *Register* is available for free searching from the federal Patent and Trademark Office's website. Go to www.uspto.gov for information. If you wish to search the *Register* in printed form, go to a large public library or special business and government library in your area that carries the *Register*.

Reserve Your LLC Name

Let's say you have decided on an LLC name and checked that it is available by checking online or calling your LLC filing office. Most states allow you to reserve available LLC names. During the reservation period, only you—the person who reserved a name—may file articles of organization using this name. The reservation period and the fees vary, but generally an available LLC name can be reserved for 30 to 120 days for $10 to $50. In many states, you can reserve the same name more than once if you don't get around to filing your articles of organization during the first reservation period. We show your state's LLC name reservation rules in your state sheet in Appendix A.

It makes sense to reserve your name if you will not be filing your articles of organization immediately. Start by checking your state's online information or the materials mailed from your state LLC filing office. A sample or fill-in-the-blank reservation of LLC name form may be included, or you may find instructions for preparing one from scratch. Also note: Some states now let you reserve a name online. Filing a name reservation online is the quick and easy way to reserve a name, and we suggest you use this method if your state provides it.

Your state's online fee schedule should show how much you must pay for a name reservation, as well as indicate the period of reservation.

If a reservation form is not available online, call your state LLC filing office and ask the clerk to send you instructions and a form to reserve your proposed LLC name. If the state LLC filing office requires a written name reservation, but does not provide a form, you can use the tear-out reservation of LLC name letter included in Appendix B. Following is a sample with instructions.

Sample LLC Reservation of Name Letter

[date]

[name and address of your state's LLC filing office]

LLC Filings Office:

Please reserve the following proposed limited liability company name for my use for the allowable period specified under state law:

[insert your proposed LLC name; make sure it conforms to your state's name

requirements as shown in your state sheet in Appendix A]   .

☐ If the above name is not available, please reserve the first available name from the following list of alternative names: ❶

Second Choice: _____

Third Choice: _____

I enclose a check in payment of the reservation fee.❷ Please send a certificate, receipt for payment, or other acknowledgment or approval of my reservation request to me at my address shown below.

Thank you for your assistance,

[your signature]   ❸

[your name, address, and phone number]

_____

Enclosures: check for reservation fee; stamped, self-addressed envelope

---

 CD-ROM

The LLC Reservation of Name letter is included on the CD-ROM at the back of this book.

Special Instructions

❶ You may wish to include alternative names in case your first choice is not available. In that case, check the box and fill in the names in the blanks below.

❷ Include a check or money order for fees.

❸ Make sure that the person signing this letter will be available to sign articles of organization on behalf of your LLC. The LLC name is reserved for this person's use only. (If the requesting person drops out of the LLC, some states will allow that individual to file a transfer of reservation of name form.)

Check Your State's Procedures for Filing Articles

We cover the general procedures and rules below for preparing and filing articles of organization for LLCs. Make sure you check your state sheet in Appendix A for important rules or procedures that may apply in your state.

> **TIP**
>
> **File online.** If you have the option of filing your articles online (check Appendix A), you should use it because it's much easier and eliminates the time and trouble of printing, filling in, and mailing paper articles.

Additional Filing Procedures

The laws and regulations of some states include special requirements when filing LLC articles of organization. Most common are:

- **Supplemental forms.** An additional legal or tax form may be required to be filed with your articles. For example, a separate designation of registered agent and office, a standard industry code form that you check to show the LLC's primary business, or a state tax form may be included in your LLC materials to be completed and submitted with your articles. These extra forms may be available for downloading from your state website.

- **Publication of notice.** Some states require a pre- or post-filing publication in a legal newspaper of your intention to do business as a limited liability company. A local legal newspaper can handle this.

Your state sheet in Appendix A will alert you to extra formalities that apply when filing articles of organization in your state.

Special Requirements for Licensed Professionals

In some states, licensed professionals can form LLCs as long as they comply with additional requirements or filing formalities. For example, some states allow licensed professionals to form an LLC as long as they file a special form of articles of organization for a Professional LLC and the LLC name ends with the words "Professional Limited Liability Company" or the abbreviations "PLLC" or "P.L.L.C." Your state sheet and state materials should alert you to special requirements, but double check with your profession's state licensing board to be sure.

The special state rules that apply to professional LLCs typically limit LLC membership to licensed professionals only (and, generally, to the particular licensed profession only). Other rules may apply as well—for example, minimum malpractice insurance coverage or bonding may be required for each practicing member.

Typically, lawyers, doctors, accountants, engineers, and health care professionals must abide by these extra rules, but other licensed professions may be subject to these rules, too. To find out whether any special professional LLC rules apply to your licensed profession, call the state board or agency that regulates your profession and ask, "May I form a limited liability company in this state to render licensed professional services of [your field]?" If the answer is yes, ask whether any special requirements apply to operating your professional LLC in the state. If so, ask to be sent a copy of these special rules.

Prepare LLC Articles of Organization

The articles of organization form is your primary formation document: Your LLC comes into existence on the date you successfully file the articles with your state LLC filing office. Here's how to go about preparing it.

Locate Articles for Your State LLC Materials

Most state LLC filing office websites provide LLC articles of organization forms that meet the state's basic statutory requirements. Unless you plan to organize an LLC with a complicated organizational structure (with the help of a lawyer, accountant, or other specialist), the basic state form will work fine. If your state's website does not provide a downloadable form, call your state office to have it mailed to you.

If Your State Does Not Provide Forms: Check the State Sheets

If your state does not provide a fill-in-the-blank form or sample articles or certificate of organization, look at the "Special Instructions and Filing Requirements" section of your state sheet in Appendix A. It lists the required contents of articles and gives you specific wording to use for any tricky items. If you read this information and draft your articles or certificate according to our instructions in "How to Prepare Articles From Scratch," below, we're sure you'll do fine.

> ⓘ **CAUTION**
> **Make sure the statutory requirements are up to date.** Though our state sheets are updated annually, laws change quickly. If you are drafting your own articles or certificate of organization, make sure the statutory requirements listed for your state

are current. To do this, look up the section of your state's LLC act titled "Articles (or "Certificate") of Organization." To check your state's LLC act, use the link listed in your state sheet in Appendix A.

How to Complete Articles of Organization

The basic clauses required in most states' LLC articles of organization are similar. Below, we provide sample language and explanations for provisions you are likely to find in the articles provided by your LLC filing office and required under your state's LLC statutes. You'll find a tear-out form containing all the provisions discussed here in Appendix B.

By following the material below and referring to the specific instructions for preparing articles of organization provided by your LLC office (or the statute that lists the required contents of LLC articles in your state), you should be able to prepare your own articles without difficulty. Here are some hints to make this job easier:

- **Scan our sample articles of organization.** Glancing through the language of our sample articles below will help you get a general idea of the types of provisions included in standard LLC articles of organization. This overview will help you understand the form and instructions provided by your LLC office, or evaluate how each provision can satisfy your state's statutory requirements if you are drafting your own form.

- **Use instructions as guidance.** If you get stuck with a particular article or provision in a state-provided form, refer to our instructions below for a similar item in our sample form.

- **Use the state sheets and the information from your state LLC office.** To locate any special LLC formation requirements in your state, see your state's online information and your state sheet in Appendix A. For example, your state may require you to specify in your articles whether members of your LLC can vote to continue the legal existence of your LLC after the dissociation (the loss of membership rights) of a member; we show each state's statutory requirements for this "default continuation rule" in the state sheets.

- **Use sample articles if you are preparing your articles from scratch.** If you are crafting your own articles of organization based upon the requirements listed in your state's LLC act, you will use one or more of the sample provisions below to prepare your articles. We show how to use our sample article provisions to create articles of organization in "How to Prepare Articles From Scratch."

CD-ROM

The sample LLC articles of organization is included on the CD-ROM at the back of this book.

We'll start at the top of the articles and discuss each part of the form separately. Each provision is shown, followed by explanatory text. The bold information contains instructions for filling in blanks in a given provision.

TIP

Follow state format requirements. Most state LLC filing offices expect articles of organization to be typed or printed on one side of a page only, with letter-size (8$\frac{1}{2}$" x 11") now being the customary page size (though many will still accept 8$\frac{1}{2}$" x 14" legal-sized paper). Make sure the printed text is legible and of good contrast.

Customizing Your Articles of Organization

Although the standard articles of organization discussed in this chapter and the form normally provided by your state will be sufficient for most LLCs, you may wish to include special operating rules or provisions. Ordinarily it is preferable to cover such special rules in your operating agreement, which can be adopted and changed with relative ease, rather than in the articles (amended articles must be refiled with the state LLC office).

You may, however, need to place certain special provisions in the articles for them to be effective. For example, if an LLC wants to adopt the following types of provisions, they must often be included in its articles of organization:

- management of the LLC by designated managers
- appointment of a manager or member by a designated person or group, rather than by all members, or
- indemnification (payment of legal expenses) of LLC members or managers under special provisions of state law.

You won't normally have reason to be concerned with provisions of this sort—but if you do, your state's articles instructions may indicate any special provisions that must be included in the articles to be effective. (The state LLC statute that contains the list of required information in articles almost always lists special items of information that need to be placed in articles, rather than in the operating agreement, if the LLC wishes to adopt them. For further information and for help customizing your articles with special provisions, check your state's LLC statutes or consult an LLC business lawyer.)

Heading of Articles

Articles of Organization
of
_____ [*Name of LLC*] _____

State law does not normally specify any format for the heading of the articles, but it's common practice to give the title of the document, usually "Articles of Organization," followed by the proposed name of the LLC. Some states use a different title for this document—for example, the "Certificate of Formation." If a name other than "Articles of Organization" is used for this form, it will be shown on your state sheet and in your state's articles or articles instructions.

In the blank, fill in the correct, full name of your LLC. Make sure the name you list is exactly the way you want your LLC to be named. As discussed above, we suggest you check the availability of your proposed name and, if appropriate, reserve it prior to filing your articles.

Statement of Statutory Authority

The undersigned natural person(s), of the age of eighteen years or more, acting as organizer(s) of a limited liability company under the State of __*[name of state]*__ Limited Liability Company Act, adopt(s) the following articles of organization __*[or other title for form, such as "Certificate of Formation"]*__ for such limited liability company.

Although not required, it is traditional in many states to include a preliminary statement of statutory authority after the heading to the articles of organization and before the first article. This statement just means that you are filing the articles under the state's laws and intend them to be legally recognized. You will normally see language of this sort on state-provided forms.

Name of Limited Liability Company

Article 1. Name of Limited Liability Company. The name of this limited liability company is __*[name of LLC]*__.

Insert the proposed name of your LLC in the blank. This should be identical to the name listed in the heading.

TIP

Numbering or lettering of articles of organization. State law does not normally specify any particular numbering or lettering scheme for articles. We employ Arabic numerals, but other number or letter sequences are permissible—such as "Article One," "Article I," or "Article A."

Name and Address of Initial Registered Office and Agent

Article 2. Registered Office and Registered Agent. The initial registered office of this limited liability company and the name of its initial registered agent at this address are: __*[name and address of LLC initial registered agent and office]*__.

Most states require that articles of organization include both of the following:

- **The name of the LLC's initial registered agent.** The agent is sometimes called the "agent for service of process." He or she is authorized to receive legal papers on behalf of the LLC. Typically, the agent must be a resident of the state and at least 18 years of age.

- **The address of the initial registered office.** The registered office is the address where the agent maintains a place of business—where papers may be mailed, and where service of process (the delivery of official legal papers) can be personally performed on the agent. The registered office address must be located in the state.

Although the registered office may be different from the principal office of the LLC (the actual office or business location of the LLC) in many states, most LLCs keep things simple and appoint one of the members as the initial agent, showing the principal address of the LLC as the registered office address. Usually, this must be a street address, not a post office box.

Some states supply a separate "Designation of Registered Agent" form (or one with a similar title) to be filed with the articles, which the agent signs to show his or her consent to act as registered agent for the LLC. Other states require only a simple statement at the end of the articles, signed by the initial agent— such as, "The undersigned hereby accepts appointment as registered agent for the above named limited liability company."

TIP

Don't needlessly hire a registered agent company. Most states allow you to designate another business as a registered agent, and some companies specialize in acting as registered agents for an annual fee. Because acting as a registered agent simply involves being available to receive mail (and personal service), most readers will handle this task themselves and need not bother to hire an outside firm.

Some states also require an LLC to designate the Secretary of State or another state official as the person who is entitled to receive legal notices on behalf of the LLC in case the registered agent resigns, cannot be located, or is otherwise unable or unavailable to act as agent for the LLC in the future. In some states, this designation of state official as alternate agent happens automatically as a matter of law; in other states, specific language to this effect must be inserted in the articles. The sample articles provided by your state should include any required language.

Statement of Purposes

Article 3. Statement of Purposes. The purposes for which this limited liability company is organized are:

[list purposes of the LLC business, for example, "to operate a computer repair and retail store, and to engage in any other lawful business for which limited liability companies may be organized in this state."]

Many states require a statement of purposes in the articles of organization. Some say that a general statement of purposes is sufficient—that is, "to engage in any lawful business for which limited liability companies may be organized in this state." Others states require a brief statement of the specific business purposes of the LLC—usually a short and straightforward description of the particular type of business to be operated by the LLC.

If a specific statement of business purposes is required, it is often a good idea to follow it with a general statement of purposes—allowing the LLC "to engage in any other lawful business for which limited liability companies may be organized in this state." Adding this general language makes it clear to the organizers, future LLC members, and others who may read your articles that your LLC, while formed for one particular purpose, can engage in other business activities (but your LLC can engage in any lawful business whether or not you include this language). The sample language above contains a dual-purpose statement of this sort.

Here are some other examples of how to complete this statement:

- "to open and operate a car stereo and security alarm sales and service facility, and to engage in any other lawful business for which limited liability companies may be organized in this state"

- "to purchase, sell, and otherwise invest in real property and commercial interests in real property, and to engage in any other lawful business for which limited liability companies may be organized in this state," or

- "to provide financial consulting services to individuals and businesses, and to engage in any other lawful business for which limited liability companies may be organized in this state."

Management of the LLC

Article 4. Management and Names and Addresses of Initial _["Members" or "Managers"]_ . The management of this limited liability company is reserved to the _["members" or "managers."]_ . The names and addresses of its initial _["members" or "managers."]_ are: _[names and addresses of members or managers]_ .

Articles of organization usually state whether the LLC will be member-managed or manager-managed (discussed in detail in Chapter 2). Here's a recap of what these terms mean:

- **Member-managed LLC.** This means the LLC's members will manage the business. It is the default rule in most states—if you don't specify how your LLC will be managed in your articles, your LLC will be managed by all the members.

- **Manager-managed LLC.** Some LLCs decide to specifically appoint some of the members and/or nonmembers as managers of the

LLC. If so, the articles must usually state that management is reserved to managers, and list the names and addresses of the specially designated managers. Normally, just one manager is required. If managers are listed, members' names and addresses usually are not required, but in some states, you may be asked to list the names and addresses of members and managers separately (even if some individuals function in both capacities).

In each of the first sets of blanks, indicate whether your LLC will be run by "members" or "managers." All states now allow an LLC to be formed with just one member. You may of course have more members. In the indicated space, list the names and addresses of the LLC's initial members or managers. Normally, street (not post office box) addresses must be shown.

Principal Place of Business

Article 5. Principal Place of Business of the Limited Liability Company. The principal place of business of the limited liability company shall be: _[street address of principal office of LLC]_ .

The articles of organization often specify the principal place of business of the LLC. Though this location may be within or outside the state, most LLCs will show the address of its main office located in the state. Technically, the principal place of business listed in the articles is one of the places where the business may be sued (brought to court), not necessarily the place where most of the business operations of the LLC are performed. For most smaller LLCs, there's only one place of business, and you will list it here.

Duration of the LLC

Article 6. Period of Duration of the Limited Liability Company. The period of duration of the limited liability company shall be: ___ [*"perpetual" or "from the date these articles of organization are filed through and including (give future date or state a period of years)"*] ___.

As explained earlier, in some states, the articles of organization must include a provision specifying the duration of the LLC. Your state's articles form, articles instructions, or statute for the contents of articles will tell you if this provision is required for your state, and if so, how you must fill it in.

In most states that require you to state the duration of the LLC, it's permissible to provide for a "perpetual" (unlimited) duration in this provision. If you have this option, you probably will want to take it—so your LLC automatically continues into the future until your members vote to dissolve it.

Some states won't let you provide a perpetual duration for your LLC. Instead, you must limit its duration to a number of years from the date the articles are filed or to a specific date in the future. Some states even say that this date can't be more than 30 or 50 years into the future. Don't worry about any of these limitations. If you must limit the life of your LLC in your articles under state rules, choose a date that is as far in the future as you can. If your LLC is still around after whatever termination date you are forced to select, you or your LLC successors can file an amendment extending the legal life of the LLC for as long as your state's laws allow.

Signatures of Persons Forming the LLC

In Witness Whereof, the undersigned organizer(s) of this limited liability company has (have) signed these articles of organization on the date indicated.

Date: _____

Signature(s):

[typed or printed name] , Organizer

[typed or printed name] , Organizer

[typed or printed name] , Organizer

[typed or printed name] , Organizer

[typed or printed name] , Organizer

States have various signature requirements for LLC articles of organization. In most states, one person may act as organizer of the LLC by signing the form and submitting the articles for filing. The usual practice is to have one of the initial members who is listed in the articles of organization date and sign the form as the LLC organizer. If managers are listed instead of members in the articles, a manager will usually sign the form and act as organizer of the LLC.

TIP

If your LLC's name was reserved, the person who reserved your LLC name with the state should sign your articles as one of its organizers. If he or she is not available, check with your LLC filing office, which may allow you to file a transfer of reservation of name or similar form, signed by the person who reserved your LLC name.

The signature statement on your state articles of organization may look a little different from the sample form. For example, in some states, people must sign under penalty of perjury.

In a few states, the articles must be notarized—signed in the presence of a notary public, who fills out a concluding notarization statement and impresses a notarial seal at the bottom of the form (notary statements vary from state to state). Notaries are found in real estate offices and other businesses, or simply by looking up "Notary" in a local telephone directory. Notary fees are usually modest.

If your state does not provide a fill-in-the-blank form, the articles instructions posted on your state's website should tell you who needs to sign your articles and how this should be done, including any required language or notary procedure.

LLC Organizer Does Not Have to Be a Member or Manager

Typically, the organizer does not need to be a member or associated with the LLC in any way; in most states he or she must be at least 18 years of age. What the states have in mind here is to allow a lawyer to prepare, sign, and file your articles for you—but you will usually tend to this task yourself by selecting at least one of your initial members or managers as your organizer.

Sample Completed Articles of Organization

To help you tie all this information together, we include a sample completed articles of organization form below. The articles are prepared for a fictitious business, "Luxor Light LLC," a three-member LLC for a lighting fixture business. The sample is relatively standard; note that in Article 4, Luxor Light has opted to be managed by members (the option most LLCs will choose).

Articles of Organization
of

__Luxor Lighting LLC__

The undersigned natural persons, of the age of eighteen years or more, acting as organizers of a limited liability company under the Anystate Limited Liability Company Act, adopt the following articles of organization for such limited liability company.

Article 1. Name of Limited Liability Company. The name of this limited liability company is

Luxor Light LLC.

Article 2. Registered Office and Registered Agent. The initial registered office of this limited liability company and the name of its initial registered agent at this address are:

Robert Johnston, 1515 San Estudillo, Anycity, Anystate, 00000.

Article 3. Statement of Purposes. The purposes for which this limited liability company is organized are:

to operate a custom home and commercial lighting and fixture store, and to engage in any other lawful business for which limited liability companies may be organized in this state.

Article 4. Management and Names and Addresses of Initial Members. The management of this limited liability company is reserved to the members. The names and addresses of its initial members are:

Robert Johnston, 1515 San Estudillo, Anycity, Anystate, 00000

Rebecca Johnston, 1515 San Estudillo, Anycity, Anystate, 00000

Gregory Luxor, 3021 Los Avenidos, Anycity, Anystate, 00000.

Article 5. Principal Place of Business of the Limited Liability Company. The principal place of business of the limited liability company shall be:

56 Rue de Campanille, Anycity, Anystate, 00000.

Article 6. Period of Duration of the Limited Liability Company. The period of duration of the limited liability company shall be: _perpetual_ .

In Witness Whereof, the undersigned organizer of this Limited Liability Company has signed these articles of organization on the date indicated.

Date: _11/05/20xx_

Signature(s): _Gregory Luxor_

_____ Gregory Luxor _____ , Organizer

How to Prepare Articles From Scratch

As we've noted, not all states provide blank forms or sample articles of organization. If your state does not provide one, we list the required contents of articles or a certificate of organization in the "Special Instructions and Filing Requirements" section of your state sheet in Appendix A. This information is drawn from each state's LLC statute, which contains the technical requirements for articles or a certificate—we translate any technical or tricky terms for you. Here is an example of how to use your state's requirements for articles, together with our sample articles, to craft your own LLC articles of organization.

Hypothetical LLC articles statute:

Formation of a Limited Liability Company

To form a liability company, you must file articles of organization pursuant to Article 12.16 of the Limited Liability Company Act. The articles of organization must minimally set forth:

1. The name of the limited liability company. The name must contain the words "Limited Liability Company" or "Limited Company" or the abbreviations "L.L.C.," "LLC," "LC," "L.C.," or "Ltd. Co." The name of a limited liability company cannot be the same as or deceptively similar to that of another limited liability company, corporation, limited partnership, name reservation, or registration.

2. The period of duration, which may be perpetual, or a specific date of termination.

3. The purpose for which the limited liability company is organized, which may be stated to be, or include, the transaction of any or all lawful business for which limited liability companies may be organized.

4. The street address of its initial registered office in this state and the name of its initial registered agent at such address.

5. If the limited liability company is to be managed by a manager or managers, a statement that the company is to be managed by a manager or managers and the names and addresses of the initial manager or managers. If the management of a limited liability company is reserved to the members, a statement that the limited liability company will not have managers and the names and addresses of its initial members.

6. The name and address of each organizer.

Here is a summary of how we used the sample articles of the previous section to craft articles to meet the requirements of the hypothetical statute, above.

Note that in Article 4, below, we add a statement that the LLC shall not have managers. The statute says that this language is necessary if management is reserved to the members (normally, a statement that the management is reserved to members is enough). This is the only substantive change necessary to make our sample articles fit the hypothetical statute.

Articles of Organization
of

[name of LLC]

The undersigned natural persons, of the age of eighteen years or more, acting as organizers of a limited liability company under the Hypothetical Limited Liability Company Act, adopt the following articles of organization for such limited liability company.

Article 1. Name of Limited Liability Company. The name of this limited liability company is

[name of LLC]   .

Article 2. Registered Office and Registered Agent. The initial registered office of this limited liability company and the name of its initial registered agent at this address are:

[name and address of registered agent and office]   .

Article 3. Statement of Purposes. The purposes for which this limited liability company is organized are:

["to engage in any lawful business for which limited liability companies may be

organized in this state"]   .

Article 4. Management and Names and Addresses of Initial Members. The management of this limited liability company is reserved to the members, and it shall not have managers. The names and addresses of its initial members are:

[name(s) and address(es) of initial members]   .

Article 5. Period of Duration of the Limited Liability Company. The period of duration of the limited liability company shall be: *"perpetual"*   .

Article 6. Names and Addresses of Organizers. The names and addresses of the organizers of this LLC are:

[name(s) and address(es) of organizer(s), typically one or more of the initial members] .

In Witness Whereof, the undersigned organizer(s) of this Limited Liability Company has (have) signed these articles of organization on the date indicated.

Date: _____ [date] _____

Signature(s): _____ [signature(s) of organizer(s)] _____

_____ [typed or printed name] _____ , Organizer

Finalize and File Your Articles of Organization

Read over your articles of organization one last time to make sure they're correct and have been properly signed.

If you downloaded an articles form, it is normally provided in Adobe Acrobat pdf format. You may need to print the form out and then fill in the blanks with a typewriter or by printing neatly. Alternatively, you may be able to fill the form in online and then print and mail it. As a third alternative, an increasing number of states now allow you to fill in and submit the form online without printing or mailing.

File your articles of organization with your state LLC filing office following your state's official instructions. (Again, any special filing requirements or procedures are also listed in your state sheet.) Filing is usually done by mail, although many offices will accept articles in person. If you mail your articles, remember to keep an extra copy in case the original is lost in the mail.

TIP

Check your state website for online filing (see Appendix A). Some states now let you fill in and file your articles online. If you have the option, you should use it because it's much easier and eliminates the time and trouble of printing, filling in, and mailing paper articles to your state.

In Appendix B, we include a filing letter that you may wish to use to submit your articles of organization to the state LLC filing office (if you file by mail); if your state office website provides a cover letter, use it instead of our form cover letter. If you use our form cover letter, complete it following the sample and special instructions below. The address of your state LLC filing office and the amount of the required filing fee are shown on your state sheet in Appendix A, but your state website will have the most current fee information.

CD-ROM

The articles filing letter is included on the CD-ROM at the back of this book.

TIP

If you have problems filing your articles. The filing office may return your articles and indicate which items need correction (your check should be held until you fix the problem). Often the problem is technical, not substantive, and easy to fix. If the problem is more complicated, such as an improper or insufficient LLC purpose clause, you may be able to solve the problem by rereading the instructions earlier in this chapter and those provided online for preparing articles. If you get stuck, you will need to do a little research or obtain further help from an LLC lawyer who's experienced in drafting and filing LLC articles of organization in your state. (See Chapter 8.)

Sample LLC Articles Filing Letter

[date]

[name and address of your state's LLC filing office]

LLC Filings Office:

I enclose an original and ___ _[number]_ ___ ❶ copies of the proposed Articles of Organization of _____ _[name of LLC]_ _____, ❷ a proposed domestic limited liability company.

Please file the Articles of Organization and return a file-stamped copy of the original Articlesor other receipt, acknowledgment, or proof of filing to me at the address below.

A check/money order in the amount of $ _[filing fee amount—see your state sheet]_ , ❸ made payable to your office, for total filing and processing fees is enclosed.

☐ The above LLC name was reserved for my use ___ _[if applicable, insert "according_ ___ ___ to reservation number" _and the reservation number]_ ___, issued on ___ _[date of issuance]_ ___ . ❺

Sincerely,

[your signature]

[your printed or typed name] ___, Organizer

[your address and phone number]

Enclosures: articles of organization; check

Special Instructions

❶ In some states, you need only submit an original of the articles—the LLC office will file the original and send you a file-stamped copy or file receipt. In other states, you need to submit the original and one or more copies. The LLC filing office will file the original and file-stamp and return one or more copies to you.

Depending on the state, an additional fee may be charged for submitting more than one copy of your articles for file-stamping. One copy (plus the original) should be sufficient in most cases; you can always make copies of this file-stamped copy to keep in your LLC records book or give to others as the need arises.

❷ Enter the proposed name for your LLC (the name stated in your articles of organization). As explained above, it can be risky to file articles with a name that you haven't checked ahead of time. We recommend checking the availability of your proposed name before filing articles or reserving the name for your exclusive use. If you don't, and the desired name is unavailable, your articles will be returned unfiled.

❸ Include a check (or money order) for the total fees, made payable to the state or state office. Remember to consult your state sheet in Appendix A and your state website for particulars.

❹ If you reserved your LLC name, check the box. Then fill in the blanks to show the certificate number and/or date of issuance of your reservation of LLC name. In some states, the LLC filing office simply sends you a file-stamped copy of your reservation letter—if so, just fill in the file-stamped date of the name reservation letter in the second blank, and include a copy of your file-stamped reservation certificate with this cover letter.

❺ The person (or one of the persons) who is acting as organizer of your LLC—by signing your articles—should sign this filing letter. If an LLC name was reserved, the person who reserved the name should sign this letter—and the articles of organization as well—since the LLC name is reserved for this person's use.

What to Do After Filing Articles of Organization

Once you've sent in your articles for filing, your next step is to wait. The LLC filing office will make sure the LLC name is available for use and that your articles conform to law. If there are no problems, the office will mail you a file-stamped copy of your articles or a filing receipt.

Don't forget to congratulate yourself. Once your articles of organization have been successfully filed, your business is a legally recognized limited liability company.

Although filing articles of organization is all you are legally required to do to establish the legal existence of your LLC, make sure you go at least one step further and prepare an operating agreement for your LLC—see Chapter 5 if your LLC will be member-managed or Chapter 6 if your LLC will be manager-managed. This agreement sets out the basic legal rules for operating your LLC.

Finally, don't miss Chapter 7, where we cover some of the ins and outs of tending to your new LLC. ●

Prepare an LLC Operating Agreement for Your Member-Managed LLC

If you've turned to this chapter, we assume you have already formed or are in the process of forming your LLC by preparing and filing articles of organization with your state LLC filing office, as explained in Chapter 4. Here, you'll learn how to prepare a fill-in-the-blanks operating agreement for a member-managed LLC.

SKIP AHEAD

Manager-managed LLCs. Most LLCs will be member-managed—that is, managed by all members. If, however, you plan to adopt a manager-managed LLC (one managed by only some LLC members and/or by nonmembers), you'll need an operating agreement that provides for manager-management. Chapter 6 will cover that in detail, but you'll need to read the first two sections of this chapter first—they discuss areas of LLC operation not covered elsewhere, as well as information about how to customize your operating agreement.

Scope of Our Basic LLC Operating Agreements

The tear-out operating agreements we supply in this book are relatively straightforward forms that cover basic LLC issues. Our agreements simply help you set up your LLC under sensible ground rules and contain necessary reminders about restrictions that apply to most LLCs under state law. You may discover that they are considerably shorter than the longer LLC agreements available commercially or from a lawyer, so you may want to hire one if you think you need to significantly customize the agreement.

There are two major areas of LLC operations that our agreements do not cover, however. Let's briefly look at each.

Special Capital Account Provisions

Capital account provisions set forth the types and amounts of capital contributed by your original members. If you read a lawyer- or accountant-prepared LLC operating agreement, you'll usually see lists of complicated capital account definitions and provisions (language that specifies how members' capital contributions and distributions are to be handled under a range of circumstances). This special language can be important if you decide to split profits and losses among your LLC members in ratios that are different from the percentage of capital each member contributes to your LLC. (For a fuller discussion of this issue, see Chapter 3.)

For our purposes, and for most readers of this book, adding special provisions to handle these "special allocations" of profits and losses is not necessary, so we do not include them in our tear-out operating agreements. If you think you'd like to include special allocation provisions in your operating agreement, ask your tax adviser for help.

SEE AN EXPERT

Consider getting help drafting other special financial provisions. A legal or tax adviser can also help you prepare special financial provisions of any sort—for example, to set up a special class of membership that gets a guaranteed share of LLC profits or losses or to establish a special schedule for distribution of LLC profits to members before liquidation.

Buy-Sell Provisions

An important and sometimes complicated aspect of forming any business is deciding what happens when a member wants to sell his or her interest. Here are some examples of the kinds of issues that may arise:

- **"Right of first refusal" issues.** Does an owner who wishes to sell out have to offer to sell his or her interest to the other owners before selling to an outsider? Must the other owners buy that interest for the amount an outsider is ready to pay?

- **Valuation questions.** When a member (or the member's estate) wishes to sell to other members, how will the interest be valued? Should an appraiser resolve this issue at the time of sale? Or should the value of membership interests be established ahead of time in the LLC operating agreement—if so, should the value be based upon the book (net asset) value of the business, a multiple of the earnings of the business, or some other formula?

- **When and how should a departing LLC member who is being bought out be paid?** Should payment be made all in a lump sum or in installments? This is an important question, since your LLC or its other members may not have sufficient cash or borrowing power to come up with the needed buyout funds right away. On the other hand, a departing LLC member (or the member's estate) will want to be paid as soon as possible. If the buyout is paid in installments, should the LLC be charged interest?

- **Life insurance.** Should the buyout of a deceased owner be funded with life insurance purchased ahead of time by the LLC or each of the other members?

- **Does it matter why or when a member is being bought out?** For example, if a member calls it quits and wishes to transfer his or her interest back to the LLC after only six months with the LLC, should he or she receive a smaller buyback price than a member who stays with the LLC for five years? What about a member who is expelled? What about a member who suffers a debilitating illness or dies?

Most businesses decide to tackle these issues down the road. They reason that, for now, it's enough to know that an appraiser can be called in to establish a fair value of a member's interests if a member wishes to sell out. (You don't even need to say this in your operating agreement; you can just call in an appraiser when the time comes.) Our operating agreements do include basic transfer restrictions, which may be adequate, at least in the short term. These transfer restrictions require the approval of all or a majority of the nontransferring members before admitting a new person as a member in the LLC.

However, other detail-oriented business owners decide to ask and answer all these questions and spell out their conclusions as part of the membership restrictions in their initial operating agreement. If you decide to go the extra distance and include buy-sell or buyout provisions in your initial operating agreement, you can ask your LLC legal adviser to put together provisions that will work for you. Alternately, you can consult Nolo's book *Business Buyout Agreements: A Step-by-Step Guide for Co-Owners,* by Bethany Laurence and Anthony Mancuso, which provides step-by-step instructions and forms for preparing your buy-sell, or buyout, provisions.

Customizing Your LLC Operating Agreement

As you create your own LLC operating agreement, you may want to add or change provisions to suit your needs. Modifying or writing LLC operating agreement provisions is not akin to brain surgery, and you can ordinarily do much of it yourself—just use common sense and your own sound business judgment.

If you wonder whether state law has established any guidelines you must follow in an area of your LLC's operation, simply check your state's LLC act to make sure your rule does not conflict with a specific statute (use the link shown in your state sheet in Appendix A). You may also want to ask a legal or tax adviser about the validity or effect of your custom-crafted provisions. We think this is a good idea for any changes you feel are important—such as special voting rights for certain members or special voting requirements to amend your articles of organization or to approve the dissolution of the LLC. (For guidance on self-help research and finding an LLC legal or tax adviser, see Chapter 8.)

Here's a brief summary of the different types of changes you can make to the included agreement, and a quick assessment of how safe you are in making them on your own:

- **Internal matters.** Internal LLC housekeeping provisions are your own business. For example, you may choose to specify how and when member or manager meetings will be held or who qualifies to be an officer or employee in your LLC. If you want to put rules such as these in your operating agreement, you should be safe doing so; state LLC statutes and the tax rules have little or nothing to say about internal issues of this sort.

- **Legal procedures.** If you wish to change a legal procedure—such as the number of votes necessary to dissolve your LLC, amend your articles of organization or effect a similar structural change—check to see if legal rules affect your desired change. If you browse your state's LLC act online, it should take just a few minutes to see if state law has placed limitations or restrictions on the provisions you are thinking of adopting.

- **Tax matters.** Tax matters are a little trickier. We recommend showing your LLC tax adviser any changes to your operating agreement that may have tax effects—for example, provisions dealing with the sale of assets, allocation or distribution of profits, and the like. A tax adviser can tell you if your proposed operating agreement changes are good, bad, or neutral from a tax perspective.

EXAMPLE 1:

Hank forms an LLC with friend and former business partner Max. Hank has cash and Max doesn't. Max signs a note, promising to pay his investment to the LLC (together with interest) over time. It's decided that even though each person ultimately will contribute equally to the capitalization of the LLC, Hank should get an extra share of the profits for putting up cash in one lump sum at the start of the business operations and that Max's capital account probably should be handled differently because he hasn't contributed anything to the LLC yet. They ask their tax adviser to check their operating agreement, because special allocations (a disproportionate division) of profits may have tax consequences and require the addition of special provisions to their operating agreement. Their tax adviser adds IRS special allocations language to the agreement that restates technical tax regulations related to sharing profits and losses disproportionately. The adviser also tells them that IRS regulations say that Max's capital account should be credited only if and when, and to the extent, that he makes payments to the LLC under the terms of his promissory note. In other words, his capital account—and his basis in his LLC interest—will start at zero.

EXAMPLE 2:

Kenneth and Francine decide to lower the membership vote requirement in their LLC member-managed operating agreement to approve the transfer of LLC interests to outsiders. First, they check their state sheet in Appendix A, where we provide the basic state rules and whether the state lets LLC organizers change these rules. They ask their legal adviser to make sure their changes comport to any recent changes made to their state's LLC act (or they go online to check the relevant code section in their state LLC act themselves).

How to Prepare a Member-Managed LLC Operating Agreement

Appendix B contains a basic operating agreement for a member-managed limited liability company (the first of two agreements in Appendix B). If you wish to prepare this form, tear it out now so you can follow along, making sure that you don't miss any pages or inadvertently take pages from the other (manager-managed) operating agreement, also in Appendix B.

We'll start at the top of the agreement and work our way through it. We provide instructions for filling out items in the sample agreement, below. To help you complete some of the more complicated information, we provide additional instructions in the special instructions that accompany the sample operating agreement. Special instructions are numbered sequentially as they occur in the sample agreement. The first page of the sample agreement appears on the next page.

Special Instructions

❶ Insert the name of your LLC exactly as shown in your articles of organization.

❷ Insert a date that is on or after the date all your members sign this operating agreement (you'll have your operating agreement signed as the last step in preparing this form). If you aren't sure how long it will take to do this, simply insert the words "the last date of signing shown at the end of this agreement."

❸ All members will sign the agreement at the end of this process.

❹ Insert the date and year your articles of organization or certificate of formation was filed with your state LLC filing office. In most cases, this date will be shown as the "file-stamped" date on the first page of the filed articles or certificate, or on a filing receipt mailed to you from the state LLC filing office.

❺ This paragraph states that your LLC is allowed to do business under another name—one that is different from the formal LLC name stated in your articles of organization and operating agreement. In that event, you may need to register a fictitious or assumed business name with the state, as well as each county where you will use the fictitious business name. (See Chapter 7 for more information.)

❻ Most articles of organization specify the LLC's registered office and agent—if yours do, just copy the information from your articles of organization into this blank. (We cover this in Chapter 4.) Typically, the registered office address must be a street address (not a post office box) located in the state. Most states require the agent to be at least 18 years of age and a state resident. Usually, a founding member of the LLC will act as initial agent and show the principal office address of the LLC as the registered office address.

Operating Agreement for
Member-Managed Limited Liability Company

I. Preliminary Provisions

[*Here we address preliminary matters, such as the effective date of the agreement, the name of the LLC, and other basic information.*]

(1) **Effective Date:** This operating agreement of ____[*name of LLC*] ❶ ____ _____ , effective ____[*date*] ❷ _____ , is adopted by the members whose signatures appear at the end of this agreement. ❸

(2) **Formation:** This limited liability company (LLC) was formed by filing articles of organization, a certificate of formation, or a similar organizational document with the LLC filing office of the state of ____[*state of formation*]____ on ____[*date of filing articles of organization, certificate of formation, or similar organizational document*]____ ❹ . A copy of this organizational document has been placed in the LLC's records book.

(3) **Name:** The formal name of this LLC is as stated above. However, this LLC may do business under a different name by complying with the state's fictitious or assumed business name statutes and procedures. ❺

(4) **Registered Office and Agent:** The registered office of this LLC and the registered agent at this address are as follows: ____[*name and address of registered agent and office*]____ _____ .

The registered office and agent may be changed from time to time as the members may see fit, by filing a change of registered agent or office form with the state LLC filing office. It will not be necessary to amend this provision of the operating agreement if and when such a change is made. ❻

(5) **Business Purposes:** The specific business purposes and activities contemplated by the founders of this LLC at the time of initial signing of this agreement consist of the following: [*state the specific business purposes and activities you foresee for your LLC*] ❼ _____ _____ _____ .

It is understood that the foregoing statement of purposes shall not serve as a limitation on the powers or abilities of this LLC, which shall be permitted to engage in any and all lawful business activities. If this LLC intends to engage in business activities outside the state of its formation that require the qualification of the LLC in other states, it shall obtain such qualification before engaging in such out-of-state activities.

As this paragraph specifies, you may change your LLC's registered agent and office by filing a form with your state LLC filing office (and paying a small fee). If and when you do so, there is no need to go back and change this information in your operating agreement.

❼ In plain English, specify the business purposes of your LLC. You may have listed specific business purposes in your articles of organization. If so, you can copy that information into these blanks.

Mostly, this statement is meant to let your own members know what your plans are for the LLC's business operations, so feel free to expand your statement of purposes to provide as much detail as you want. Here are some examples:

- "to open and operate a car stereo and security alarm sales and service facility"
- "to purchase, sell, and otherwise invest in real property and commercial interests in real property," or
- "to provide financial consulting services to individuals and businesses."

❽ Many states require the articles of organization to specify the duration of the legal existence of the LLC, as discussed in Chapter 4. If so, insert this same time period here. If you had to specify a limited duration for your LLC under state law, remember: You can always amend your articles to extend the legal life of your LLC as the termination date approaches.

If your articles are silent on this issue, your state most likely does not require you to limit the duration of your LLC's legal existence, and you can insert the word "perpetual" in the blank. Your state's LLC information should indicate if your state has any special rules for limiting the life of your LLC.

Finally, notice that the concluding sentence of this provision makes it clear that the LLC can always be terminated by a vote of the membership and as otherwise allowed by law. (See "VI. Dissolution Provisions: (1) Events That Trigger Dissolution of the LLC," in this operating agreement, and the corresponding special instructions ❸❽ through ❹❶, below.) We include this sentence as a reminder that members have the ultimate say as to when the LLC will wind up its affairs and dissolve.

❾ Although there is no legal requirement that you insert this statement of nonliability in your agreement, we think it's a good idea to include it as a basic restatement of this important state law protection.

❿ This paragraph authorizes the LLC to reimburse its founders for LLC formation expenses advanced by members, such as filing fees, legal fees, and tax fees.

Also included is a reminder that Sections 195 and 709 of the Internal Revenue Code allow businesses to deduct up to $5,000 each of organizational and start-up expenses, respectively, in their first year, then to amortize (deduct over time) the remainder of the expenses over the next 15 years. There are special rules that kick in if the expenses exceed $50,000. Your tax adviser can tell you more about these important tax elections and how to implement each of them on your first and subsequent LLC informational tax return.

⓫ This provision makes it clear that all members will manage your LLC. If you want to provide for management by some, but not all, members, you need to adopt the management agreement covered in Chapter 6, not this agreement. For a discussion of this important management decision, see "Responsibility for Managing an LLC" in Chapter 2.

(6) **Duration of LLC:** The duration of this LLC shall be   ["*perpetual*" *or any specific*
termination date or term of years for the LLC, as specified in the articles of organization] .
Further, this LLC shall terminate when a proposal to dissolve the LLC is adopted by the
membership of this LLC or when this LLC is otherwise terminated in accordance with law. **8**

II. Membership Provisions

[*Here we cover provisions that deal with the rights and responsibilities of your
LLC's members.*]

(1) **Nonliability of Members:** No member of this LLC shall be personally liable for the
expenses, debts, obligations, or liabilities of the LLC; or for claims made against it. **9**

(2) **Reimbursement for Organizational Costs:** Members shall be reimbursed by the LLC
for organizational expenses paid by the members. The LLC shall be authorized to elect to
deduct and amortize organizational expenses and start-up expenditures as permitted by
the Internal Revenue Code and as may be advised by the LLC's tax adviser. **10**

(3) **Management:** This LLC shall be managed exclusively by all of its members. **11**

(4) **Members' Percentage Interests:** A member's percentage interest in this LLC shall be
computed as a fraction, the numerator of which is the total of a member's capital account
and the denominator of which is the total of all capital accounts of all members. This
fraction shall be expressed in this agreement as a percentage, which shall be called each
member's "percentage interest" in this LLC. **12**

(5) **Membership Voting:** Except as otherwise may be required by the articles of
organization, certificate of formation, or a similar organizational document; by other
provisions of this operating agreement; or under the laws of this state, each member
shall vote on any matter submitted to the membership for approval in proportion to the
member's percentage interest in this LLC. Further, unless defined otherwise for a particular
provision of this operating agreement, the phrase "majority of members" means the vote
of members whose combined votes equal more than 50% of the votes of all members in
this LLC, and a majority of members, so defined, may approve any item of business brought
before the membership for a vote unless a different vote is required under this operating
agreement or state law. **13**

(6) **Compensation:** Members shall not be paid as members of the LLC for performing
any duties associated with such membership, including management of the LLC. Members
may be paid, however, for any services rendered in any other capacity for the LLC, whether
as officers, employees, independent contractors, or otherwise. **14**

12 This paragraph defines an important LLC formula: the calculation of each member's percentage interest in the LLC. This percentage will be used later in the agreement to:

- allocate profits and losses of the LLC to members

- allocate voting rights among the members

- distribute assets of the LLC when it is liquidated, and

- value a member's interest when it is sold to an outsider or back to the LLC.

This percentage is arrived at by computing a fraction that reflects the proportion of each member's capital account to the total of all members' capital accounts. Each member's capital account starts with the amount of money or value of property he or she contributed at the outset of the LLC, plus any additions to or minus any distributions from or other adjustments to this account.

EXAMPLE:

Barbara, Bill, Fred, Francis, and Mike start their LLC by each contributing $5,000 cash. Each member's capital account currently shows a positive $5,000 balance and each member has a 20% percentage interest in the LLC. This figure is the result of dividing each member's $5,000 capital account balance by the $25,000 total capital account balance for all members, resulting in the fraction 1/5, expressed as a percentage interest of 20%. The percentage interests of the members will be listed in Section IV (Capital Provisions) of the agreement (see Instruction **25**, below). (According to subsequent provisions in the agreement, each person is allocated 20% of the profits and losses of the LLC and is entitled to a 20% share of the LLC's total voting power.)

SEE AN EXPERT

You may base interests in your LLC disproportionately. For example, you could decide that anyone who contributes cash to your LLC is entitled to a 10% increase in the standard percentage interest (with other members' interests reduced accordingly). If you wish to come up with your own method, ask your tax adviser to make sure that you will meet the requirements of IRS regulations relating to special allocations of profits and losses discussed in detail in Chapter 3.

13 This provision gives each member voting power equal to his or her percentage interest in the LLC—for instance, a 10% member gets a 10% vote on any matter. This is standard practice, although you can base voting rights on some other measure if you wish. Here are some possibilities:

- each member gets one vote on all membership matters—known as per capita voting

- members get different numbers of votes each—you can even decide to make one or more members nonvoting members by specifying that they have zero votes, or

- each member's vote depends on his or her share in the profits of the LLC (if the members' share of profits, or "profits interests" differ from percentage interests).

If you decide to opt for your own membership voting scheme, delete this paragraph and substitute your own wording. For example, if a four-member LLC wishes to specify specific voting power for three members, and make the fourth a nonvoting member, it could replace the standard provision in the agreement with the following wording:

(7) Members' Meetings: The LLC shall not provide for regular members' meetings. However, any member may call a meeting by communicating his or her wish to schedule a meeting to all other members. Such notification may be in person or in writing, or by telephone, facsimile machine, or other form of electronic communication reasonably expected to be received by a member, and the other members shall then agree, either personally, in writing, or by telephone, facsimile machine, or other form of electronic communication to the member calling the meeting, to meet at a mutually acceptable time and place. Notice of the business to be transacted at the meeting need not be given to members by the member calling the meeting, and any business may be discussed and conducted at the meeting.

If all members cannot attend a meeting, it shall be postponed to a date and time when all members can attend, unless all members who do not attend have agreed in writing to the holding of the meeting without them. If a meeting is postponed, and the postponed meeting cannot be held either because all members do not attend the postponed meeting or the nonattending members have not signed a written consent to allow the postponed meeting to be held without them, a second postponed meeting may be held at a date and time announced at the first postponed meeting. The date and time of the second postponed meeting shall also be communicated to any members not attending the first postponed meeting. The second postponed meeting may be held without the attendance of all members as long as a majority of the percentage interests of the membership of this LLC is in attendance at the second postponed meeting. Written notice of the decisions or approvals made at this second postponed meeting shall be mailed or delivered to each nonattending member promptly after the holding of the second postponed meeting. **⓯**

Written minutes of the discussions and proposals presented at a members' meeting, and the votes taken and matters approved at such meeting, shall be taken by one of the members or a person designated at the meeting. A copy of the minutes of the meeting shall be placed in the LLC's records book after the meeting. **⓰**

(8) Membership Certificates: This LLC shall be authorized to obtain and issue certificates representing or certifying membership interests in this LLC. Each certificate shall show the name of the LLC and the name of the member, and state that the person named is a member of the LLC and is entitled to all the rights granted members of the LLC under the articles of organization, certificate of formation, or a similar organizational document; this operating agreement; and provisions of law. Each membership certificate shall be consecutively numbered and signed by one or more officers of this LLC. The certificates shall include any additional information considered appropriate for inclusion by the members on membership certificates.

Except as otherwise may be required by the articles of organization, certificate of formation, or a similar organizational document; by other provisions of this operating agreement; or under the laws of this state, the members of this LLC shall have the following voting power:

Member 1: 1 vote

Member 2: 2 votes

Member 3: 2 votes

Member 4: 0 votes

Further, unless defined otherwise for a particular provision of this operating agreement, the phrase "majority of members" means the vote of members whose combined votes equal more than 50% of the votes of all members in this LLC, and a majority of members, so defined, may approve any item of business brought before the membership for a vote unless a different vote is required under this operating agreement or state law.

TIP

Special voting rules may apply to transfers of membership or when agreeing to continue the LLC when a member leaves. Some states still require specific membership approval procedures, even though they no longer matter under the federal tax rules. These special voting rules in your operation agreement will take precedence if they conflict with any of the provisions of the basic LLC membership voting rule specified here.

⓮ This paragraph says that members will not be paid in their capacity as members or member-managers of the LLC. It does, however, allow compensation in any other capacity—for example, the LLC may pay members who also serve as LLC officers, staff, salaried personnel, or independent contractors.

Sally and Joe are the only two members of their member-managed LLC. Both actively operate the LLC, Sally as president and Joe as sales manager. They receive salaries for their day-to-day work, but don't receive any extra compensation simply for signing up and legally functioning as members (and member-managers) of their LLC.

⓯ Especially if you have previously been involved in a small corporation, you may be surprised that the operating agreement doesn't require regular membership meetings. We don't require meetings for two reasons:

- Most LLC members naturally will prefer to spend their time taking care of business, not holding and documenting formal LLC meetings. After all, you and your business associates can schedule and hold meetings for any purpose when and as you need, without having to treat them as formal LLC membership meetings.

- When you do need a formal meeting to approve an important legal formality that should be recorded in your LLC records, you can call one as provided in this clause.

Most state statutes are silent as to whether and how members' meetings are called and held. If your state law does deal with this, the state law LLC meeting provisions are usually default rules only, so you are usually free to change them in your LLC operating agreement. To learn what, if anything, your state has to say on this subject, scan your state's LLC act. Particularly, look for a section of law titled "Meetings of Members." Be aware, however, that many meeting requirements only concern meetings by managers in *manager*-managed LLCs (the type of LLC that uses the operating agreement covered in Chapter 6). Manager-meeting provisions of this sort do not apply to a member-managed LLC.

When it comes to calling meetings, we've kept things simple and in line with the kind of flexibility normally accorded LLCs under state law: Members can decide to meet at any time with a minimum of premeeting formality. Further, our provision says that all members must either attend a meeting or, alternatively, that any nonattending members must agree in writing to the holding of the meeting ahead of time. This is the approach most small, closely held LLCs will wish to take—after all, the holding of a formal membership meeting is infrequent and is usually enough of a big deal to warrant attendance by everyone, or at least to require the premeeting consent of any member who can't attend.

We have also added an escape hatch in this provision, which allows the holding of a formal LLC membership meeting with less than unanimous attendance or consent. This provision says that a meeting may be held with only a majority of the membership (percentage) interests in attendance, if it is a second postponed meeting and the time and date was announced at the first postponed meeting. You can change this postponement procedure to suit your preference—for example, you could require two postponements (instead of one) before permitting a meeting with less than unanimous attendance or consent. Similarly, you may wish to change the quorum requirement of such a meeting, such as to two-thirds of the per capita membership in the LLC rather than our majority of percentage interests requirement.

Some LLCs will wish to provide alternatives to face-to-face member meetings. For example, you can allow for membership action by unanimous written consent of the members (without a meeting), or provide for conference call, computer network, or video hookups and other technology-assisted ways to hold virtual meetings over the phone lines or the Internet. Frankly, we think worrying about all of this is probably a bit much for most smaller LLCs. Formal membership meetings are not commonly needed in the first place, unless big structural changes are in the works, such as amending the LLC articles of organization or approving a dissolution of the LLC. If you are considering approving a major proposal of this sort, meeting face-to-face makes the most sense anyway.

If the subject of LLC meetings sparks your interest and you want to include more detailed rules, let your imagination and good sense be your guide. Following are some examples of issues you may want to address—but before you make any changes, do take a quick look at your state LLC act to be sure there are no special rules to consider:

- You can set a time limit for calling meetings (a meeting may be held no more than 60 days or fewer than 10 days from the date of the call, for example).

- You may want to require oral or written notice of meetings (our provision allows all sorts of methods for giving and acknowledging notice, including the use of fax machines and other electronic means).

- You may limit the business to be conducted at a meeting to matters stated in the notice.

- You may wish to set lower quorum requirements to hold member meetings (less than the unanimous presence or consent of members).

16 In Chapter 7, we show you how to document meetings and discuss the importance of keeping good records, preferably in a well-organized LLC records book.

17 There is no statutorily required form for LLC membership certificates, and you are not even legally required to issue them. Many LLCs don't. However, if you prepare your own certificates, you can follow the basic format for the contents of the certificates as stated in this provision, or you can modify the provision to require additional information on each certificate, such as the date of issuance and the percentage interest each member holds. Also, you should put a legend on each of the certificates—see "How to Prepare a Membership Certificate Legend," below.

You do not have to obtain and impress a seal of the LLC on each certificate—and, in fact, seals are becoming a bit outdated now that formal documents are routinely faxed or emailed to recipients. If you want to order an LLC seal from a local stamp maker, you can design one to your liking—state law does not contain mandatory requirements for LLC seals. Most seals in use are circular and contain the name of the LLC and year and state of formation of the LLC.

How To Prepare a Membership Certificate Legend

If you adopt and use one of the two operating agreements included with this book without making modifications, you will require the vote of all nontransferring members to admit a new member into LLC membership. See Instruction **36**, below, which covers "V. Membership Withdrawal and Transfer Provisions: (2) Restrictions on the Transfer of Membership," in this operating agreement.

This operating agreement's "II. Membership Provisions: (8) Membership Certificates," requires your LLC to put members on notice of the existence of these transfer restrictions—as well as any others you may adopt in your operating agreement or articles—by including a statement (a "legend") on any membership certificates you issue. You don't need to spell out exact transfer restrictions in your LLC membership certificate legend. Instead, you can summarize the restrictions and tell people how to get a copy of the restrictions from the LLC.

Below is a sample of a simple membership certificate legend that accomplishes these purposes. To use this legend, type or print the language below on the front of each membership certificate prior to issue; printing it in all caps and/or in boldface is a good way to ensure that it is conspicuous and will be noticed and read by anyone who looks at the certificate:

THE MEMBERSHIP INTEREST REPRESENTED BY THIS CERTIFICATE IS SUBJECT TO RESTRICTIONS ON TRANSFER, AND MAY NOT BE OFFERED FOR SALE, SOLD, TRANSFERRED, OR PLEDGED EXCEPT ACCORDING TO, AND ONLY IF ALLOWED BY, THESE TRANSFER RESTRICTIONS. TO OBTAIN A COPY OF THESE TRANSFER RESTRICTIONS, CONTACT AN OFFICER OF THIS LLC AT THE FOLLOWING ADDRESS: _[insert main address of LLC]_ .

In addition to the above information, all membership certificates shall bear a prominent legend on their face or reverse side stating, summarizing, or referring to any transfer restrictions that apply to memberships in this LLC under the articles of organization, certificate of formation, or a similar organizational document, and/or this operating agreement; as well as the address where a member may obtain a copy of these restrictions upon request from this LLC.

The records book of this LLC shall contain a list of the names and addresses of all persons to whom certificates have been issued, show the date of issuance of each certificate, and record the date of all cancellations or transfers of membership certificates. **17**

(9) Other Business by Members: Each member shall agree not to own an interest in, manage, or work for another business, enterprise, or endeavor, if such ownership or activities would compete with this LLC's business goals, mission, profitability, or productivity, or would diminish or impair the member's ability to provide maximum effort and performance in managing the business of this LLC. **18**

III. Tax and Financial Provisions

[*These provisions deal with tax and financial aspects or organizing and running your LLC.*]

(1) Tax Classification of LLC: The members of this LLC intend that this LLC be initially classified as a ["partnership" *or* "sole proprietorship of the sole member" *or* "corporation"] for federal and, if applicable, state income tax purposes. It is understood that, subject to federal and state law requirements, all members may agree to change the tax treatment of this LLC by signing, or authorizing the signature of, IRS Form 8832, Entity Classification Election, and filing it with the IRS and, if applicable, the state tax department within the prescribed time limits. **19**

(2) Tax Year and Accounting Method: The tax year of this LLC shall be ["the calendar year" *or specify a noncalendar year period, such as* "July 1 to June 30th"]. The LLC shall use the ["cash" *or* "accrual"] method of accounting. Both the tax year and the accounting period of the LLC may be changed with the consent of all members if the LLC qualifies for such change, and may be effected by the filing of appropriate forms with the IRS and state tax authorities. **20**

(3) Tax Matters Partner: If this LLC is required under Internal Revenue Code provisions or regulations, it shall designate from among its members a "tax matters partner" in accordance with Internal Revenue Code Section 6231(a)(7) and corresponding regulations, who will fulfill this role by being the spokesperson for the LLC in dealings with the IRS as required under the Internal Revenue Code and Regulations, and who will report to the members on the progress and outcome of these dealings. **21**

❶❽ This noncompetition provision limits the ability of members to own interests in, manage, or work in competing outside businesses. We don't specify exactly what a competing business is, so you may want to add language that addresses this issue.

EXAMPLE:

"Each member shall agree not to own an interest in, manage, or work for another computer retail sales or service business, enterprise, or endeavor…"

You can be more liberal if you wish, and allow members to own, manage, or be employed by competing businesses, but we think our provision states a basic restriction that will match the wishes of most smaller LLC owners.

RESOURCE

If you want to expand the noncompete provision, take a look at noncompetition provisions for LLCs, partnerships, corporations, and other businesses in a local law or business library. Noncompetition clauses can be found in law texts in your local law library or online. Or, you may wish to ask your LLC legal adviser to help you craft a noncompetition clause that complies with any state law restrictions.

❶❾ Fill in this blank to specify the IRS income tax classification you wish to obtain for your LLC (look through Chapter 3 again first). There are three choices for filling in this blank:

Choice #1: Insert "partnership" if you are forming an LLC with more than one member, and you do not wish to be classified as a corporation for income tax purposes—this is the response most multi-member LLCs will make.

Choice #2: Insert "sole proprietorship of the sole member" if you are forming a one-

member LLC and do not wish to be classified as a corporation. This is the choice most one-member LLCs will make.

Choice #3: Insert "corporation" if you are forming a one-member or a multi-member LLC and wish to be classified as a corporation for income tax purposes. Most LLC organizers will not wish to start out with their LLC classified as a corporation, but if you do, make sure to check the "A domestic eligible entity electing to be classified as an association taxable as a corporation" box on IRS Form 8832 and file it on time as explained in Chapter 3.

❷⓿ The tax year and accounting period options available to LLCs are the same as those available to partnerships. There are several places to look for the most current information on these rules, including IRS publications and commercial tax guides at the local law or business library. (See IRS Publication 538, *Accounting Periods and Methods*, and IRS Publication 541, *Partnerships*, available on the IRS website at www.irs.gov.) Of course, your tax adviser should be on top of any recent rules in these areas, and can help you make the right choices for your LLC tax year and its accounting method.

Here is the basic information on options for tax years and accounting methods for your LLC:

- **Generally, LLCs that are treated as pass-through entities (partnerships or sole proprietorships) must select a tax year that is the same as a majority of its members** (members with a greater than 50% interest in the profits and capital of the LLC; or the sole member of a one-member LLC). For most LLCs, this means selecting a calendar tax year (from January 1 to December 31), which is the normal tax year for individual members.

- **If your LLC elects corporate tax treatment,** it should be able to choose a calendar tax year or a "fiscal year"—one which ends on the last day of any month except December.

- **An LLC classified as a partnership can also qualify for a fiscal tax year** other than the calendar year if it can show a good business purpose, or if it results in the deferral of not more than three months of income for LLC members. For further information, see IRS Publication 538, *Accounting Periods and Methods.*

- **LLCs may elect a cash or accrual method of accounting.** Under the cash method, the business deducts expenses when paid and reports income when received. This is the way most individual taxpayers handle income and expenses on their tax returns. Under the accrual method, the business deducts expenses when it becomes legally obligated to pay them, and reports income when the LLC becomes legally entitled to receive the income. Small, closely held LLCs may benefit from the cash method of accounting because it may allow them to defer the reporting of income and give them added flexibility in claiming deductions, so most choose this option.

However, your LLC may not be able to use the cash method of accounting if:

- it has a corporation as a member (with some exceptions)

- it is considered a "tax shelter" under IRS rules.

- it stocks an inventory of items to sell to the public, or

- it has sales of more than $5 million per year.

Tax shelters include businesses that sell securities that are registered with the SEC (your LLC should be exempt from registration; those set up with the principal purpose of avoiding the payment of federal income taxes (most LLC founders will have a primary purpose of making money from active business operations, not tax avoidance); and those that fall under the definition of a "syndicate" (your LLC will be considered a syndicate—and therefore unable to elect the cash accounting method—if more than 35% of its losses are allocable to members who do not actively participate in the business).

SEE AN EXPERT

Select a tax year and accounting method with the help of your tax adviser. Because these are important tax decisions with significant financial and tax repercussions, it's important to check your conclusions on picking a tax year and accounting method with your tax adviser.

㉑ Generally, if you have ten or more LLC members (or if any member uses more than one percentage to figure his or her shares in LLC profits, losses, credits, deductions, or other tax items—for example, a member with a 10% profits interest gets a 20% share of losses), you will need to select a "tax matters partner" and file a designation of tax matters partner with the IRS. This is a partner who will deal with the IRS if tax issues arise, and will keep the other members apprised of what is going on. (You designate a tax matters partner on the LLC's annual Form 1065 informational return. Remember, LLCs are treated like partnerships under federal tax law.)

This provision simply reminds you that your LLC may have to designate a tax matters partner. You do not have to specify in your operating agreement who will act in this capacity. You may designate someone later as a tax matters partner, and may change this designation when and as needed. There are technical rules on who may serve as a tax matters partner for an LLC (if interested,

(4) Annual Income Tax Returns and Reports: Within 60 days after the end of each tax year of the LLC, a copy of the LLC's state and federal income tax returns for the preceding tax year shall be mailed or otherwise provided to each member of the LLC, together with any additional information and forms necessary for each member to complete his or her individual state and federal income tax returns. If this LLC is classified as a partnership for income tax purposes, this additional information shall include a federal (and, if applicable, state) Schedule K-1 (Form 1065, Partner's Share of Income, Deductions, Credits) or equivalent income tax reporting form. This additional information shall also include a financial report, which shall include a balance sheet and profit and loss statement for the prior tax year of the LLC. **㉒**

(5) Bank Accounts: The LLC shall designate one or more banks or other institutions for the deposit of the funds of the LLC, and shall establish savings, checking, investment, and other such accounts as are reasonable and necessary for its business and investments. One or more members of the LLC shall be designated with the consent of all members to deposit and withdraw funds of the LLC, and to direct the investment of funds from, into, and among such accounts. The funds of the LLC, however and wherever deposited or invested, shall not be commingled with the personal funds of any members of the LLC. **㉓**

(6) Title to Assets: All personal and real property of this LLC shall be held in the name of the LLC, not in the names of individual members or managers. **㉔**

IV. Capital Provisions

[*These provisions deal with capital contributions, allocations, and distributions by and to LLC members, as well as related matters.*]

(1) Capital Contributions by Members: Members shall make the following contributions of cash, property, or services as shown next to each member's name below. Unless otherwise noted, cash and property described below shall be paid or delivered to the LLC on or by _____*[final date or period for contributions]*_____. The fair market values of items of property or services as agreed between the LLC and the contributing member are also shown below. The percentage interest in the LLC that each member shall receive in return for his or her capital contribution is also indicated for each member. **㉕**

Name	Contribution	Fair Market Value	Percentage Interest in LLC
_____	_____	$ _____	_____
_____	_____	$ _____	_____
_____	_____	$ _____	_____
_____	_____	$ _____	_____
_____	_____	$ _____	_____
_____	_____	$ _____	_____

see Internal Revenue Code Regulation §301.6231(a)(7)-1, (a)(7)-2, found in Title 26 of the C.F.R). Ask your tax adviser to help you pick and designate a tax matters partner if you are required to do so.

㉒ If an LLC is classified and taxed as a pass-through entity (partnership or sole proprietorship), LLC profits and losses are passed along to members. The members will need these figures at the end of each year, as well as other LLC information, to prepare their individual income tax returns. To this end, we include a paragraph requiring that within 60 days after the end of each tax year, all members must be provided with:

- LLC income tax returns (partnership or corporate)
- If the LLC is classified as a partnership for income tax purposes, a completed IRS Schedule K-1 (Form 1065, *Partner's Share of Income, Deductions, Credits*), and
- LLC financial statements (you can dispense with this requirement, but we think most members will regard this additional information as critical).

⚠ **CAUTION**

Figure out whether actual payouts will be required. Ask your tax adviser if you should add a provision to your agreement that requires the actual payout of a specified percentage of the profits allocated to each member at the end of the year. Members may need this money to pay their share of income taxes on profits allocated to them.

You can change the time frame for the LLC to provide this information—for example, within 30 days after the end of the LLC's tax year (instead of 60 days), but make sure to give your LLC enough time to prepare these forms and statements (Schedule K-1 must be given to each member of an LLC classified as a partnership on or by the date the LLC must file its annual Form 1065 partnership return—this means on or by April 15 for LLCs classified as partnerships with a calendar tax year).

㉓ This is a general authorization paragraph that allows the LLC to establish accounts with banks and other institutions. It allows one or more members to be designated to deposit and withdraw funds into and from these accounts, and to direct the investment of funds held in these accounts.

Note that unanimous consent is required to designate a person or persons to have this depositing/check-writing authority, but you can lessen this requirement if you wish by simply deleting the words "with the consent of all members" from the second sentence of this paragraph. You may also alter, rather than delete, the language, for example "with the consent of a majority of members."

Typically, each member of a small, closely held LLC will have depositing and check-writing authority—although, for added fiscal control, multiple signatures may be required for withdrawals that exceed a specified amount. You don't need to specify these arrangements in your operating agreement because such details will be spelled out on the signature cards and paperwork you must file with the bank when opening accounts on behalf of your LLC.

The final sentence in this paragraph is a reminder that personal funds of the LLC members may not be commingled (mixed) with the funds of the LLC. If you commingle funds, a state court may decide that you and the other members are not entitled to the limited liability protection normally afforded an LLC, and may hold you personally liable for its debts and claims.

㉔ This is another one of our "reminder" provisions to make it clear that the LLC will not commingle (mix) or confuse title to property. LLC property will only be owned by and in the name of the LLC.

㉕ Here is an important provision in your agreement, where you specify who pays what to the LLC to get it started.

In most states, there are no minimum capitalization requirements for LLCs. You can start an LLC with a large amount of cash or property, or on a shoestring.

Capital contributions may include cash, property, or a promise to pay cash or property in the future—for example, one member agrees to provide future services as a contribution and another to pay a specified amount of cash to the LLC within a certain time limit. The state sheets in Appendix A indicate if states place restrictions on the types of payment (consideration) that may be made for membership interests; a few prohibit the use of promises to pay money or provide future services as capital contributions. Also check your state's LLC act for restrictions on the types of consideration that may be paid as capital contributions—use the Internet link to your LLC act listed in state sheets in Appendix A.

> ⚠ **CAUTION**
>
> **Capital contributions may have tricky tax consequences.** Particularly problematic are contributions of appreciated property and the contribution of services to an LLC. We discuss potential problems that can occur with these types of capital contributions, such as increased personal income taxes for members, in Chapter 3. To avoid problems, we strongly suggest you talk to your tax adviser before settling on the particular capital contribution scenario you will follow to fund your LLC—if all members won't be paying cash up front.

If your state says a promise to pay or to work for the LLC can't be used to set one up, you may be able to find a way around this limitation. For example, if a state prohibits using promissory notes (a promise to pay money) to capitalize an LLC, one of the cash-rich members may loan funds to another member for the latter to use as his or her capital contribution.

EXAMPLE:

Warren has plenty of cash and will contribute $20,000 as his one-half interest in a new LLC. He makes a personal loan of another $20,000 to his buddy Carl, who turns around and pays this $20,000 as his contribution to the LLC. Warren trusts Carl to pay back the $20,000 (plus interest) with Carl's eventual shares in the LLC's profits. Warren asks Carl to sign a personal promissory note that carries an annual interest rate of 7%, and may even require that Carl pledge collateral for payback of the loan if he wants an extra measure of safety.

Once you've ironed out the details of members' contributions, you're ready to fill in the blanks in this provision. In the first blank, specify a date or period when capital contributions must be made by the members—such as "30 days from the signing of this agreement."

Here's how to fill in the remaining blanks:

- **Name.** On separate lines, list the name of each contributing LLC member. If you need more space than we've provided, add more lines or fill in the words "See Attachment 1" and provide the information on a separate sheet of paper labeled "Attachment 1."

- **Contribution.** Describe each member's contribution. If a member is contributing cash, fill in the amount. If a member is contributing property, describe it in plain language. If a member will make payments of money, transfer property, or contribute services to the LLC as a capital contribution in the future, you must describe the timeline and general terms for those future payments or services. If you wish, you can insert the specifics of members' future payments here (the date specified for members' contributions in the first paragraph of this provision applies only if you do not specify a later date for payment here). If you need more room, which is likely, fill in the words, "See the [schedule/bill/promissory note] attached to this agreement as Attachment 1" (or another numbered attachment, as the case may be). Then attach a separate document that spells out the details of each member's initial capital contribution to the LLC.

EXAMPLE 1:

Jeremy will contribute $10,000 in cash as his capital contribution. He can come up with only half the cash now, and agrees to pay the balance in six months. The description of his capital contribution reads as follows: "$5,000 cash on or by the date indicated above for contributions by members, and payment of an additional $5,000 on or by June 15, 20xx."

EXAMPLE 2:

John contributes a promise to pay $10,000 in cash to his LLC as his capital contribution. The description of John's contribution is: "$10,000 to be paid per the terms of a promissory note attached to this agreement as Attachment 1."

EXAMPLE 3:

Tom will pay cash of $1,000 to his LLC, plus a promise to contribute $6,000 in future services as his capital contribution. The following statement is inserted: "$1,000 in cash; $6,000 in future

services—see schedule of services attached to this agreement as Attachment 1." On a separate page, the following schedule of future services appears:

"Attachment 1—Schedule of Future Services: Tom Chan will contribute a total of 300 hours of work for the LLC, for which he normally would be compensated at the hourly rate of $20. This contributed work shall be performed between January 1, 20xx and June 30, 20xx, and shall consist of services of at least 12 hours per week during this period."

- **Fair Market Value.** For noncash payments, show the fair market value of the property or services to be contributed. You may leave this item blank for cash payments.

- **Percentage Interest in LLC.** Here you specify the percentage interest each member will receive in return for his or her capital contribution. A member's interest should be expressed as a percentage—for example, "50%." A percentage interest—also referred to as the member's capital interest—is the portion of the net assets of the LLC (total assets minus liabilities) that each member is entitled to when the business is sold or that is used to value a member's interest when a member is bought out. To compute this percentage, see Instruction **12** above. This percentage interest figure is usually also used to determine other financial and managerial rights. For example, in our agreement, it is used to determine each member's share of the LLC's profit and loss, as well as members' voting power in the LLC.

In most cases involving smaller LLCs, members will each put up a proportionate amount of cash for a membership interest—that is, each will normally receive a percentage interest in the LLC that equals his or her proportionate cash capital contribution.

EXAMPLE 1:

Judy, Ed, and Sharon each contribute $10,000 to their LLC to get it started, reasoning that $30,000 is just about right to begin operations until enough cash starts to flow into the business to make it self-supporting. Each person gets a one-third (33⅓%) percentage interest in the LLC in return for his or her initial cash capital contributions.

EXAMPLE 2:

Gail and Lilian form their own LLC. Gail puts up $10,000 in cash, plus a used computer system that will be signed over to the LLC for a fair market value of $5,000. Lilian puts up $7,500 in cash, plus signs over the pink slip to her paid-off Honda Accord with a middle blue book resale value of $7,500. Each is given a 50% membership interest in the LLC.

EXAMPLE 3:

Sam and Jerry start an LLC. Sam has the cash, Jerry the expertise. Sam puts up $75,000. Jerry agrees to forego his first $25,000 in salary from the LLC as his capital contribution. Sam is given a 75% interest in the LLC, and Jerry is given a 25% interest. (In addition, Jerry will likely have to pay personal income taxes on the value of his LLC interest in the year the operating agreement is signed, as discussed in Chapter 3.)

How much, if any, extra documentation do you need to prepare to back up your capital contributions? In most cases, just filling in these blanks in your operating agreement to describe the type, value, and timing of each member's payment will be enough. For instance, stating that a member will contribute future services worth $10,000 to the LLC on or by a particular date, or that a member will pay $10,000 to the LLC within three years of signing the agreement, plus interest at an annual rate of 9%, will ordinarily make the other members comfortable. In some cases, you may feel the need to prepare additional documentation, such as a schedule of future services that describes when and what work a member will do for the LLC, or a promissory note that specifies the repayment terms of a future cash payment.

EXAMPLE 1:

Jeff will pay $15,000 at an 8% interest rate per the terms of a two-year note to buy a one-quarter stake in a new LLC. His capital contribution is described as follows:

Name	Contribution
Jeff Billings	$15,000 per terms of note attached as Attachment 1

Fair Market Value	Percentage Interest in LLC
--	25%

RESOURCE

Use a promissory note for future cash payments. Make the note payable on demand after a certain date or number of months or years, or payable in equal or unequal installments during the term of the note. For simple promissory note forms to use for this purpose, see *Your Limited Liability Company: An Operating Manual,* by Anthony Mancuso (Nolo). Or you may wish to inventory and separately value various items of property that are being transferred by a member.

(2) **Additional Contributions by Members:** The members may agree, from time to time by unanimous vote, to require the payment of additional capital contributions by the members, on or by a mutually agreeable date. ㉖

(3) **Failure to Make Contributions:** If a member fails to make a required capital contribution within the time agreed for a member's contribution, the remaining members may, by unanimous vote, agree to reschedule the time for payment of the capital contribution by the late-paying member, setting any additional repayment terms, such as a late payment penalty, rate of interest to be applied to the unpaid balance, or other monetary amount to be paid by the delinquent member, as the remaining members decide. Alternatively, the remaining members may, by unanimous vote, agree to cancel the membership of the delinquent member, provided any prior partial payments of capital made by the delinquent member are refunded by the LLC to the member promptly after the decision is made to terminate the membership of the delinquent member. ㉗

(4) **No Interest on Capital Contributions:** No interest shall be paid on funds or property contributed as capital to this LLC, or on funds reflected in the capital accounts of the members. ㉘

(5) **Capital Account Bookkeeping:** A capital account shall be set up and maintained on the books of the LLC for each member. It shall reflect each member's capital contribution to the LLC, increased by each member's share of profits in the LLC, decreased by each member's share of losses and expenses of the LLC, and adjusted as required in accordance with applicable provisions of the Internal Revenue Code and corresponding income tax regulations. ㉙

(6) **Consent to Capital Contribution Withdrawals and Distributions:** Members shall not be allowed to withdraw any part of their capital contributions or to receive distributions, whether in property or cash, except as otherwise allowed by this agreement and, in any case, only if such withdrawal is made with the written consent of all members. ㉚

(7) **Allocations of Profits and Losses:** No member shall be given priority or preference with respect to other members in obtaining a return of capital contributions, distributions or allocations of the income, gains, losses, deductions, credits, or other items of the LLC. The profits and losses of the LLC, and all items of its income, gain, loss, deduction, and credit shall be allocated to members according to each member's percentage interest in this LLC. ㉛

(8) **Allocation and Distribution of Cash to Members:** Cash from LLC business operations, as well as cash from a sale or other disposition of LLC capital assets, may be distributed from time to time to members in accordance with each member's percentage interest in the LLC, as may be decided by _____["all" *or* "a majority"]_____ of the members. ㉜

(9) **Allocation of Noncash Distributions:** If proceeds consist of property other than cash, the members shall decide the value of the property and allocate such value among the members in accordance with each member's percentage interest in the LLC. If such noncash proceeds are later reduced to cash, such cash may be distributed among the members as otherwise provided in this agreement. ㉝

EXAMPLE 2:

Mary plans to contribute $3,000 in cash and $3,000 in property over the first year of a new LLC's life for her 40% share. Here's how she completes this provision:

Name	Contribution
Mary Ranier	$3,000 in cash and $3,000 in property as described on schedule attached as Attachment 2

Fair Market Value	Percentage Interest in LLC
$6,000	40%

㉖ This simple provision requires the unanimous vote of all members before members can be asked to contribute additional capital to the LLC. You may lower the vote requirement if you wish—for example, by specifying a majority vote (specifying a majority of members per capita or of percentage interests or profits interests), but if you do, be aware that some members may not be able to come up with the cash on time. What will you do then? Will you let the cash-rich members increase their percentage interests in the LLC while decreasing the percentage interests of the noncontributing members? This seems unfair, particularly to the members who want to contribute but can't come up with the additional capital on time. Especially for small LLCs, this is the reason we think unanimity is best when it comes to additional contributions.

㉗ This is a penalty provision for failure to pay contributions to the LLC on time. We don't address what "on time" means—it will follow the timelines established in your capital contributions clause unless you add language to this late payment provision specifying when its voting procedures kick in. For example, you may want this late payment provision to apply if a member fails to make a cash or property contribution within 30 days of its scheduled date. On the other hand, you may give a member who is to provide future services or make installment cash payments over the course of one or more years at least a month or two to remedy a missed installment payment before the late payment procedures go into effect.

You can also vary the penalty terms. Our provision requires a unanimous vote of remaining members to extend the terms for payment of a late capital contribution or terminate a delinquent member's membership. You may decide to require a lesser vote, eliminate entirely the procedure of terminating a membership for failure to pay a capital contribution on time, or make other changes or additions.

㉘ It is standard not to pay interest to members on their capital contributions—after all, members are investing money in the business with the hope of making more money, not banking it.

If, however, you wish to pay interest on members' capital contributions, you should delete this paragraph and provide for interest payments instead. You can make a general authorization, which lets members pin down the terms of the interest payments later by themselves, or spell out the terms—such as interest rate, dates, and manner of payment:

> **Sample Language:** Interest on Capital Contributions: Interest shall be paid on funds or property contributed as capital to this LLC or on funds reflected in the capital accounts of the members   ["as may be agreed by unanimous vote of the members" or specify terms (interest rate, dates, and manner of payment)]   .

㉙ This tax language requires the LLC to set up capital accounts for each member, something that is required for federal income tax purposes. We state general rules here for LLC capital account bookkeeping. We don't cite specific sections of the Internal Revenue Code that may affect your LLC's bookkeeping or lay out all the special provisions that may apply to setting up and maintaining LLC capital accounts.

As discussed in Chapter 3, if you decide to make special allocations of profits and losses, you (and your tax adviser) may decide to include additional language to make sure your allocations of profits and losses will go unchallenged by the IRS.

❸⓿ This provision reflects a standard practice of not allowing withdrawals of capital by LLC members prior to a dissolution of the company, unless approved in writing by all members. You can change this provision to allow premature withdrawals of capital in certain instances or with the consent of fewer than all members. For example, you may want to give yourself and the other members flexibility to withdraw part of the cash balance from positive capital accounts in times of personal financial emergency with less than unanimous membership consent as long as the LLC remains solvent and able to pay its bills. Your tax adviser can help you draft custom provisions of this sort.

❸❶ This paragraph makes it clear that all members have equal participation rights in the profits and losses of the LLC. The last sentence specifies that members will share in LLC profits and losses in accordance with their respective percentage interests in the business—the most common arrangement for smaller LLCs. These percentages, in turn, are established by the capital contributions listed in "IV. Capital Provisions: (1) Capital Contributions by Members" (the first paragraph of this section of the agreement) and "II. Membership Provisions: (4) Members' Percentage Interests" (the fourth paragraph of Section II).

As we've mentioned earlier, we think most smaller LLCs will not need or benefit by adopting disproportionate profit or loss provisions. But if you have special needs and your tax adviser concurs, replace this paragraph with special provisions of your own. For example, you may wish to give a member who contributes $25,000 in cash as capital a greater share of LLC profits than a member who promises to contribute $25,000 over the course of three years. Again, see Chapter 3 and consult your tax adviser to make sure any disproportionate allocations of profits will comply with IRS rules (discussed in Chapter 3).

EXAMPLE:

Dwayne, Blaine, and Jane agree to allocate their LLC profits and losses disproportionately. They change this paragraph to read: "No member shall be given priority or preference with respect to other members in obtaining a return of capital contributions, distributions, or allocations of the income, gains, losses, deductions, credits, or other items of the LLC. Items of its income, gain, loss, deduction, and credit shall be allocated to members according to each member's percentage interest in this LLC, except as follows: [here they specify any special (disproportionate) allocations of profits, losses, and any other items to particular members]. Their tax adviser adds additional language to have these special allocations respected by the IRS.

Here are other changes you can make to this provision (again, get help from your tax adviser):

• You can adopt multi-class membership provisions, with some members being first in line to receive a return of their capital investment.

• You can decide that some LLC members will be entitled to their share of profits and losses (disproportionate or otherwise) before all other members and shall continue to receive the only distributions of LLC profits until they have been paid back their initial capital contribution. The following sample provision, or one similar to it, will accomplish this.

Sample Language: Allocations of Profits and Losses: Notwithstanding any other provision in this agreement, the following members, called "priority members," shall receive all distributions of the LLC's profits and losses before any distributions are made to any other members of the LLC: ___[list priority members]___. Further, the other members of the LLC shall not receive any distributions until each of these priority members has received total distributions equal to each priority member's initial capital contribution to the LLC.

㉜ This provision gives members leeway to distribute cash profits or proceeds of the LLC to members if they vote to do so. Most smaller LLCs will require a unanimous vote, but some may prefer to allow just a majority of the membership to decide this issue—remember, a majority of members is defined earlier in this agreement ("II. Membership Provisions: (5) Membership Voting") as a majority of the percentage interests in the LLC.

Again, we assume that allocations of profits and losses will follow each member's percentage interest in the LLC, but you can vary who gets how much if you (and your tax adviser) decide to implement disproportionate (special) allocations of LLC profits.

㉝ This paragraph addresses how any non-cash LLC property will be allocated among members. Basically, property gets allocated among the members in proportion to each member's percentage interest in the LLC. If reduced to cash later, it will be distributed to members according to an earlier provision in this operating agreement ("IV. Capital Provisions: (8) Allocation and Distribution of Cash to Members").

EXAMPLE:

Second-Hand Freight and Salvage, Ltd. Liability Co., a five-member company, decides to sell a truck and allocate the current value of this asset to the members, who own the LLC in equal percentages. The truck is worth $30,000, so the capital account of each member is increased by $6,000. The members can vote to distribute this cash according to the cash distribution provision in their agreement.

㉞ This paragraph sets up a special rule to handle a distribution of the cash and other assets of the LLC when the business itself liquidates or when a member's interest is liquidated. It applies the distribution to each member's capital account, then allows for credits and deductions that may need to be made prior to a final distribution. A final distribution is then made to members with positive account balances.

CAUTION

Avoid personal liability for negative capital account balances. You may want to add special provisions to make sure your members are not personally liable for any negative balances remaining in their capital accounts when the LLC liquidates. If this is important to you, make sure to ask your tax adviser to add "qualified income offset" language to your agreement, which can help relieve members of their liability for deficits in their capital accounts while satisfying the IRS under its safe-harbor regulations for special allocations.

㉟ This is a liberal provision that lets a member bow out from the LLC by giving

(10) Allocation and Distribution of Liquidation Proceeds: Regardless of any other provision in this agreement, if there is a distribution in liquidation of this LLC, or when any member's interest is liquidated, all items of income and loss shall be allocated to the members' capital accounts, and all appropriate credits and deductions shall then be made to these capital accounts before any final distribution is made. A final distribution shall be made to members only to the extent of, and in proportion to, any positive balance in each member's capital account. **34**

V. Membership Withdrawal and Transfer Provisions

[*These provisions deal with members' deciding to leave the LLC. We specifically require a vote to admit a transferee (someone who buys or is otherwise tranferred an LLC interest from a member) as a new member of the LLC. As discussed in Chapter 3, some states impose mandatory membership vote requirements to admit transferees into membership. Our transfer restriction language below is intended to help you meet the most stringent of any such rules in effect in your state.*]

(1) Withdrawal of Members: A member may withdraw from this LLC by giving written notice to all other members at least _____*[number of days]*_____ days before the date the withdrawal is to be effective. **35**

(2) Restrictions on the Transfer of Membership: A member shall not transfer his or her membership in the LLC unless all nontransferring members in the LLC first agree to approve the admission of the transferee into this LLC. Further, no member may encumber a part or all of his or her membership in the LLC by mortgage, pledge, granting of a security interest, lien, or otherwise, unless the encumbrance has first been approved in writing by all other members of the LLC. **36**

Notwithstanding the above provision, any member shall be allowed to assign an economic interest in his or her membership to another person without the approval of the other members. Such an assignment shall not include a transfer of the member's voting or management rights in this LLC, and the assignee shall not become a member of the LLC. **37** prescribed written notice. The period required is up to you—you can allow a quick departure, say in 30 days, or require many months' prior written notice. A typical advance notice period mentioned in LLC statutes is 180 days.

If you want, you may modify this provision. For example, you may choose to limit the circumstances under which members may withdraw, or you may want to assess a monetary penalty if a member leaves too soon. (One way is to limit the price the member gets for his or her interest under mandatory buy-sell, or buyout, provisions in your agreement. We don't include buy-sell provisions of this sort in our simple agreement so you'll need to consult a lawyer or tax adviser. Or, see *Business Buyout Agreements: A Step-by-Step Guide for Co-Owners,* by Bethany Laurence and Anthony Mancuso (Nolo), for instructions and buyout provisions for your operating agreement.)

> **CAUTION**
>
> **Be careful if you decide to specify a substantial monetary penalty for leaving the LLC too soon.** Courts may not enforce limitations placed on individuals' abilities to come into and go out of a business freely if they believe the limitations unduly restrict an individual's right to transfer an LLC interest or compete freely in the marketplace. Besides, lawyers love to sue, and your departing member may hook up with a litigious lawyer (or vice versa) upon leaving your LLC.

There are other issues you may want to address in this provision—for example, what happens if a "service member" leaves the business before fully performing services promised in return for a share in the LLC.

EXAMPLE:

John received a 15% share in Fast Fries LLC in return for a promise to perform $15,000 worth of services for the LLC over a two-year period. However, John leaves prior to completing these promised capital contributions; when he gives notice of withdrawal, he has only worked off $7,500. Can John be forced to report to work for the LLC even though he is no longer a member? No—a court simply won't enforce this requirement. In short, if John is determined to leave, there is no legal remedy available to force him to keep working off his capital contribution.

The simple solution is to require departing "service members" to pay off in cash the amount of services left undone. This can be paid by way of a set-off against the departing member's capital account, with the member's agreeing to pay any deficiency in cash or over time according to the terms of a promissory note.

Sample Language: If any member leaves this LLC prior to fully performing services promised as part of the member's capital contribution, his or her capital account shall be debited in an amount equal to the dollar amount of the value of the unpaid services prior to a distribution of any capital account balance to the member. If the capital account balance prior to this deduction is less than the full amount of the value of the unperformed services, the amount of the value of the unperformed services that exceeds the positive capital account balance of the member shall be paid by the departing member as follows: _[specify terms of repayment of any deficiency, for example "in cash within 30 days of departure by the member from the LLC" or "in accordance with the terms of a promissory note payable to the LLC by the departing member, the principal amount of which shall be the value of the unperformed services that were not satisfied from the member's positive capital account balance upon his or her departure from the LLC"]_ .

EXAMPLE:

Part of Sam's contribution to Sam & Pam's Sandblasting & Plastering LLC is a promise to perform future services worth $10,000. The LLC operating agreement requires departing service members to convert any unperformed services to a promissory note if they leave the LLC prior to performing all promised services. Sam decides to leave the LLC when he still owes $5,000, and his capital account balance is at $2,000. When he departs, Sam will either be required to pay the remaining $3,000 (the amount he still owes reduced by his capital account balance) in cash or under the terms of a promissory note that he signs in favor of the LLC.

For departing members who received a share in the LLC in return for a promise to pay off a note on which they still owe money, you may choose to do nothing. Because these people are still legally bound to pay off the note, you can simply let them leave (not try to renegotiate the note or convert it to a lump-sum payment).

You may, however, decide that any type of long-distance or extended payoff would be too tenuous or uncomfortable after a member leaves the business. Accordingly, you may wish to add language here requiring all persons who owe money on their initial capital contribution to make a lump-sum cash payment to the LLC equal to the amount of the unpaid capital contribution at the time of their withdrawal from the LLC.

> **Sample Language:** If a member departs this LLC prior to full payment of his or her capital contribution, whether the unpaid capital contribution consists of cash, payments under a promissory note, the performance of future services, or the transfer of property, the member shall be bound to pay a lump sum to the LLC at the time of his or her departure equal to the amount of the unpaid cash, amount of the unpaid principal and interest under the note, value of unperformed services, or the value of the untransferred property. The lump sum shall be paid to this LLC no later than   *[number of days]*   days after the departing member leaves the LLC, and payment of the lump sum within this period shall extinguish the liability of the departing member for the amount or value of his or her unpaid capital contribution to this LLC.

Our above examples and sample provisions are suggestions only. The best way to anticipate and come to terms with handling unpaid capital contributions upon the departure of a member is to talk with all members and your tax adviser (particularly if you plan to tinker with a member's capital account balance when he or she leaves). Reaching this kind of informed consensus before you add any language to your operating agreement helps avoid bad feelings and uncooperative behavior later—when, for example, a departing member complains he or she wasn't in on the discussions on how unpaid contributions would be handled when a member leaves, and therefore didn't realize being let out of the LLC meant having to pay cash.

This operating agreement provision deals only with a member's packing up and quitting the LLC. It does not address a member who wants to sell his or her interest to a new member—we deal with this latter issue in the next provision in the agreement titled "Restrictions on the Transfer of Membership."

❸❻ This provision is intended to satisfy any requirements in your state's LLC act that require member approval of nontransferring members when a member wishes to transfer membership to a new member. As explained in Chapter 3, these state law requirements are no longer necessary for your LLC to obtain a favorable tax classification with the IRS, but

VI. Dissolution Provisions

[*This section addresses the dissolution of the LLC, or events that may trigger a dissolution. In Section 1(a), we specifically require the vote of all remaining members to continue the business of the LLC after a member is dissociated (loses his or her membership interest). Many states still require a vote in such cases, and our provision is intended to meet the most stringent of any such state rules in effect in your state.*]

(1) **Events That Trigger Dissolution of the LLC:** The following events shall trigger a dissolution of the LLC, except as provided:

(a) the death, incapacity, bankruptcy, retirement, resignation, or expulsion of a member, except that within _____ [*number of days (typically a maximum of 90 under state LLC default rules)*] of the happening of any of these events, all remaining members of the LLC may vote to continue the legal existence of the LLC, in which case the LLC shall not dissol 38

(b) the expiration of the term of existence of the LLC if such term is specified in the articles of organization, certificate of formation, or a similar organizational document, or this operating agreement; 39

(c) the written agreement of all members to dissolve the LLC; 40

(d) entry of a decree of dissolution of the LLC under state law. 41

VII. General Provisions

[*These provisions cover general items concerning operation of the LLC. You'll also find standard provisions, normally found at the end of LLC agreements, dealing with the enforceability of the agreement.*]

(1) **Officers:** The LLC may designate one or more officers, such as a president, vice president, secretary, and treasurer. Persons who fill these positions need not be members of the LLC. Such positions may be compensated or noncompensated according to the nature and extent of the services rendered for the LLC as a part of the duties of each office. Ministerial services only as a part of any officer position will normally not be compensated, such as the performance of officer duties specified in this agreement, but any officer may be reimbursed by the LLC for out-of-pocket expenses paid by the officer in carrying out the duties of his or her office. 42

(2) **Records:** The LLC shall keep at its principal business address a copy of all proceedings of membership meetings, as well as books of account of the LLC's financial transactions. A list of the names and addresses of the current membership of the LLC also shall be maintained at this address, with notations on any transfers of members' interests to nonmembers or persons being admitted into membership in the LLC.

some states will keep these requirements on the books for at least a few more years.

This provision requires the approval of *all* non-transferring members to the sale of membership interests to a new member. This requirement should not only meet any requirement still found in your state's LLC act, but also helps protect your members from having to admit an incompatible person as a new member of your LLC. After all, the new member will have to get along and work closely with the other members. If any member doesn't like or is incompatible with the new member, the LLC's business may suffer significantly and the personal enjoyment the members derive from working together may be lost.

If you wish to alter this provision to allow just a majority (or other lesser number) of non-transferring members to approve the sale of a membership to a new member, make sure your state lets you adopt the lesser membership vote rule you have in mind. Your state's requirement on this vote is summarized in your state sheet in Appendix A, in the Operating Rules section, under the heading "Default Transfer Rule." To make sure the rule listed is current, check your state LLC act—we provide the Internet link in your state sheet.

Finally, note that this paragraph requires all members to agree before a member encumbers a membership, such as putting it up as collateral for a loan or pledging it as security for the performance of some other legal obligation. You can lessen the vote requirement for encumbrances, but we think unanimous written approval works best here too.

37 This paragraph states an exception to requiring unanimous approval of transfers of interest, which is recognized under state statutes. Namely, even in states that still require membership approval to a transfer of membership, a member is allowed to transfer *economic interests in a membership* without the approval of the nontransferring members. As long as the person getting the interest—the assignee or transferee—does not become a new member with management and voting rights, the transfer is of an economic interest only, and does not require membership approval under state law.

EXAMPLE:
Katherine owns a one-third interest in a lucrative LLC. She assigns one-quarter of her profits interest in her LLC to a trust set up for the benefit of her niece, Brenda. This transfer of economic rights only is not restricted under state law.

Of course, you can decide not to permit even these transfers of economic interests by members, simply by deleting this paragraph. (By the way, you don't need to be overly concerned about the possibility of outsiders buying an economic interest in your LLC—there generally is little interest by outsiders in buying a profits-only interest in an LLC without full membership rights.)

38 This provision covers what will happen when a member's interest in the LLC is terminated—legally, when a member is *dissociated*—because he or she resigns, retires, dies, is permanently incapacitated, goes bankrupt, or is subject to any of the other conditions listed here. Some states still have requirements in their LLC acts that require a membership vote to continue the legal existence of the LLC after a member is dissociated. There is no longer any tax reason for this requirement, as explained in Chapter 3, but you will want to comply with any existing state law requirement on this issue by including this provision.

State statutes that contain this type of requirement generally mandate the vote of at least a "majority in interest" of the remaining members to continue the legal existence of the LLC after a member's interest is terminated, but some states require a vote of all remaining members. To keep things simple, and to avoid a long-winded explanation of what "majority-in-interest" means, our provision requires the vote of all remaining LLC members to continue the legal life of your LLC after a member withdraws, sells his or her interest, becomes incapacitated, dies, or is expelled. This unanimous vote requirement satisfies the most stringent of any legal requirements on this point still on the books in various states. We're sure you'll find it easy to comply with too—just meet with the remaining LLC members and ask if everyone is in agreement that the business of your LLC should continue without the dissociated member. With rare exceptions, everyone should agree (if someone doesn't, you will want to rethink your LLC business anyway, perhaps deciding to buy out the protesting member before continuing on with LLC business).

If you decide to modify the provision in our operating agreement and lessen the vote requirement, make sure your state lets you do so by checking the "Default Continuation Rule" listed in the Operating Rules section of your state sheet in Appendix A and by checking your state's current LLC act.

Notice that you must fill in the blank in our provision to specify the deadline for voting to continue the legal existence of the LLC after the occurrence of a dissolution-triggering event. In most states that require a vote to continue the LLC, this vote must be taken within 90 days from the triggering event—again, see the "Default Continuation Rule" in your state sheet in Appendix A. If your state does not specify a deadline for taking this vote, or lets you override the state requirements (most

states permit this), we suggest putting "90 days" in this blank anyway. You can always vote any time before the 90-day deadline (the language says "within [number of days]" of the happening of one of the membership terminating events). If, however, you want to insert a shorter period, we recommend specifying no fewer than 30 days to give your members a chance to meet and approve the continuance of your LLC.

㊋ Some states require the articles of organization to limit the legal existence of the LLC to a specified term of years or until a particular date. This provision simply states that the LLC will dissolve if a termination date or period is specified in the articles of organization or this operating agreement. (See our earlier discussion on filling in "I. Preliminary Provisions: (6) Duration of LLC," in Special Instruction **㊇**, above.)

㊉ Your LLC may decide to call it quits at any time by the unanimous approval of all members to dissolve. We think this makes sense—and most LLC owners wouldn't want it any other way. (In fact, most state LLC laws say you can do this even if your operating agreement doesn't specify it.)

㊀ State statutes may provide for the involuntary dissolution of an LLC should the members reach an impasse or in the case of fraud, illegality, or nonpayment of state taxes. This provision simply recognizes that the LLC may dissolve by order of a state court.

㊁ This paragraph allows, but does not require, the LLC to appoint one or more persons as officers of the LLC, who may be members or nonmembers. Some state LLC statutes mention the officer positions of president, vice president, secretary, and treasurer, but even those states don't require that the positions be filled or define the job duties and responsibilities of these offices.

Copies of the LLC's articles of organization, certificate of formation, or a similar organizational document, a signed copy of this operating agreement, and the LLC's tax returns for the preceding three tax years shall be kept at the principal business address of the LLC. A statement also shall be kept at this address containing any of the following information that is applicable to this LLC:

- the amount of cash or a description and value of property contributed or agreed to be contributed as capital to the LLC by each member;
- a schedule showing when any additional capital contributions are to be made by members to this LLC;
- a statement or schedule, if appropriate, showing the rights of members to receive distributions representing a return of part or all of members' capital contributions; and
- a description of, or date when, the legal existence of the LLC will terminate under provisions in the LLC's articles of organization, certificate of formation, or a similar organizational document, or this operating agreement.

If one or more of the above items is included or listed in this operating agreement, it will be sufficient to keep a copy of this agreement at the principal business address of the LLC without having to prepare and keep a separate record of such item or items at this address.

Any member may inspect any and all records maintained by the LLC upon reasonable notice to the LLC. Copying of the LLC's records by members is allowed, but copying costs shall be paid for by the requesting member. **43**

(3) **All Necessary Acts:** The members and officers of this LLC are authorized to perform all acts necessary to perfect the organization of this LLC and to carry out its business operations expeditiously and efficiently. The Secretary of the LLC, or other officers, or all members of the LLC, may certify to other businesses, financial institutions, and individuals as to the authority of one or more members or officers of this LLC to transact specific items of business on behalf of the LLC. **44**

(4) **Mediation and Arbitration of Disputes Among Members:** In any dispute over the provisions of this operating agreement and in other disputes among the members, if the members cannot resolve the dispute to their mutual satisfaction, the matter shall be submitted to mediation. The terms and procedure for mediation shall be arranged by the parties to the dispute.

If good-faith mediation of a dispute proves impossible or if an agreed-upon mediation outcome cannot be obtained by the members who are parties to the dispute, the dispute may be submitted to arbitration in accordance with the rules of the American Arbitration Association. Any party may commence arbitration of the dispute by sending a written request for arbitration to all other parties to the dispute. The request shall state the nature of the dispute to be resolved by arbitration, and, if all parties to the dispute agree to arbitration, arbitration shall be commenced as soon as practical after such parties receive a copy of the written request.

We suggest you not worry too much about specific officer titles ("Treasurer" vs. "Chief Financial Officer" vs. "Chief Poobah in Charge of Payroll"). Pay attention instead to making sure each LLC employee knows the scope and responsibilities of his or her position with your LLC, whether it is as a formal officer or in a regular staff position.

Feel free to modify this provision to have it reflect how you want to handle the designation and compensation of any officers in your LLC. We suggest not being too specific, to allow maximum leeway to appoint various types of LLC salaried and nonsalaried officers and personnel. You do not need to say that your LLC has the power to hire employees and compensate them for their services; this type of employment authority goes without saying.

43 Your state LLC statute may allow you to restrict when or why members are allowed to look at LLC records or access particular types of LLC legal or financial records. We don't nitpick here, and simply give all members an unrestricted right to view all records at any time. If you want to restrict member inspection rights, first take a look at your state LLC statute for any limits or rules on this.

> **Sample Language:** Any member may inspect the financial or other records of this LLC for a purpose reasonably related to the member's interest in this LLC. The Treasurer of this LLC shall make the determination within one week of the member's request and, if the Treasurer finds that the member's request is related to his or her interest in the LLC, the requesting member shall be allowed to inspect the records during regular business hours of the LLC at its principal place of business.

44 This housekeeping provision says that the secretary of the LLC or other LLC officers or its members may sign a statement that certifies to other businesses or outside persons the capacity of one or more LLC members or officers to engage in particular business on behalf of the LLC. A bank, escrow, or title company, or other outside person or business may wish to obtain a statement certifying such authority prior to entering into a contract or business transaction with an LLC member or officer. (We provide a Certification of Authority form to use for this purpose in Chapter 7; a blank form is also provided in Appendix B and on the CD-ROM.)

45 Mediation, followed if necessary by arbitration, is a usually a quicker and less expensive way to settle disputes than litigation—for example, arguments over the valuation of LLC interests incident to a buyout or disagreements over who gets to use the LLC's name after the business is formally dissolved.

This bare-bones provision says unresolved disputes among LLC members should first be submitted to mediation. Mediation is a voluntary, nonbinding process in which an impartial mediator tries to get the parties to agree to a settlement. (For an excellent, in-depth coverage of the mediation process, see *Mediate, Don't Litigate: Strategies for Successful Mediation,* by Peter Lovenheim and Lisa Guerin (Nolo).)

In our provision, if mediation cannot be undertaken or is unsuccessful, the dispute may be submitted to binding arbitration by the parties. Even this procedure—an out-of-court, informal hearing before an impartial arbitrator that produces a legally enforceable decision—is both quicker and less expensive than going to court.

You may want to make some minor changes, such as choosing a different association as a model for the arbitration rules, requiring three arbitrators instead of one (opposing sides of a dispute each pick one arbitrator, and these two arbitrators pick a third), and other changes you deem appropriate.

All parties shall initially share the cost of arbitration, but the prevailing party or parties may be awarded attorney fees, costs, and other expenses of arbitration. All arbitration decisions shall be final, binding, and conclusive on all the parties to arbitration, and legal judgment may be entered based upon such decision in accordance with applicable law in any court having jurisdiction to do so. **45**

(5) Entire Agreement: This operating agreement represents the entire agreement among the members of this LLC, and it shall not be amended, modified, or replaced except by a written instrument executed by all the parties to this agreement who are current members of this LLC as well as any and all additional parties who became members of this LLC after the adoption of this agreement. This agreement replaces and supersedes all prior written and oral agreements among any and all members of this LLC. **46**

(6) Severability: If any provision of this agreement is determined by a court or arbitrator to be invalid, unenforceable, or otherwise ineffective, that provision shall be severed from the rest of this agreement, and the remaining provisions shall remain in effect and enforceable. **47**

VIII. Signatures of Members and Spouses

[*The final section of the agreement contains signature lines for the members, plus a series of lines for their spouses to sign.*]

(1) Execution of Agreement: In witness whereof, the members of this LLC sign and adopt this agreement as the operating agreement of this LLC.

Date: _____ **48**

Signature: _____

Printed Name: _____ , Member

Date: _____

Signature: _____

Printed Name: _____ , Member

Date: _____

Signature: _____

Printed Name: _____ , Member

Date: _____

Signature: _____

Printed Name: _____ , Member

(2) **Consent of Spouses:** The undersigned are spouses of the members of this LLC who have signed this operating agreement in the preceding provision. These spouses have read this agreement and agree to be bound by its terms in any matter in which they have a financial interest, including restrictions on the transfer of memberships and the terms under which memberships in this LLC may be sold or otherwise transferred. **49**

Date: _____

Signature: _____

Printed Name: _____

Spouse of: _____

Date: _____

Signature: _____

Printed Name: _____

Spouse of: _____

Date: _____

Signature: _____

Printed Name: _____

Spouse of: _____

Date: _____

Signature: _____

Printed Name: _____

Spouse of: _____

㊻ This is a boilerplate legal provision that negates any prior agreements among the members, whether oral or written. This can be important because the general rule is that LLCs, like partnerships, may legally be based on oral agreements.

This provision also requires future changes to the agreement, or the adoption of a new operating agreement, to be signed by all original parties to the agreement who are current members of the LLC, plus any new members. You can change this provision to allow less than unanimous approval of operating agreement changes, but we think these changes are usually important enough to warrant unanimous approval of all current members. (We cover how to amend your operating agreement in Chapter 7.)

㊼ This is a standard legal provision that directs a court or arbitrator to enforce the balance of the agreement even if one or more provisions are held invalid, ambiguous, or otherwise unenforceable.

㊽ Before the members sign the agreement, have them initial crossed-out language and changes that were made to the agreement, if any. (However, they don't need to initial filled-in lines.)

Have each member date and sign the operating agreement. Type or print the name of each member under the corresponding signature line, after the words "Printed Name." Make sure each member signs the operating agreement.

SEE AN EXPERT

Get sign-off from a tax adviser. Before you sign your final agreement, let your tax adviser review your choices, particularly those related to the financial (capital) provisions and tax options (for example, whether to have your LLC taxed as a pass-through entity or as a corporation, and whether to require minimum payouts of a percentage of profits each year to help members pay income taxes they owe on LLC profits allocated to them at the end of the year).

㊾ This standard provision shows spousal consent to the provisions of the operating agreement. We strongly suggest that each married LLC member have his or her spouse date and sign on one of the sets of lines following this spousal consent provision. Doing this can help avoid disputes later, should spouses separate, divorce, or die, or should one spouse decide to sell or transfer his or her membership in the LLC.

SEE AN EXPERT

Leaving interests by means of estate planning devices. You may add provisions that permit spouses of members to use a will or other estate planning device, such as a living trust, to leave their half- or other co-interest in an LLC membership to outsiders. See your tax or legal adviser for guidance if you wish to address issues of this sort in your agreement.

Distribute Copies of Your Operating Agreement

Congratulations! You are done with another important organizational task, and your LLC is well on its legal way. Make photocopies of the completed, signed operating agreement and give each member a copy. Finally, place the original, signed operating agreement in your LLC records book. ●

Prepare an LLC Operating Agreement for Managers

Some LLCs wish to set up a special management structure that does not consist of all LLC members. The management team may be made up of:

- some, but not all, LLC members
- both outside managers and some LLC members, or
- only outside managers.

If your LLC is structured in one of these ways, you have a manager-managed LLC. We'll show you how to prepare an operating agreement here. We assume you are in the process of forming, or have already formed, your LLC by preparing and filing articles of organization with your state LLC filing office, as explained in Chapter 4.

SKIP AHEAD

If yours is a member-managed LLC, turn to Chapter 5. In Chapter 5, we cover the first LLC operating agreement contained in Appendix B, which provides for management of the LLC by all members. If you're unsure which agreement you need, read on.

Choosing a Manager-Managed LLC

Although most smaller LLCs will choose to be managed by all members, a minority will find a manager-managed LLC more suitable. LLCs that decide on manager-management usually do so for one or both of these reasons:

- At least one member wishes to be a "passive" investor and to hand over the reins and responsibilities of management to others.

EXAMPLE:

Sole Sisters is a shoe design and distribution partnership owned and operated by three sisters, Julie, Laurie, and Ginny. Ginny contributed the cash to get the partnership started, leaving all business management and day-to-day operations to Julie and Laurie, whose capital contributions are portions of their past (unpaid) services performed for the partnership. All three sisters decide that converting the business to an LLC makes sense, but they wish to keep the same management arrangement among themselves. What's the solution? Simple. They decide to adopt a manager-management agreement—the kind discussed in this chapter—with Julie and Laurie designated as the managers of the LLC. Ginny will be a nonmanaging member, thus avoiding all management responsibilities.

- The members believe that the LLC will be handled better by outsiders (nonmembers) who have special expertise in managing the business.

EXAMPLE:

Power-Packed Peanut Products LLC (PPPP), a food wholesaler, is formed and funded by Tina and Kay, entrepreneurs with an eye for a promising business venture, but with little expertise or interest in managing or running it on a day-to-day basis. They decide to shell out substantial salaries to experienced food wholesalers Jason and Charlotte, who will manage and run the business as its nonmember managers. Jason and Charlotte bring years of prior experience to the newly formed business, having just sold their co-owned food distribution business, J & C Wholesalers, at a substantial profit. They are ready to get involved growing another successful company in exchange for chunky salaries on PPPP's payroll.

Limited Liability for All Members of Manager-Managed LLC

In their roles as LLC members, all members—whether managing or nonmanaging—qualify for personal legal immunity from business debts and legal claims made by outsiders against the LLC.

Limited Liability for Managers of Manager-Managed LLC

State law may impose slightly stricter standards on LLC managers (regardless of whether they're also members). That is, managers will receive the normal personal immunity from business debts and liabilities that the LLC provides, but they may suffer exposure to personal liability if they participate in making exceptionally bad or illegal business decisions in their roles as managers.

Don't get too concerned here if you plan to be an LLC manager. The circumstances where a manager may be found personally liable are the exceptions, not the rule. Circumstances that breed such personal liability tend to involve decisions that are self-interested (where a manager takes personal advantage of a business deal with the LLC without proper disclosure of his or her interest) or situations where the manager acts in an extremely reckless or illegal manner.

EXAMPLE 1:

Suits of Amoré, LLC, a haberdasher of formal men's attire for weddings, parties, and other black-tie affairs, is on the lookout for top-quality Italian suits it can offer its customers. In the course of his research, Fredo, an LLC manager, spots a phenomenal opportunity to purchase top-of-the-line Santoro suits (normally $2,500 plus retail per unit) at an unheard of discount. He decides to cash out his personal bank account savings and buy up the suits, rather than mention his find to the other LLC managers, who would jump at the chance to acquire the merchandise. Fredo will find a private buyer for the suits. If another LLC manager gets wind of Fredo's find, and the LLC sues him for lost profits—the amount the LLC could have made had it been allowed to buy and resell the suits—a court would likely find Fredo personally liable. The normal rule is that a manager has a duty of loyalty to disclose opportunities discovered in the course of his or her work that might benefit the business (unless it is obvious that the business would have no interest in the opportunity); only after the business decides not to act is the manager allowed to go ahead and personally pursue the opportunity.

EXAMPLE 2:

The managers of Lowball Construction Ltd. Liability Co. are warned repeatedly by the VP of operations that an electrical panel box installation being performed by the company at one of its worksites is not up to code. The LLC managers disregard his advice to order the substandard work to be redone, insisting that the company can't afford to miss another performance deadline under its contract with the owner of the building. After Lowball completes the installations, the owner rents the building to a computer manufacturer, which moves in and sets up sensitive electronic measurement and test equipment it uses in its operation. When the computer firm flips the switch to fire up its equipment, a short circuit due to faulty ground wiring in the service panel box sends a voltage spike through the outlets on the circuit—and destroys all the computer maker's expensive test equipment. The building owner is sued for the loss, and she immediately sues Lowball and its managers. Lowball's lawyer advises the managers that it is unlikely that their commercial insurance carrier will cover this loss—the electrical panel box at fault was never inspected and approved by the local building inspector. The managers may be held personally liable for the loss due to their gross negligence in not heeding the warnings of their VP to redo the faulty service panel wiring.

Of course, these are extreme examples, mostly used to make the following points. First, the LLC will protect you and your comanagers personally for normal negligence—the kind of business judgment errors humans without 20-20 foresight may make. But don't be lulled into an unassailable sense of security by the normal limited liability protection afforded by the LLC form. If you engage in truly foolish conduct that is obviously reckless to the safety of other people or their property, or you act illegally or underhandedly in your own self-interest, then the mantle of personal protection that your LLC normally provides may be lifted. In that case, you and the other LLC managers will be exposed to personal liability for the reckless or illegal decisions.

TIP

Provide managers with indemnification and/or insurance. If you want to attract outside managers to help run your LLC, you may need to take extra measures to make them feel more comfortable in these lawsuit-happy times. One way is to offer an LLC indemnity agreement, guaranteeing direct payment by the LLC for any legal expenses or judgments arising out of a manager's work for the LLC. Another personal safeguard is to cover managers personally with an errors and omissions insurance policy for their managerial duties. The two can be combined for complete legal coverage:

Indemnification can kick in for all amounts not covered by insurance.

One final point about managers: State law typically invests each manager of a manager-managed LLC with "agency" authority. That is, each manager has legal authority to bind the LLC to contracts and business deals made with outsiders. You will want to make sure to select managers you can trust.

Exception: State law normally says a manager's acts will not bind the LLC if 1) the acts were not the type of business the LLC normally would transact or, 2) even if the acts were the type of business the LLC would normally transact, the manager did not have the actual authority to enter into the deal and the outsider knew the manager didn't. These exceptions are rare—don't expect to be able to rely on either them if a manager commits your LLC to a bad business deal.

How to Prepare an LLC Management Operating Agreement

Now let's look at the LLC management operating agreement. Note that this is the second operating agreement in Appendix B, titled Limited Liability Company Management Operating Agreement. You can tear the agreement out now to follow along with the instructions if you wish. Make sure you pick the right agreement and don't miss any pages.

CD-ROM

The Limited Liabilitty Company Management Operating Agreement is included on the CD-ROM at the back of this book.

Read Chapter 5 Material on Basic Operating Agreement Issues

The management operating agreement is similar to the operating agreement provided in Chapter 5, but it is customized to include LLC manager provisions. Before you begin filling in your LLC management operating agreement, read these two sections of Chapter 5, which apply to both member-managed and manager-managed LLCs:

- **"Scope of Our Basic LLC Operating Agreements."** There, you'll find information about capital account provisions and buy-sell and right-of-first-refusal provisions.

- **"Customizing Your LLC Operating Agreement."** This covers general rules on when and how to make changes to your agreement.

How to Use Instructions for LLC Management Operating Agreement

Below, we provide instructions in the sample agreement to help you fill in the blanks. In addition, we use two different kinds of references to alert you to special instructions:

- **Lettered references** accompany provisions that are unique to this management operating agreement. Special Instructions **A** through **N** accompany the management operating agreement in this chapter.

- **Numbered references** apply to provisions that are the same as (or almost identical to) those found in the Chapter 5 agreement. Special instructions **1** through **49** are in Chapter 5. Because certain provisions in Chapter 5 apply only to member-managed LLCs, they are not carried over to this management operating agreement, and the numbers are not consecutive.

Line-by-Line Instructions for Management Operating Agreement

We'll start at the top of the Limited Liability Company Management Operating Agreement and work our way through it.

Special Instructions

A Fill in the name(s) and address(es) of the manager(s) of the LLC—you only need one manager, but many LLCs have more than one person on their management teams. Check the appropriate box to show whether each manager is a member or nonmember.

B This paragraph reiterates the basic legal rule that managers (like members) are not personally liable for LLC debts and claims.

C In the blank, specify how many management votes are necessary to pass or approve decisions submitted to the managers. You may select "all" or "a majority," or specify a particular number or percentage of votes needed to make a management decision, such as "two-thirds, "51%," or "three." We recommend specifying percentages or fractions, rather than numbers, because a specified number may turn out to be too small if you increase the size of your management team later. For example, if you require three management votes for a management team currently consisting of five persons, and you later add one more manager to your LLC, this number will represent less than a majority.

Note that this provision states the standard rule that each manager gets one vote, regardless of any percentage interest he or she may hold in the LLC as a member.

D You may wish to use your operating agreement to state procedures for the removal of LLC managers. You may want to specify the membership votes needed for removal of a manager, or the automatic grounds for such

Limited Liability Company
Management Operating Agreement

I. Preliminary Provisions

[*Here we address preliminary matters, such as the effective date of the agreement, the name of the LLC, and other basic information. These provisions are almost identical to those provided in the basic LLC operating agreement in Chapter 5.*]

(1) **Effective Date:** This operating agreement of _____ [*name of LLC*] ❶ _____

_____ ,

effective _____ [*date*] ❷ _____ , is adopted

by the members whose signatures appear at the end of this agreement. ❸

(2) **Formation:** This limited liability company (LLC) was formed by filing articles of organization, certificate of formation, or a similar organizational document with the LLC filing office of the state of _____ [*state of formation*] _____ on _____ [*date of filing articles of organization, certificate of formation, or similar organizational document*] . ❹ A copy of this organizational document has been placed in the LLC's records book.

(3) **Name:** The formal name of this LLC is as stated above. However, this LLC may do business under a different name by complying with the state's fictitious or assumed business name statutes and procedures. ❺

(4) **Registered Office and Agent:** The registered office of this LLC and the registered agent at this address are as follows: _____ [*name and address of registered agent and office*]

_____ .

The registered office and agent may be changed from time to time as the members or managers may see fit, by filing a change of registered agent or office form with the state LLC filing office. It will not be necessary to amend this provision of the operating agreement if and when such a change is made. ❻

(5) **Business Purposes:** The specific business purposes and activities contemplated by the founders of this LLC at the time of initial signing of this agreement consist of the following:

_____ [*state the specific business purposes and activities you foresee for your LLC*] ❼ _____

_____

_____ .

It is understood that the foregoing statement of purposes shall not serve as a limitation on the powers or abilities of this LLC, which shall be permitted to engage in any and all lawful business activities. If this LLC intends to engage in business activities outside the state of its formation that require the qualification of the LLC in other states, it shall obtain such qualification before engaging in such out-of-state activities.

(6) Duration of LLC: The duration of this LLC shall be ___*["perpetual" or any specific*___ *termination date or term of years for the LLC, as specified in the articles of organization]* . Further, this LLC shall terminate when a proposal to dissolve the LLC is adopted by the membership of this LLC or when this LLC is otherwise terminated in accordance with law. **❽**

II. Management Provisions

[*These provisions address the unique management structure of a manager-managed LLC. The lettered special instructions for these provisions accompany the agreement in this chapter.*]

(1) Management by Managers: This LLC will be managed by the managers listed below. All managers who are also members of this LLC are designated as "members"; nonmember managers are designated as "nonmembers." **Ⓐ**

Name: _____ ☐ Member ☐ Nonmember
Address: _____

Name: _____ ☐ Member ☐ Nonmember
Address: _____

Name: _____ ☐ Member ☐ Nonmember
Address: _____

Name: _____ ☐ Member ☐ Nonmember
Address: _____

Name: _____ ☐ Member ☐ Nonmember
Address: _____

Name: _____ ☐ Member ☐ Nonmember
Address: _____

(2) Nonliability of Managers: No manager of this LLC shall be personally liable for the expenses, debts, obligations, or liabilities of the LLC, or for claims made against it. **Ⓑ**

(3) Authority and Votes of Managers: Except as otherwise set forth in this agreement, the Articles of Organization, Certificate of Organization, or similar organizational document, or as may be provided under state law, all management decisions relating to this LLC's business shall be made by its managers. Management decisions shall be approved by _____["all" *or* "a majority"]_____ of the current managers of the LLC, with each manager entitled to cast one vote for or against any matter submitted to the managers for a decision.   **Ⓒ**

(4) Term of Managers: Each manager shall serve until the earlier of the following events:

    (a) the manager becomes disabled, dies, retires, or otherwise withdraws from management;

    (b) the manager is removed from office; or **Ⓓ**

    (c) the manager's term expires, if a term has been designated in other provisions of this agreement.

Upon the happening of any of these events, a new manager may be appointed to replace the departing manager by _["a majority of the members of the LLC" *or* "a majority of the remaining managers"]_____ . **Ⓔ**

(5) Management Meetings: Managers shall be able to discuss and approve LLC business informally, and may, at their discretion, call and hold formal management meetings according to the rules set forth in the following provisions of this operating agreement.

Regularly scheduled formal management meetings need not be held, but any manager may call such a meeting by communicating his or her request for a formal meeting to the other managers, noting the purpose or purposes for which the meeting is called. Only the business stated or summarized in the notice for the meeting shall be discussed and voted upon at the meeting.

The meeting shall be held within a reasonable time after a manager has made the request for a meeting, and in no event, later than _____[*period*]_____ days after the request for the meeting. A quorum for such a formal managers' meeting shall consist of _["all" *or* "a majority of"]_ managers, and if a quorum is not present, the meeting shall be adjourned to a new place and time with notice of the adjourned meeting given to all managers. An adjournment shall not be necessary, however, and a managers' meeting with less than a quorum may be held if all nonattending managers agreed in writing prior to the meeting to the holding of the meeting. All such written consents to the holding of a formal management meeting shall be kept and filed with the records of the meeting. **Ⓕ**

The proceedings of all formal managers' meetings shall be noted or summarized with written minutes of the meeting and a copy of the minutes shall be placed and kept in the records book of this LLC.

removal. You can even specify a procedure to have a vote of the managers themselves decide the removal of a manager.

Sample Language: Removal of Managers: Managers may be removed by the vote of [_"a majority of the members" or "all of the members"_], not counting the vote of any manager to be removed. _[You may also specify one or more automatic reasons for removal of a manager; for example:_ "A member-manager shall be removed automatically from office upon missing two or more consecutive meetings of the managers without giving reasonable written notice of such expected absence to the other managers of the LLC prior to the meeting."]

E Our provision gives an unspecified term for managers—that is, it doesn't contain a periodic election procedure for managers. This provision does specify a procedure to fill a vacancy on the management team. In the blank, indicate the vote requirement necessary for the remaining managers or members to accomplish this. If you require a majority vote of members, keep in mind that a majority vote will be defined in "III. Membership Provisions: (4) Membership Voting" as the vote of a majority of the percentage interests of the members—unless you provide a special formula to use for filling a vacancy by members. Conversely, a majority of managers under paragraph (3) of this section of the agreement means the per capita (one person, one vote) majority vote of the remaining LLC managers.

You may wish to limit the terms of managers by providing for their periodic election. Here is an optional management election provision you can add to this provision to require the annual election of managers by the members.

Sample Language: Election of Managers: The membership of this LLC shall meet every year on ___[date]___ to nominate and elect ___[number]___ member-managers and ___[number]___ nonmember-managers of the LLC. _[You may specify a procedure for voting and how the number of votes to be cast are to be calculated; for example:_ "Voting by the membership at this election shall be as follows: according to "capital interests" or "per capita voting." _You may want to exclude member-managers from voting in this election or add other provisions to suit your needs.]_

Written or electronic notice of this annual membership meeting, its purpose, and the name of anyone nominated as of the date of the notice, shall be mailed, delivered, or personally given to each member of this LLC no later than ___[period, typically "30 days"]___ prior to the date of the annual meeting.

The term of office for each manager so elected shall be for one year, and until his or her successor is elected by the membership at the next annual membership meeting and such successor accepts his or her office.

F This provision explains that management decisions may be made either informally or at a formal meeting of managers. This is a flexible provision with the following key points:

• **Managers don't have to call formal meetings to make ordinary business decisions.** A formal meeting is only necessary if you want the managers to meet in person at a prearranged time or if you want to make a written record of a decision.

• **Only the business communicated in the call for the formal meeting by the manager may be taken up at the meeting.** We think this makes sense for formally called and held management meetings, to give all managers fair opportunity to prepare for the discussion. But you can change our language to allow any business to be discussed and voted upon at a formal meeting. For example, you can change the language to read "Any business may be discussed and voted upon at a formal managers' meeting, whether or not stated or summarized in the notice for the meeting or written consent signed by a nonattending member."

- **Formal management decisions—those you wish to record in your LLC records book— should be approved by the vote requirement specified in the manager voting provision of your agreement.** The vote requirement is covered in "II. Management Provisions: (3) Authority and Votes of Managers."

- **Formal management meetings may be called by any manager.** Formal meetings must be held "within a reasonable time" of the call (request) for the meeting, subject to a final date (no later than a specified number of days after the request for the meeting—for example, 30 or 60 days). You may change these provisions to specify minimum and maximum timelines—for example, requiring the holding of a meeting no less than 10 or more than 60 days after a request for a meeting.

- **You can set the quorum requirement—the number or percentage of managers who must be present to hold a formal management meeting.** You may specify "all," "a majority," or some other portion of the managers as a quorum. If you specify a quorum requirement and a quorum is not in attendance, the meeting must be adjourned unless all nonattending managers give written consent ahead of time, agreeing to the holding of the meeting for one or more specified purposes even though they can't attend. A simple signed note to this effect is enough.

RESOURCE

Learn more about manager meetings. See Chapter 7 for details on when and how to conduct and document formal LLC meetings.

Our provisions are adequate for most smaller LLCs. If the formal management meeting provisions don't suit your needs, you are free to change them. For example, even though the managers of most smaller LLCs should normally meet and make decisions face-to-face at a formal managers' meeting, you can add language allowing technologically assisted participation—such as through a networked meeting via online interactive chats, video, or telephone conferences. You also can allow your managers to make decisions by unanimous written consent (unanimity is typically required for written management decisions under state law, so check your state LLC act if this interests you).

Again, bear in mind that if an issue is important enough to require the time and consideration of your managers to make and record a formal decision, it's probably best for the managers to talk with one another in person, not just to mail, fax, or email in their votes.

G This provision expresses the desire of the LLC to obtain maximum energy and effort from each LLC manager, and prohibits managers from working in or for outside businesses that compete with the LLC's business or in any business if doing so detracts from the manager's ability to perform properly for the LLC.

This is a general noncompetition provision, and you may wish to tighten it up a little. For example, we've carefully avoided saying that managers must work full-time for the LLC (as managers or in other capacities), since this is not always the case. You can add language

(6) Managers' Commitment to LLC: Managers shall devote their best efforts and energy working to achieve the business objectives and financial goals of this LLC. By agreeing to serve as a manager for the LLC, each manager shall agree not to work for another business, enterprise, or endeavor, owned or operated by himself or herself or others, if such outside work or efforts would compete with the LLC's business goals, mission, products, or services, or would diminish or impair the manager's ability to provide maximum effort and performance to managing the business of this LLC. **G**

(7) Compensation of Managers: Managers of this LLC may be paid per-meeting or per diem amounts for attending management meetings, may be reimbursed actual expenses advanced by them to attend management meetings or attend to management business for the LLC, and may be compensated in other ways for performing their duties as managers. Managers may work in other capacities for this LLC and may be compensated separately for performing these additional services, whether as officers, staff, consultants, independent contractors, or in other capacities. **H**

III. Membership Provisions

[*The membership provisions are nearly identical to those provided in Section II of the member-managed LLC operating agreement; where indicated, see the corresponding numbered instructions in Chapter 5.*]

(1) Nonliability of Members: No member of this LLC shall be personally liable for the expenses, debts, obligations, or liabilities of the LLC, or for claims made against it. **9**

(2) Reimbursement for Organizational Costs: Members shall be reimbursed by the LLC for organizational expenses paid by the members. The LLC shall be authorized to elect to deduct and amortize organizational expenses and start-up expenditures as permitted by the Internal Revenue Code and as may be advised by the LLC's tax adviser. **10**

(3) Members' Percentage Interests: A member's percentage interest in this LLC shall be computed as a fraction, the numerator of which is the total of a member's capital account and the denominator of which is the total of all capital accounts of all members. This fraction shall be expressed in this agreement as a percentage, which shall be called each member's "percentage interest" in this LLC. **12**

(4) Membership Voting: Except as otherwise may be required by the articles of organization, certificate of formation, or a similar organizational document, by other provisions of this operating agreement, or under the laws of this state, each member shall vote on any matter submitted to the membership for approval in proportion to the member's percentage interest in this LLC. Further, unless defined otherwise for a particular provision of this operating agreement, the phrase "majority of members" means the vote of members whose combined votes equal more than 50% of the votes of all members in this LLC, and a majority of members, so defined, may approve any item of business brought before the membership for a vote unless a different vote is required under this operating agreement or state law. **13**

(5) Compensation: Members shall not be paid as members of the LLC for performing any duties associated with such membership. Members may be paid, however, for any services rendered in any other capacity for the LLC, whether as officers, employees, independent contractors, or otherwise. ⓮

(6) Members' Meetings: The LLC shall not provide for regular members' meetings. However, any member may call a meeting by communicating his or her wish to schedule a meeting to all other members. Such notification may be in person or in writing, or by telephone, facsimile machine, or other form of electronic communication reasonably expected to be received by a member, and the other members shall then agree, either personally, in writing, or by telephone, facsimile machine, or other form of electronic communication to the member calling the meeting, to meet at a mutually acceptable time and place. Notice of the business to be transacted at the meeting need not be given to members by the member calling the meeting, and any business may be discussed and conducted at the meeting.

If all members cannot attend a meeting, it shall be postponed to a date and time when all members can attend, unless all members who do not attend have agreed in writing to the holding of the meeting without them. If a meeting is postponed, and the postponed meeting cannot be held either because all members do not attend the postponed meeting or the nonattending members have not signed a written consent to allow the postponed meeting to be held without them, a second postponed meeting may be held at a date and time announced at the first postponed meeting. The date and time of the second postponed meeting shall also be communicated to any members not attending the first postponed meeting. The second postponed meeting may be held without the attendance of all members as long as a majority of the percentage interests of the membership of this LLC is in attendance at the second postponed meeting. Written notice of the decisions or approvals made at this second postponed meeting shall be mailed or delivered to each nonattending member promptly after the holding of the second postponed meeting. ⓯

Written minutes of the discussions and proposals presented at a members' meeting, and the votes taken and matters approved at such meeting, shall be taken by one of the members or a person designated at the meeting. A copy of the minutes of the meeting shall be placed in the LLC's records book after the meeting. ⓰

(7) Membership Certificates: This LLC shall be authorized to obtain and issue certificates representing or certifying membership interests in this LLC. Each certificate shall show the name of the LLC and the name of the member, and state that the person named is a member of the LLC and is entitled to all the rights granted members of the LLC under the articles of organization, certificate of formation, or a similar organizational document, this operating agreement, and provisions of law. Each membership certificate shall be consecutively numbered and signed by one or more officers of this LLC. The certificates shall include any additional information considered appropriate for inclusion by the members on membership certificates.

In addition to the above information, all membership certificates shall bear a prominent legend on their face or reverse side stating, summarizing, or referring to any transfer restrictions that apply to memberships in this LLC under the articles of organization, certificate of formation, or a similar organizational document, and/or this operating agreement; as well as the address where a member may obtain a copy of these restrictions upon request from this LLC.

The records book of this LLC shall contain a list of the names and addresses of all persons to whom certificates have been issued, show the date of issuance of each certificate, and record the date of all cancellations or transfers of membership certificates. **17**

IV. Tax and Financial Provisions

[*The tax and financial provisions below are very similar to those provided in Section III of the member-managed LLC operating agreement, but they are extended to apply to LLC managers. Where indicated, see the corresponding numbered instructions in Chapter 5.*]

(1) **Tax Classification of LLC:** The members of this LLC intend that this LLC be initially classified as a ["partnership" *or* "sole proprietorship of the sole member" *or* "corporation"] for federal and, if applicable, state income tax purposes. It is understood that, subject to federal and state law requirements, all members may agree to change the tax treatment of this LLC by signing, or authorizing the signature of, IRS Form 8832, Entity Classification Election, and filing it with the IRS and, if applicable, the state tax department within the prescribed time limits. **19**

(2) **Tax Year and Accounting Method:** The tax year of this LLC shall be ["the calendar year" *or specify a noncalendar year period, such as* "July 1 to June 30th"]. The LLC shall use the ["cash" *or* "accrual"] method of accounting. Both the tax year and the accounting period of the LLC may be changed with the consent of all members or all managers if the LLC qualifies for such change, and may be effected by the filing of appropriate forms with the IRS and state tax authorities. **20**

(3) **Tax Matters Partner:** If this LLC is required under Internal Revenue Code provisions or regulations, it shall designate from among its members or member-managers a "tax matters partner" in accordance with Internal Revenue Code Section 6231(a)(7) and corresponding regulations, who will fulfill this role by being the spokesperson for the LLC in dealings with the IRS as required under the Internal Revenue Code and Regulations, and who will report to the members and managers on the progress and outcome of these dealings. **21**

that requires such full-time effort, or go the other way and permit involvement with outside businesses or personal projects by your managers as long as they don't compete with the LLC's business.

EXAMPLE:

Ted and Jill found Bird Nest Bed & Breakfast, LLC. They have the money and energy to buy, set up, and maintain a few scenically situated bed and breakfast cottages in their home town—a suburban location outside a major metropolitan area. The two members are new to the B & B business and decide to bring in Elaine, an experienced B & B consultant, to help organize and operate the LLC. Elaine will work part-time on a consulting basis, plus be given a small stake in LLC profits for joining Ted and Jill as a formal manager of the LLC. Their operating agreement allows Elaine to do consulting work for other businesses, whether in the B & B or unrelated areas of operation, as long as this outside work does not interfere with her ability to provide best management efforts for the LLC.

Don't make changes to this provision that further restrict the activities of managers. Courts are often reluctant to enforce restrictions on how hard individuals work, and for whom. You may be able to sue a manager who strays from the fold in contravention of your noncompetition provision or for nonperformance of his or her duties under an employment agreement, but don't expect a court to order a person to return to work for you, or work harder for your LLC—this just won't happen.

Also realize that provisions of this sort are really best viewed as an expression of the parties' expectations, rather than ironclad legal language. If a manager wishes to stray or stay away from your LLC, your best solution is to acquiesce—and find a more suitable replacement on your management team.

❶ This broad provision says managers may receive per-meeting, per-diem, or other payment or compensation for serving as managers. It allows managers to serve and be paid for performing work for the LLC in other capacities as officers, employees, and independent contractors.

Even though this provision allows for a multitude of arrangements, typically managers also work for the LLC on a day-to-day basis in officer or employee positions (for example, as president, sales manager, or chief financial officer) and do not receive payment for also serving as managers. But you may wish to make other arrangements if you bring in nonmember managers who only work part-time as managers. That is, if they do not work in other capacities for your LLC, you may want to pay your managers as managers. The details of these arrangements are up to you; this provision allows you to pay managers in any capacity you wish.

Note that managers may not wish to receive direct payment for managing an LLC. If the manager is an investor in the LLC, for example, she can look to her capital and/or profits interest in the LLC for a payback, rather than to direct payment for intermittent or part-time management services.

EXAMPLE:

Sals' Berry Farms, a two-person LLC owned and operated by a married couple, Salvatore and Sally, owns and operates a California berry-growing business. The spouses bought the business from the prior owners, who have been kept on as managers of the LLC. Sally and Sal are on the management team too, but they receive compensation as vice presidents of operations, not as managers. The prior owners sold the business for a lump-sum buyout payment plus a 20% share in future profits for the next five years. These nonmember managers of the LLC are not paid in their capacities as managers—they are content to let their management efforts pay off in a more important and lucrative fashion—namely, by boosting the value of their 20% profits interest in the business.

Finally, note that managers of smaller management-run LLCs normally approve the amount of payment, if any, each person gets for performing management duties. You may, however, let LLC members decide the compensation issue. By adding the following sample language to the end of this provision, you allow members who are not managers to approve payments to managers. The managers are still allowed to approve smaller amounts, such as reimbursements or per-meeting or per diem payments.

> **Sample Language:** Except for per-meeting or per diem amounts, or reimbursement of actual expenses paid to managers, the nonmanaging members of this LLC shall approve compensation and other payments to managers for performing management duties for this LLC.

❶ This is a general authorization paragraph that allows the LLC to establish accounts with banks and other institutions. It allows the managers to unanimously designate one or more LLC employees to deposit into and withdraw funds from these accounts, and to direct the investment of funds held in these accounts.

Note that unanimous consent is required to designate a person or persons to have this depositing/check-writing authority, but you can lessen this requirement if you wish by simply deleting the words "with the consent of all managers" from the second sentence of this paragraph. You may also alter, rather than delete, the language, for example, "with the consent of the majority of members."

In many businesses, multiple signatures may be required for withdrawals that exceed a specified amount. You don't need to specify these arrangements in your operating agreement. The details of these check-writing and investment-directing arrangements will be spelled out on the bank's signature cards and paperwork you must fill in when opening bank accounts on behalf of your LLC.

The final sentence in this paragraph is a reminder that personal funds of the LLC members and managers may not be commingled (mixed) with the funds of the LLC. If you commingle funds, a state court may decide that you and the other members and/or managers are not entitled to limited liability protection normally afforded an LLC, and may hold members and managers personally liable for LLC debts and claims.

❿ This provision gives members or managers leeway to distribute cash profits or proceeds of the LLC to members if they vote to do so. Many smaller LLCs will trust their managers to make these allocations and distributions, but some may wish to leave important financial decisions of this sort strictly to the members themselves, or require the approval of both managers and members.

Most smaller LLCs will specify a unanimous vote, but some may prefer to allow just a majority of the members and/or managers to decide this issue. Remember, a majority of members is defined in "III. Membership Provisions: (4) Membership Voting," as a majority of the percentage interests in the LLC, whereas a majority of managers is

(4) Annual Income Tax Returns and Reports: Within 60 days after the end of each tax year of the LLC, a copy of the LLC's state and federal income tax returns for the preceding tax year shall be mailed or otherwise provided to each member of the LLC, together with any additional information and forms necessary for each member to complete his or her individual state and federal income tax returns. If this LLC is classified as a partnership for income tax purposes, this additional information shall include a federal (and, if applicable, state) Schedule K-1 (Form 1065, Partner's Share of Income, Deductions, Credits) or equivalent income tax reporting form. This additional information shall also include a financial report, which shall include a balance sheet and profit and loss statement for the prior tax year of the LLC. ㉒

(5) Bank Accounts: The LLC shall designate one or more banks or other institutions for the deposit of the funds of the LLC, and shall establish savings, checking, investment, and other such accounts as are reasonable and necessary for its business and investments. One or more employees of the LLC shall be designated with the consent of all managers to deposit and withdraw funds of the LLC, and to direct the investment of funds from, into, and among such accounts. The funds of the LLC, however and wherever deposited or invested, shall not be commingled with the personal funds of any members or managers of the LLC. ㉓

(6) Title to Assets: All personal and real property of this LLC shall be held in the name of the LLC, not in the names of individual members or managers. ㉔

V. Capital Provisions

[*Most of the capital provisions in this management operating agreement are almost identical to those provided in Section IV of the member-managed LLC operating agreement in Chapter 5. These provisions should work fine for smaller manager-run LLCs.*]

(1) Capital Contributions by Members: Members shall make the following contributions of cash, property, or services as shown next to each member's name below. Unless otherwise noted, cash and property described below shall be paid or delivered to the LLC on or by ___*[final date or period for contributions]*___. The fair market values of items of property or services as agreed between the LLC and the contributing member are also shown below. The percentage interest in the LLC that each member shall receive in return for his or her capital contribution is also indicated for each member. ㉕

Name	Contribution	Fair Market Value	Percentage Interest in LLC
_____	_____	$ _____	_____
_____	_____	$ _____	_____
_____	_____	$ _____	_____
_____	_____	$ _____	_____
_____	_____	$ _____	_____
_____	_____	$ _____	_____

(2) Additional Contributions by Members: The members may agree, from time to time by unanimous vote, to require the payment of additional capital contributions by the members, on or by a mutually agreeable date. **㉖**

(3) Failure to Make Contributions: If a member fails to make a required capital contribution within the time agreed for a member's contribution, the remaining members may, by unanimous vote, agree to reschedule the time for payment of the capital contribution by the late-paying member, setting any additional repayment terms, such as a late payment penalty, rate of interest to be applied to the unpaid balance, or other monetary amount to be paid by the delinquent member, as the remaining members decide. Alternatively, the remaining members may, by unanimous vote, agree to cancel the membership of the delinquent member, provided any prior partial payments of capital made by the delinquent member are refunded by the LLC to the member promptly after the decision is made to terminate the membership of the delinquent member. **㉗**

(4) No Interest on Capital Contributions: No interest shall be paid on funds or property contributed as capital to this LLC, or on funds reflected in the capital accounts of the members. **㉘**

(5) Capital Account Bookkeeping: A capital account shall be set up and maintained on the books of the LLC for each member. It shall reflect each member's capital contribution to the LLC, increased by each member's share of profits in the LLC, decreased by each member's share of losses and expenses of the LLC, and adjusted as required in accordance with applicable provisions of the Internal Revenue Code and corresponding income tax regulations. **㉙**

(6) Consent to Capital Contribution Withdrawals and Distributions: Members shall not be allowed to withdraw any part of their capital contributions or to receive distributions, whether in property or cash, except as otherwise allowed by this agreement and, in any case, only if such withdrawal is made with the written consent of all members. **㉚**

(7) Allocations of Profits and Losses: No member shall be given priority or preference with respect to other members in obtaining a return of capital contributions, distributions or allocations of the income, gains, losses, deductions, credits, or other items of the LLC. The profits and losses of the LLC, and all items of its income, gain, loss, deduction, and credit shall be allocated to members according to each member's percentage interest in this LLC. **㉛**

(8) Allocation and Distribution of Cash to Members: Cash from LLC business operations, as well as cash from a sale or other disposition of LLC capital assets, may be distributed from time to time to members in accordance with each member's percentage interest in the LLC, as may be decided by _____["all" *or* "a majority"]_____ of the __["members," "managers," "members and managers," *or* "members or managers"]__ . **Ⓙ**

(9) Allocation of Noncash Distributions: If proceeds consist of property other than cash, the ["members," "managers," "members and managers," *or* "members or managers"] shall decide the value of the property and allocate such value among the members in accordance with each member's percentage interest in the LLC. If such noncash proceeds are later reduced to cash, such cash may be distributed among the members as otherwise provided in this agreement. **Ⓚ**

(10) Allocation and Distribution of Liquidation Proceeds: Regardless of any other provision in this agreement, if there is a distribution in liquidation of this LLC, or when any member's interest is liquidated, all items of income and loss shall be allocated to the members' capital accounts, and all appropriate credits and deductions shall then be made to these capital accounts before any final distribution is made. A final distribution shall be made to members only to the extent of, and in proportion to, any positive balance in each member's capital account. **㉞**

VI. Membership Withdrawal and Transfer Provisions

[*These provisions, which are the same as those provided in Section V of the member-managed LLC operating agreement in Chapter 5, deal with members deciding to leave the LLC. We specifically require a vote to admit a transferee (someone who buys or is otherwise transferred an LLC interest from a member) as a new member of the LLC.*]

(1) Withdrawal of Members: A member may withdraw from this LLC by giving written notice to all other members at least _____[*number of days*]_____ days before the date the withdrawal is to be effective. **㉟**

(2) Restrictions on the Transfer of Membership: A member shall not transfer his or her membership in the LLC unless all nontransferring members in the LLC first agree to approve the admission of the transferee into this LLC. Further, no member may encumber a part or all of his or her membership in the LLC by mortgage, pledge, granting of a security interest, lien, or otherwise, unless the encumbrance has first been approved in writing by all other members of the LLC. **㊱**

Notwithstanding the above provision, any member shall be allowed to assign an economic interest in his or her membership to another person without the approval of the other members. Such an assignment shall not include a transfer of the member's voting or management rights in this LLC, and the assignee shall not become a member of the LLC. **㊲** determined on a per capita basis (according to "II. Management Provisions: (3) Authority and Votes of Managers").

Again, we assume that allocations of profits and proceeds will follow each member's percentage interest in the LLC, but you can vary who gets how much if you (with help from your tax adviser) decide to implement disproportionate (special) allocations of LLC profits.

K This paragraph addresses how any non-cash LLC property will be allocated among members. As with the previous provision, you may want to leave these decisions to just members or managers, or have either or both approve them.

Whoever decides, this provision says that property gets allocated among members in proportion to each member's percentage interest in the LLC. If reduced to cash later, it will be distributed to members according to the previous provision in this operating agreement.

EXAMPLE:

Second-Hand Freight and Salvage, Ltd. Liability Co., a five-member company with three member-managers, decides (by a unanimous manager vote as provided in its operating agreement) to sell a truck and allocate the current value of this asset to all five members, who own the LLC in equal percentages. The truck is worth $30,000, so the capital account of each member is increased by $6,000. The members and/or managers can vote to distribute this cash according to the cash distribution provision in their agreement.

L Your state LLC statute may allow you to restrict when or why members or managers are allowed to look at LLC records, or restrict access to particular types of LLC legal or financial records. We don't nitpick here, and simply give all members and managers an unrestricted right to view all records at any time.

If you want to restrict inspection rights, take a look at your state LLC statute to see how restrictive you are allowed to be under state law, then insert your own provisions. Normally, you will not wish to limit manager's rights— managers may need to look at LLC legal or financial records on a moment's notice to make a management decision—but you may wish to restrict members' inspection rights. Here's some sample language to accomplish this:

Sample Language: Any member may inspect the financial or other records of this LLC for a purpose reasonably related to the member's interest in this LLC. The Treasurer of this LLC shall make the determination within one week of the member's request and, if the Treasurer finds that the member's request is related to his or her interest in the LLC, the requesting member shall be allowed to inspect the records during regular business hours of the LLC at its principal place of business.

M Have each of your managers (one or more) sign and date at the bottom of the form. If a manager is also a member, he or she should sign and date the operating agreement in two places: once as member on the members' lines (Section 1), and a second time here as a manager on the manager lines (Section 3).

VII. Dissolution Provisions

[This section addresses the dissolution of the LLC, or events that may trigger a dissolution. It is identical to Section VI of the member-managed operating agreement in Chaper 5. In Section 1(a), we specifically require the vote of all remaining members to continue the business of the LLC after a member is dissociated (loses his or her membership interest).]

(1) **Events That Trigger Dissolution of the LLC:** The following events shall trigger a dissolution of the LLC, except as provided:

(a) the death, permanent incapacity, bankruptcy, retirement, resignation, or expulsion of a member, except that within ___*[number of days (typically a maximum of 90 under state LLC default rules)]*___ of the happening of any of these events, all remaining members of the LLC may vote to continue the legal existence of the LLC, in which case the LLC shall not dissolve; ❸❽

(b) the expiration of the term of existence of the LLC if such term is specified in the articles of organization, certificate of formation, or a similar organizational document, or this operating agreement; ❸❾

(c) the written agreement of all members to dissolve the LLC; or ❹⓿

(d) entry of a decree of dissolution of the LLC under state law. ❹❶

VIII. General Provisions

[The housekeeping and miscellaneous provisions here are almost identical to those provided in Section VII of the member-managed LLC operating agreement; see the corresponding instructions in Chapter 5.]

(1) **Officers:** The managers of this LLC may designate one or more officers, such as a president, vice president, secretary, and treasurer. Persons who fill these positions need not be members or managers of the LLC. Such positions may be compensated or noncompensated according to the nature and extent of the services rendered for the LLC as a part of the duties of each office. Ministerial services only as a part of any officer position will normally not be compensated, such as the performance of officer duties specified in this agreement, but any officer may be reimbursed by the LLC for out-of-pocket expenses paid by the officer in carrying out the duties of his or her office. ❹❷

(2) **Records:** The LLC shall keep at its principal business address a copy of all proceedings of membership meetings, as well as books of account of the LLC's financial transactions. A list of the names and addresses of the current membership of the LLC also shall be maintained at this address, with notations on any transfers of members' interests to nonmembers or persons being admitted into membership in the LLC. A list of the current managers' names and addresses shall also be kept at this address.

Copies of the LLC's articles of organization, certificate of formation, or a similar organizational document, a signed copy of this operating agreement, and the LLC's tax returns for the preceding three tax years shall be kept at the principal business address of the LLC. A statement also shall be kept at this address containing any of the following information that is applicable to this LLC:

- the amount of cash or a description and value of property contributed or agreed to be contributed as capital to the LLC by each member;
- a schedule showing when any additional capital contributions are to be made by members to this LLC;
- a statement or schedule, if appropriate, showing the rights of members to receive distributions representing a return of part or all of members' capital contributions; and
- a description of, or date when, the legal existence of the LLC will terminate under provisions in the LLC's articles of organization, certificate of formation, or a similar organizational document, or this operating agreement.

If one or more of the above items is included or listed in this operating agreement, it will be sufficient to keep a copy of this agreement at the principal business address of the LLC without having to prepare and keep a separate record of such item or items at this address.

Any member or manager may inspect any and all records maintained by the LLC upon reasonable notice to the LLC. Copying of the LLC's records by members and managers is allowed, but copying costs shall be paid for by the requesting member or manager. **Ⓛ**

(3) All Necessary Acts: The members, managers, and officers of this LLC are authorized to perform all acts necessary to perfect the organization of this LLC and to carry out its business operations expeditiously and efficiently. The Secretary of the LLC, or other officers, or one or more managers, or all members of the LLC, may certify to other businesses, financial institutions, and individuals as to the authority of one or more members, managers, or officers of this LLC to transact specific items of business on behalf of the LLC. **㊹**

(4) Mediation and Arbitration of Disputes Among Members: In any dispute over the provisions of this operating agreement and in other disputes among the members, if the members cannot resolve the dispute to their mutual satisfaction, the matter shall be submitted to mediation. The terms and procedure for mediation shall be arranged by the parties to the dispute.

If good-faith mediation of a dispute proves impossible or if an agreed-upon mediation outcome cannot be obtained by the members who are parties to the dispute, the dispute may be submitted to arbitration in accordance with the rules of the American Arbitration Association. Any party may commence arbitration of the dispute by sending a written request for arbitration to all other parties to the dispute. The request shall state the nature of the dispute to be resolved by arbitration, and, if all parties to the dispute agree to arbitration, arbitration shall be commenced as soon as practical after such parties receive a copy of the written request.

All parties shall initially share the cost of arbitration, but the prevailing party or parties may be awarded attorney fees, costs, and other expenses of arbitration. All arbitration decisions shall be final, binding, and conclusive on all the parties to arbitration, and legal judgment may be entered based upon such decision in accordance with applicable law in any court having jurisdiction to do so. **㊺**

(5) Entire Agreement: This operating agreement represents the entire agreement among the members of this LLC, and it shall not be amended, modified, or replaced except by a written instrument executed by all the parties to this agreement who are current members of this LLC as well as any and all additional parties who became members of this LLC after the adoption of this agreement. This agreement replaces and supersedes all prior written and oral agreements among any and all members of this LLC. **㊻**

(6) Severability: If any provision of this agreement is determined by a court or arbitrator to be invalid, unenforceable, or otherwise ineffective, that provision shall be severed from the rest of this agreement, and the remaining provisions shall remain in effect and enforceable. **㊼**

IX. Signatures of Members, Members' Spouses, and Managers

[*The signature lines for members and their spouses are the same as those provided in Section VIII of the LLC member-managed operating agreement in Chapter 5 (see the corresponding instructions), but we also include date and signature lines for your manager(s).*]

(1) Execution of Agreement: In witness whereof, the members of this LLC sign and adopt this agreement as the operating agreement of this LLC.

Date: _____ **㊽**

Signature: _____

Printed Name: _____ , Member

Date: _____

Signature: _____

Printed Name: _____ , Member

Date: _____

Signature: _____

Printed Name: _____ , Member

Date: _____

Signature: _____

Printed Name: _____ , Member

(2) Consent of Spouses: The undersigned are spouses of the members of this LLC who have signed this operating agreement in the preceding provision. These spouses have read this agreement and agree to be bound by its terms in any matter in which they have a financial interest, including restrictions on the transfer of memberships and the terms under which memberships in this LLC may be sold or otherwise transferred. **㊾**

Date: _____

Signature: _____

Printed Name: _____

Spouse of: _____

Date: _____

Signature: _____

Printed Name: _____

Spouse of: _____

Date: _____

Signature: _____

Printed Name: _____

Spouse of: _____

Date: _____

Signature: _____

Printed Name: _____

Spouse of: _____

(3) Signatures of Managers: The undersigned managers of this limited liability company have read this agreement and agree to be bound by its terms in discharging their duties as managers. Ⓜ

Date: _____

Signature: _____

Printed Name: _____ , Manager

Date: _____

Signature: _____

Printed Name: _____ , Manager

Date: _____

Signature: _____

Printed Name: _____ , Manager

Date: _____

Signature: _____

Printed Name: _____ , Manager

Distribute Copies of Your Operating Agreement

Congratulations! You are done with another important organizational task, and your LLC is well on its legal way. Make photocopies of the completed, signed management operating agreement and give each member and manager a copy. Finally, place the original, signed agreement in your LLC records book. ●

After Forming Your LLC

In this chapter, we discuss legal and proce-
dural formalities that you may need to tend
to after setting up your limited liability
company. We suggest you skim through the
chapter and get a general sense of the work you
may need to do. If any topic seems pertinent,
carefully read the discussion.

It's important to keep in mind that LLCs
are relatively new, so trying to anticipate the
ongoing issues and concerns particular to LLCs
is a bit of a guessing game. For now, we cover
operational tasks and issues we believe are
most likely to apply. We're sure you'll be on the
lookout for other LLC matters, and should be
able to handle them successfully using common
sense and good business judgment (backed
up, if necessary, by a consultation with a small
business legal or tax adviser, as discussed in
Chapter 8).

RESOURCE

Get general business information. This
book can't possibly cover all the ins and outs of
small business law. You'll find a wealth of helpful
information in *Legal Guide for Starting & Running
a Small Business*, by Fred S. Steingold (Nolo). For
tax guidance, see *Tax Savvy for Small Business*, by
Frederick W. Daily (Nolo).

If You Converted an Existing Business to an LLC

If you converted an existing sole proprietorship
or partnership to an LLC, you'll need to take a
few extra steps, as discussed in this section. (The
aftermath of converting a corporation to an
LLC is beyond the scope of this book.)

SKIP AHEAD

If yours is a new business. If you did not
convert a preexisting business to an LLC, skip to
"Basic Tax Forms and Formalities," below.

Notifying Agencies and Businesses

Make sure you notify the IRS, your state taxing
authority, and other governmental agencies that
you've changed your legal status to an LLC,
and provide them with your new LLC name.
As part of this process, you may need to obtain
some of the following in your new LLC name:

- federal employer identification number
(Co-owned LLCs need their own federal
employer identification number, or EIN.
Sole owner LLCs can use the owner's Social
Security number.)
- state employer identification number
- fictitious or assumed business name
statement if you run your LLC under a
name different from its formal name listed
in its articles
- sales tax permit
- business license, and
- professional license or permit, if the LLC
members engage in a licensed profession.

Of course, you'll want to immediately get
to work changing your stationery, business
cards, brochures, advertisements, signs, and
other marketing and business miscellany to
reflect your new LLC name. In addition, let
your bank, suppliers, customers, and business
associates know your new business name and
LLC status.

TIP
Review your files and other papers for organizations to contact. If you go through the tax returns and other papers for your prior business, you'll likely discover the names and addresses of additional agencies and businesses that should be notified of your new business name and form.

Converting a Partnership to an LLC

If you converted an existing general or limited partnership to an LLC, you will probably need to do a little extra paperwork to end the legal existence of the partnership. If you neglect to take these steps, the general partner(s) may remain personally liable for any unpaid partnership business debts (we assume your LLC will pay off any unpaid debts of the prior business anyway; see "Liability for Previous Partnership Debts," below):

- **Converting a general partnership to an LLC.** State law may require you to publish a notice of dissolution of partnership. Call a local paper that publishes legal notices and ask if it provides this service. Not only should the newspaper be able to tell you whether this notice is required in your state, it should be able to mail you a summary of your state's requirements if you want to read them yourself. When you publish your notice, the newspaper should send you a copy of the published notice and an affidavit of publication to place in your files.

- **Converting a limited partnership to an LLC.** This conversion usually is not legally effective until you file a cancellation or termination of limited partnership form with your Secretary of State's office. The state filing office should have a fill-in-the-

blanks or sample form you can use for this purpose, similar to the sample provided below. Your LLC filing office will normally handle the filing for terminating a limited partnership. You generally must attend to this formality unless your state LLC office supplied a special form of articles of conversion to convert a partnership to an LLC. In this latter case, the articles of conversion normally also legally terminate the existence of the limited partnership, so you don't have to separately file a termination or cancellation of limited partnership form.

Liability for Previous Partnership Debts

If your general or limited partnership has outstanding claims or debts owing at the time of its conversion to an LLC, the general partners of the preexisting partnership will remain personally liable for these debts. Of course, your new LLC probably plans to assume and pay these bills as they come due. As a courtesy, and to make sure all partnership creditors have personal notice of your new business structure, we recommend you send a personal letter to notify each one of the conversion of the partnership to an LLC, and provide the LLC's name and business address where future correspondence may be sent.

If there are significant disputed debts or claims of your prior partnership that your LLC will not automatically pay when it begins doing business, we strongly urge you to check with a business lawyer. You will obviously want to know your legal rights and responsibilities as to these disputed amounts.

Sample Cancellation of Limited Partnership

Prescribed by
Bob Taft, Secretary of State
30 East Broad Street, 14th Floor
Columbus, Ohio 43266-0418
Form LPC (July 1994)

Registration #_____
Approved_____
Date_____
Fee $10

CERTIFICATE OF CANCELLATION OF
LIMITED PARTNERSHIP

Pursuant to the provisions of Ohio Revised Code Section 1782.10(B), the undersigned,_____

(name of limited partnership)

bearing registration number _____, does hereby certify the following:

1.   The name of the limited partnership:_____

_____

2.   The registration number of the limited partnership:_____

3.   The date of the initial filing of its certificate of limited partnership:_____

month   day   year

4.   The date of the filing of its certificate of limited partnership with the Ohio Secretary of State (if different from the date listed in line #3):_____

month   day   year

5.   The reason for filing the certificate of cancellation is as follows:

(If insufficient space for this item, please attach a separate sheet)

6.   The effective date of cancellation: (please check/complete one of the following)

[ ] Upon Filing of Certificate of Cancellation   [ ]_____

month   day   year

(Please note that the effective date of cancellation cannot precede or be earlier than the date of filing)

7.   Is a person other than any general partner reflected on the certificate of limited partnership winding up the limited partnership's affairs?

[ ] Yes   [ ] No   *(please check the applicable box)*

Filing a Bulk Sales Notice

Some states require the publication and mailing of a Notice of Bulk Sales when certain types of businesses—such as retail, wholesale, and manufacturing businesses—are sold or converted to another form. The idea behind the requirement is to prevent debtor businesses (those owing money when they "go out of business") from changing their business form without arranging to pay their debts.

A local paper that publishes legal notices should know the rules for making this publication if it is required in your state. Ask the newspaper for a copy of your state's bulk sales act rules if you want to read them yourself. If the newspaper can't help you, a business or law library should have information and forms that you can use to handle any state requirements.

TIP

Your conversion to an LLC may be exempt from notice of bulk sales rules. In many states, bulk notice requirements are simplified or even waived if a business is simply being converted to a new form—such as the conversion of a partnership or sole partnership to an LLC—and the new business will assume and pay off the prior business's debts.

Basic Tax Forms and Formalities

Let's look at some tax issues and tasks you will need to keep in mind and tend to when the time comes.

Federal Income Taxes

If you wish your LLC to start out being treated by the IRS as a corporation, make sure to file IRS Form 8832 on time (within 75 days of the formation of your LLC). A tear-out Form 8832

is provided in Appendix B, and can be found on the IRS website at www.irs.gov. For further information, see Chapter 3.

If your LLC is classified as a partnership or a corporation (and not as the sole proprietorship of your sole member), it will need to file partnership or corporate tax returns each year. If it is classified as a partnership, make sure to provide Schedule K-1s to each member after the close of the LLC tax year as well.

Tax Resources for LLCs

Like many small business owners, you may plan to turn your annual tax preparation work over to your tax adviser, rather than handle it yourself. But you should still keep yourself informed of tax matters.

Whether you plan to prepare your own tax returns or simply want more information, you'll want to take advantage of the free tax forms and publications provided by the IRS. Go to www.irs.gov and download the forms and publications, or call 1-800-TAX-FORM and request copies of:

- IRS Form 1065, *U.S. Return of Partnership Income*
- Schedule K-1 of Form 1065, and
- IRS Publication 334, *Tax Guide for Small Business*. This is one of the best guides for finding and filling in the latest annual tax return form for different types of businesses, including LLCs (which are treated as partnerships).

State Income Taxes

Most states follow the federal lead and classify your LLC the same as the IRS does. This normally means the LLC doesn't pay any entity (business) level state income tax (unless you elect to have your LLC classified and taxed as a corporation). The LLC may still have to file a state informational return, or annually submit a copy of the federal partnership tax return.

SEE AN EXPERT

If your state doesn't impose corporate or personal income taxes. The states of Nevada, South Dakota, Washington, and Wyoming do not impose either personal or corporate state income taxes. Alaska, Florida, New Hampshire, Tennessee, and Texas do not impose state tax on individual income (although New Hampshire and Texas impose a special personal tax on interest and dividend income).

Being treated as a partnership in a state without a personal income tax ordinarily means that the LLC and its members do not pay state income tax on LLC profits. However, don't forget that even if your LLC and members avoid income taxes on profits earned in your state, out-of-state taxes may be imposed if profits are earned in other states. This is a technical issue, and subject to state-by-state variations. Ask your tax adviser or check your state's tax office website (see your state sheet in Appendix A for the link to your state's tax office website).

Some state tax offices require LLCs to pay a minimum annual tax each year, sometimes euphemistically called an LLC "renewal fee." Some states go whole hog and subject LLCs to the same income or franchise tax that is levied on corporations.

If your LLC must pay state franchise or income tax, make sure you make required estimated payments. Franchise and income taxes must usually be prepaid in four installments during the tax year, with the first payment consisting of any minimum amount charged. If you miss estimated tax payments,

you will be charged penalties and interest. In some states, your LLC can be suspended if you fail to pay these taxes for a few years.

The best source for current information on how your state handles the income taxation of LLCs is your state tax office website (listed in the state sheets in Appendix A).

Employment Taxes

Your LLC will need to register as an employer. For salaried workers, your LLC must withhold, report, and pay:

- federal and, if applicable, state income taxes
- federal employment taxes (unemployment, Social Security, and Medicare taxes), and
- state payroll taxes (state unemployment, disability, and workers' compensation insurance).

And don't forget, LLC members may have to pay self-employment taxes on their allocated share of your LLC's profits—see Chapter 3 for more information.

RESOURCE

Get more information on federal payroll tax requirements. Go to www.irs.gov or call 1-800-TAX-FORM and download or request IRS Form SS-4 (to get a federal employer identification number for your LLC), IRS Publication 15, *Circular E, Employer's Tax Guide* and the IRS Publication 15 *Supplement* (for federal payroll tax information). For state payroll tax requirements, go to the state tax office online (typically, the Department of Revenue) or call the state tax office at its main information number (see your state sheet in Appendix A) and ask to be transferred to the state employment tax division.

Other State and Local Taxes

State sales, use, and county property taxes apply to LLCs. Counties and cities also may impose local and regional taxes. Check with your county and city tax offices for current information.

Ongoing LLC Legal Paperwork and Procedures

Now let's cover a few legal formalities that may come up during the life of your LLC.

Changing Your Operating Agreement

During the life of your LLC, you may want to make changes to your operating agreement or draw up a new agreement—for example:

- If a new member joins the LLC, you will want a new agreement to include the new member's capital, profits and losses, and voting percentages.

- A prospective new member, or his or her legal or tax adviser, may ask for a change to one or more provisions in your old agreement to suit the needs of the new member.

Of course, you can decide to update your operating agreement at any time, not just when a new member joins your LLC. It's a good idea to sit down with your fellow LLC members at least once every two or so years and go over your agreement to see if it continues to meet your needs. If it doesn't, perhaps it is time to make a few changes.

EXAMPLE:

The Pig in a Poke Ltd. Liability Company, a mail-order lottery subscription and award notification service, wants to enlarge its membership base. The current members reason that it will be easier to attract new LLC members if they can be allowed to transfer their membership to others more easily than their operating agreement currently allows. They meet and decide to lessen the unanimous vote requirement in their agreement to allow transfers to new members by a per capita majority vote of the members. They then amend their operating agreement to reflect this change.

How to Update Your Operating Agreement

There are three steps to updating an LLC operating agreement:

- First, have your members formally meet, discuss, and approve the changes you plan to make to the operating agreement.

- Next, prepare a new operating agreement. Simply recreate your old agreement, revising it to reflect your LLC's new needs.

- Finally, have all members and their spouses sign the updated operating agreement, which contains the new provisions plus all unchanged provisions carried over from your previous agreement.

> **CAUTION**
>
> **Watch out for state law restrictions on changes to your agreement.** Your state's LLC act may contain restrictions or requirements. For example, some states prevent you from lowering the voting requirements necessary to amend the articles or certificate of organization or to approve the transfer of a membership to a new member.

We alert you to your state's statutory rule on membership approval of transfers, and whether you can change it, in the "Default Transfer Rule" paragraph of the Operating Rules section of your state sheet in Appendix A. We do the same for your state's voting requirements when a member is dissociated (when a member retires, dies, is disabled, expelled, or otherwise loses his or her membership interest) in the "Default Continuation Rule" paragraph of the same section. To get the most current version of these and other state rules, scan your state's LLC act online (find the link to your state's LLC act in the state sheets in Appendix A).

How to Prepare a New Agreement for a New Member

As we've said, preparing and signing a new LLC operating agreement ensures each new member agrees to all rights and responsibilities of LLC membership and that each current member agrees to the new division of capital, profits, losses, and voting.

When you prepare a new operating agreement, make sure to change the capital contributions clause and other provisions that are affected by admitting the new member. All current members plus the new member must sign the new agreement. Place the original in your LLC records book.

EXAMPLE:

Shortly after its formation, Tried & True Triad Music Promotions LLC, a three-owner company, decides to admit a fourth member. The new member will pay $20,000 to the LLC, the same amount each of the original members paid. The company adopts a new operating agreement and changes the ownership percentages of the original three members in the capital contribution clause from 33⅓% to 25%, also showing a 25% interest for the newly admitted fourth member. No other changes are required, because splitting of profits and losses and voting rights follow the percentage interests shown in the capital contributions clause. The three initial members and the new member sign the new agreement and place it in the LLC records book.

! CAUTION

Get tax advice. Adding a new member is one of the times when tax help may be needed to make important LLC tax elections. For example, a tax election may be necessary to make sure that the relative capital accounts balances of the original members are adjusted to properly reflect their correct ratios after the admission of a new member.

Minutes of Meetings

If your LLC wishes to approve and formally document an important legal, tax, or business transaction, you'll normally hold a meeting of your members (or managers, if you have opted for manager control by adopting the operating agreement covered in Chapter 6).

Your members or managers may decide to hold a formal LLC meeting to take actions such as the following:

- vote on any matters that require a membership (or manager) vote, as set out in your operating agreement
- change your LLC operating agreement (even in manager-managed LLCs, the members normally are asked to ratify any changes to the operating agreement)
- amend the LLC's articles of organization
- make significant capital outlays, such as to purchase real property

- fund a major, recurring LLC expense, such as contributions to an employee pension or profit-sharing plan
- sell real estate or other major capital items
- sell or purchase an operating division within the company, or expand or discontinue a product line or services
- pursue or settle a lawsuit, or
- approve other important legal, business, financial, or tax decisions.

You should prepare minutes of formal LLC meetings during or after the meeting, recording the discussions and decisions made. After the meeting, place the signed minutes in your LLC records book.

TIP

You don't always have to meet face-to-face to record a formal LLC decision. Even if your LLC operating agreement requires that all or a certain percentage of members or managers approve a particular decision formally, you don't usually need to get together in person to do so. You may hold meetings on paper if all members or managers agree. You do this by preparing minutes that record a decision as though it had been made at a formal meeting. You then circulate these minutes for formal approval (signing and dating) by each member or manager. This sort of "paper meeting" is fine if everyone agrees to approve a decision this way.

Give Adequate Notice of Meeting to All Members or Managers

We don't cover all the ins and outs of calling, providing notice of, and holding formal LLC meetings in our standard operating agreement. Most state laws are very flexible and allow LLCs to handle these matters in any way the members or managers wish. If, however, you have specified meeting rules in your operating agreement or articles of organization, make sure you follow them.

To make sure everyone involved knows the time, date, and purpose of each upcoming meeting, notify all members or managers (or both groups if both will attend the meeting) well in advance. Normally, two to four weeks' mailed notice is adequate. Providing adequate notice is particularly important if some members are not active in the LLC and not part of your LLC's normal network of memos, discussions, and verbal feedback. Taking the extra step to provide notice of an upcoming meeting may not be legally necessary under your operating agreement or state law, but it can avoid a lot of aggravation later—for example, if a controversial decision is adopted at a meeting without the approval of one or more members or managers.

RESOURCE

See *Your Limited Liability Company: An Operating Manual,* by Anthony Mancuso (Nolo), for a comprehensive treatment of LLC meetings, with tear-out and CD-ROM minutes forms plus more than 80 resolutions to show approval of various legal, tax, and business transactions by LLC members and managers.

How to Complete Minutes of Meeting Form

On the next page, we provide a sample of the simple, ready-to-use LLC Minutes of Meeting form included in Appendix B. You can make a copy of the tear-out form and fill it in as you follow the sample and instructions.

CD-ROM

The LLC Minutes form is included on the CD-ROM at the back of this book.

Minutes of Meeting of the

["Members" *or* "Managers"] ❶

of

[*Name of LLC*]

A meeting of the _____ ["members" *or* "managers"] _____ of the above named limited liability company was held on ___ [*date ,including year*] ___, at [*time*] ___ .M., at ___ [*address*] ___ , State of _____ [*state*] _____, for the following purpose(s): [*list the items of business discussed or considered by the members or managers*] ❷ _____

_____ .

[*name and title*]_____ acted as chairperson, and

[*name and title*]_____ acted as secretary of the meeting. ❸

The chairperson called the meeting to order.

The following ___ ["members" *or* "managers"] ___ were present at the meeting: [*names of members or managers*] ❹ _____ .

The following persons were also present at the meeting, and any reports given by these persons are noted next to their names below: ❺

Name and Title   Reports Presented, If Any

_____   _____

_____   _____

After discussion, on motion duly made and carried by the affirmative vote of ["all," "a majority of the percentage interests," *or whatever voting requirement is used for members or managers in your LLC*] _____ of the ["members" *or* "managers"] ___ , the following resolution(s) was/were adopted: [*insert language of proposal(s) passed by members or managers*] ❻ _____ .

There being no further business to come before the meeting, it was adjourned on motion duly made and carried.

Date: [*date*] _____

Signature(s): [*signature of LLC Secretary, officer, or member*] ❼

[*typed or printed name*] _____

Title: [*LLC title or status*] _____

Special Instructions

❶ In the first blank, indicate whether the minutes are being prepared for a meeting of members or managers. Because most smaller LLCs are managed by members, formal meetings will usually be convened as membership meetings.

❷ Include a brief statement of the nature of the resolutions that are raised for approval at the meeting. For example: "to approve the purchase of property by the LLC" or "to approve a proposed employment contract to be offered to the CEO of the LLC" or "to accept the terms of a construction loan obtained by the treasurer of the LLC."

❸ Insert the name and title of the persons designated as chairperson and secretary of the meeting. Normally, the CEO or president of the LLC acts as chairperson. The person preparing these minutes will typically be the secretary of the meeting (often the secretary of the LLC).

If you have not designated officers for your LLC (see Special Instruction ㊷ in the operating agreement instructions in Chapter 5), simply appoint one of the attending members or managers to serve in each of these capacities.

❹ This paragraph indicates which members or managers attended the meeting. Check your operating agreement to see if it states that a minimum number of members or managers must attend meetings—technically, this number is called a "quorum." Our standard operating agreement provisions require:

- **Member-managed LLC:** All members must attend meetings unless a nonattending member agrees in writing prior to the meeting that it may be held in his or her absence (or unless the meeting is a second postponed meeting; see Chapter 5, Special Instruction ⓯).

- **Manager-managed LLC:** You may pick the number of managers who must attend an LLC managers' meeting—see Chapter 6, Special Instruction ❺).

❺ List any nonmembers or nonmanagers who attend the meeting. Also show to the right of an attendee's name any report presented by this person (such as an "annual written financial report by the LLC treasurer," "an insurance availability and premium quote report by a vice president," or "an oral report by the president on the negotiations that led to the drafting of a proposed lease agreement being presented at the meeting for approval by members"). Attach to your minutes a copy of any written reports handed out at the meeting.

❻ Here you take care of the primary reason for preparing minutes of your meeting: to show the vote taken and the language of the proposals approved by your members or managers. If different votes are obtained on different resolutions, repeat this preliminary paragraph before each resolution.

LLC members are normally given voting power equal to their percentage interests in the LLC. So, for example, a member who owns 25% of the LLC will normally have 25% of the voting power of the LLC. Managers, on the other hand, normally are given one vote per person in reaching management decisions. Check your operating agreement to be sure of your voting rules for members and managers.

Show the vote obtained in favor of the proposal in the first blank. For more significant or controversial decisions, where members or managers dissent or abstain, you may wish to insert a paragraph that shows how each person voted on every individual proposal—for, against, or abstained.

> **! CAUTION**
>
> **On special matters, your operating agreement may have stricter voting requirements.** For example, unanimous voting approval of members or managers may be required for:
> - the approval of structural changes to the LLC, such as a sale of assets
> - the admission or departure of members
> - continuance or dissolution of the business after a member leaves, or
> - amendments to the articles of organization.

In the last blanks of the paragraph, insert the wording of each resolution approved at the meeting. The language should be nontechnical and clearly state the decision the members or managers reached. If you wish to back up your description, you can attach additional information to your minutes and refer to the attachments here.

> **Example of Contract Approval:** "The members approved a long-term contract for the supplying of goods to the LLC by [*name of company*]. A copy of the contract approved is attached."

Although routine business contracts are normally not formally approved at a membership meeting, such approval may be sought to avoid the appearance of a conflict of interest—for example, if the supply company is owned or managed by a member's spouse.

> **Example of Lease Approval:** "The managers approved the terms of a ten-year lease of premises by the LLC. A copy of the lease agreement is attached."

> **Approval of Tax Matter:** "The members approved the following tax proposal, recommended for passage by the LLC's accountant, [*name of accountant*]. Copies of correspondence with the accountant and other relevant documents considered by members before approval of this proposal are attached."

❼ Have the secretary of the meeting, or any other designated LLC officer or member, date and sign the minutes. Type or print the person's name and title under the signature line. Finally, place a copy of the signed minutes in your LLC records book together with any attachment pages.

Special Approvals for New or Departing Members

When a member joins or leaves an LLC, it is important to comply with the voting requirements in the LLC's operating agreement, especially if state law sets the requirements. This may mean obtaining formal approval of members to:

- continue the legal existence of the LLC after a member's interest is terminated, and
- admit new members who have received a transferred interest in the LLC from a prior member.

The specific vote requirements for each of these events is in your operating agreement, as discussed below.

Check Vote Required to Approve Transfer or Continuance of LLC

You'll need to determine who has to vote, when, and by how many votes, to approve the transfer of membership by a former member to a new member, or to continue the existence of the LLC after a member dies, retires, resigns, goes bankrupt or insane, or is expelled.

The accompanying sidebar, "Standard Voting Requirements in Our LLC Operating Agreements," lists the requirements for these two formal matters under provisions in our tear-out operating agreements in Appendix B.

Prepare Minutes Approving Transfer of Membership or Continuance of LLC

Once you know the voting rules you must follow, hold a meeting and obtain the required membership (or member-manager) approval. Then prepare written minutes of the meeting to place in your LLC records book.

Below is language you can use in your minutes to show the approval of either of these formal matters at a membership or member-manager meeting:

Special Instruction

❶ If your agreement requires (as ours do) a per capita vote to approve these special matters (this means a simple head count for each member or member-manager), leave this "LLC Interest" column blank.

If your operating agreement requires voting approval of these matters by capital and/or profits interests in the LLC, indicate in this column the appropriate percentage(s) for each member. If, for instance, your agreement requires a majority of the LLC's capital and profits interests to approve the continuance of your LLC after a member resigns, you would fill out this column to show these two percentages for each remaining member who attends the meeting and votes. For example, if a remaining voting member holds both a 50% capital and profits interest in your LLC, this column would state "50% capital and 50% profits interest" for the member.

Prepare New Operating Agreement

Follow the instructions in "Changing Your Operating Agreement," above, and have all members (old and new) sign the new agreement.

Sample Language: The members of ____[name of LLC]____ met to approve the ["transfer of membership by (name of former member) to (name of new member)" or "continuance of the LLC following the (insert dissociation event, such as "resignation," "retirement," "death," "bankruptcy," "mental incompetence," or transfer of membership or dissociation of member]___, which occurred on ____[date of tranfer of membership or dissociation of member]___. The ____["nontransferring" (use this word to approve transfers)] or "remaining" (use this word instead to approve a continuance of the LLC)]____ ____["members" or "member-managers"]____ of the LLC voted to approve the matter by the following vote:

Name of Member	LLC Interest ❶	Vote
[list each nontransferring or remaining member]		["approve," "against" or "abstain"]

Keep LLC Records

You will want to keep your important LLC documents in a safe, convenient place. We recommend setting up an organized system for keeping your LLC records, whether in manila envelopes, file folders, or a specially ordered LLC records book available from legal stationers.

Other Ongoing LLC Formalities

In this section, we cover a number of additional ongoing legal, tax, and practical formalities that apply to LLCs.

How to Sign Papers on Behalf of Your LLC

We're sure the separate legal existence of your LLC is important to you, particularly to avoid personal liability for business debts and claims. To make sure you and other LLC members will enjoy this limited liability, members should always sign LLC papers, documents, contracts, and other commitments clearly in the name of the LLC, not in their own names.

The best way to do this is to first state the name of the LLC, then sign your name on its behalf.

EXAMPLE:

Tom is one of two members of Park Place Plasterers, Ltd. Liability Co. He enters into a long-term contract to refurbish apartments in a high-rise condominium. Tom signs the contract as follows:

Date: November 3, 20xx

Park Place Plasterers, Ltd. Liability Co.

By: _____[Tom's signature]_____,

Tom Park, LLC Member/Manager

> ⚠ **CAUTION**
>
> **Signing in your own name could lead to personal liability.** If you don't follow our advice, the other party to a contract you sign may be able to hold you personally liable. To avoid confusion and legal problems, make this simple signing procedure a regular part of your day-to-day business routine.

Sample State LLC Annual Report

STATE OF MONTANA

ANNUAL LIMITED LIABILITY COMPANY REPORT

Prepare, sign and submit with fee.

(For use by the Secretary of State only)

MAIL TO: **MIKE COONEY**
Secretary of State
PO Box 202801
Helena, MT 59620-2801
Phone: (406)444-3665

Filing Fee: Before April 15 $10 -- After April 15 $20
After September 1 $30   Form: ART-L

In compliance with Section 35-8-208, MCA, the undersigned limited liability company submits the following report:

Exact Name of Limited Liability Company: _____

_____

Registered Agent Information

Name of Registered Agent: _____

Street Address of Registered Office: _____

PO Box or Mailing Address: _____

City, State, Zip: _____

If there is any change in the registered agent or registered office location, please complete a statement of change form and send an additional $5 filing fee. (A PO Box number may be added without the form or fee.)

1. **State of Organization:** _____

2. **Address of Principal Office** in state of organization: _____

_____

3. **Limited liability company is managed by** *(members or member/managers):* _____

4. **The last date when the limited liability company will be dissolved:** _____

5. **Names and addresses** (street name and number) **of Individual Managers or Member/Managers of company:**

Sample State LLC Annual Report (cont'd.)

6. **Names and addresses of registered business** *(managers or member/managers): These businesses must be registered with the Montana Secretary of State's Office.*

_____   _____
_____   _____
_____   _____
_____   _____
_____   _____
_____   _____
_____   _____
_____   _____

7. ☐ **Professional Limited Liability Companies only.** *(Please check)* All the members and not less than one-half of the managers are qualified with the proper licensing authority in Montana or meet higher standards as specified by that licensing authority.

8. By my signature below, I, a member of the above limited liability company authorized to execute documents on its behalf, do state that any and all statements contained herein are true and based upon actions taken by the LLC in accordance with the statutes or its articles of organization or operating agreement.

And I further state that the LLC remains in existence and has taken the necessary actions during the past year to preserve the status.

_____
Exact Name of Limited Liability Company

✓_____   _____
Signature of Member   Printed Name of Member Signing

_____
Address of Member Signing Report

File Annual State LLC Reports

Most states require LLCs to file one-page annual report forms. These forms are supplied by and filed with the state LLC filing office where you filed your LLC articles of organization, typically, the Secretary of State's office.

You usually need to provide minimal information on this form, such as the names and addresses of current LLC members and/or managers, and the name and address of the LLC's registered agent and office for service of legal process. Often, you can leave items blank if there is no change in the information from the previous annual report filing.

Typically, you must mail a small fee with the form, in the $10 to $50 range. Some states require significantly more. We alert you on your state sheet in Appendix A if your state asks for more than a small amount.

Filing a Fictitious or Assumed Business Name Statement

You may wish to operate your LLC locally under a name that's different from the formal name of your LLC listed in your articles of organization.

EXAMPLE:

The Solar Plexus Flex and Fitness Center Ltd. Liability Co. decides to operate its three franchise locations under the fictitious name Flex and Fitness Center. The LLC owners want to continue to keep the formal name stated in the state-filed LLC articles of organization, but prefer operating their fitness centers under this second, shortened version.

Most states let you use a new name by filing a fictitious or assumed business name statement form and paying a small fee. You normally file this paperwork with the Secretary of State's office or the local county clerk or another county office. In some states, both a state and county filing are required. Find out your state's rules by checking your state's LLC filing office website or calling your Secretary of State's or your local county clerk's office.

Some states also require that a notice of use of, or intention to use, the fictitious name be published in a newspaper of general circulation one or more times in each county where the name is or will be used. Newspapers with legal notice classified sections will do this for you for a moderate fee and file any statements of publication required under your state's fictitious business name statute. The easiest way to find out if your state requires publication, and what the requirements are, is to call a local newspaper.

Amending Articles of Organization

Your original LLC articles of organization contain basic information and ordinarily will stay the way they are for a long time to come. But if you need to make a major change to your LLC that alters the information in this document—such as changing the formal name of your LLC or changing whether your LLC is managed by members or managers—you will need to file amended articles with your state's LLC filing office. The filing fee for amended articles is typically the same as the fee paid to file original articles of organization.

Most LLC filing offices provide an amendment form online, which you can fill in—doing so is usually an easy task. On the following page is a standard amendment form, typical of the type of filing necessary to register amendments to LLC articles of organization with the state.

Sample Amendment of Articles

ARTICLES AMENDING OR RESTATING ARTICLES OF ORGANIZATION
DOMESTIC LIMITED LIABILITY COMPANY
LLC   Rev. 10/93

Secretary of the State
30 Trinity Street
Hartford, CT 06106

1. Name of the limited liability Company:

_____

2. Date of filing Articles of Organization (month, day, year): _____

3. The Articles of Organization Are: (Check One Only)

_____A. Amended only, pursuant to P.A. No. 93-262 §12(b).

_____B. Amended and Restated, pursuant to P.A. No. 93-262 §12(c).

_____C. Restated only, pursuant to P.A. No. 93-262 §12(c).

If 3A or 3B checked, complete #4.

4. The amendment is as follows: (Attach plain sheet of 8½x11 paper, if additional
    space required)

If 3C is checked, read #5.
5. If the Articles of Organization are restated set forth each article including
    all prior amendments.   (Attach plain sheet of 8½x11 paper, if additional space
    required.)

EXECUTION

6. Dated this_____day of_____, 19_____

7. _____   8. _____
    Name and capacity of signatory (print or type   Signature

_____
For Official Use Only |Rec; CC:
                                       |_____
                                       |
                                       |_____
                                       |
                                       |_____
                                       |
                                       |_____
                                       |
                                       |_____
                                       |
                                       |_____

J150.6

! CAUTION

Hold a formal membership meeting to approve amendments. Before filing an amendment with the state, your membership should approve any amendment to the LLC's articles of organization at a formal meeting. See "Minutes of Meetings," above, on how to prepare minutes of an LLC meeting.

Changing Registered Agent or Office

The initial registered agent and registered office of your LLC are usually specified in your articles of organization. The registered agent is the person your LLC authorizes to receive legal documents from the state as well as the public on behalf of the LLC. The registered office is the business address of the agent where legal papers may be served.

It's in your LLC's best interests that the state have the most current registered agent and office information—you don't want to miss any important legal papers sent by the state to an old address. Moreover, if you change the name or address of the registered agent, you are normally required to notify the state. In most states, the LLC filing office provides a standard form (titled "Change of Registered Agent or Address" or something similar) online. There may be a small filing fee.

Note that the change of registered agent or office is a routine task so you don't need to hold a formal LLC meeting, amend your articles of organization, or revise your operating agreement. Just fill in and file the state-supplied form—that's all there is to it.

Certification of LLC Existence

Outside businesses, financial institutions, creditors, and individuals may want to see formal legal paperwork that establishes the existence of your LLC before deciding to transact other business with it (enter into a contract, sign a lease, agree to sell or buy property, and the like). Normally, a copy of your articles of organization or operating agreement sufficiently establishes that your LLC has handled all the necessary organizational formalities.

Occasionally, you may have to be even more formal and show a *certified* copy of your LLC articles of organization. A certified copy, which should be available for a small fee from your state LLC filing office, may not only show the file stamp of the office, but also formal language stating that your LLC has met all necessary state formalities to begin doing business in your state.

Some outsiders may be sticklers for detail and insist that you show them that your legal status is still valid—after all, articles of organization and operating agreements only show that you met legal requirements on a past date. Most states will help you with this. One way is to call the status or legal section of the LLC filing office and ask if you can obtain a current certificate of status or good standing for your LLC. Some states provide a standard certification form, which shows your LLC meets all state legal and tax requirements on the date of the status request.

Sample Change of Registered Agent or Address

	For Office Use Only
State of Tennessee	
Department of State	**CHANGE OF REGISTERED**
Corporations Section	**AGENT/OFFICE**
18th Floor, James K. Polk Building	**(BY A LIMITED LIABILITY COMPANY)**
Nashville, TN 37243-0306	

Pursuant to the provisions of § 48A-8-102(a) of the Tennessee Limited Liability Company Act, the undersigned Limited Liability Company hereby submits this application:

1. The name of the Limited Liability Company is: _____

_____

2. The street address of its current registered office is: _____

_____

3. If the current registered office is to be changed, the street address of the new registered office, the zip code of such office, and the county in which the office is located is:

_____

_____

4. The name of the current registered agent is: _____

_____

5. If the current registered agent is to be changed, the name of the new registered agent is:

_____

6. After the change(s), the street addresses of the registered office and the business office of the registered agent will be identical.

Signature Date _____   **Name of Limited Liability Company** _____

Signer's Capacity _____   **Signature** _____

Name (typed or printed) _____

SS-4225   RDA Pending

Certification of Authority of LLC Members or Officers

It's possible that an outsider may raise a question about the legal authority of your LLC members, managers, and/or officers, and want to be sure they really have official status or specific authority for a transaction before proceeding. Typically, this occurs with real estate transactions involving title (and escrow companies that are paid to be fussy), particularly if the property is located in another state.

Complying with a request of this sort involves more than simply checking the legal status of your LLC as discussed above. You also will need to document that the person acting on behalf of the LLC is properly authorized by the LLC to enter into the transaction. There are a few ways to handle this, as discussed in detail below, namely by providing a:

- copy of your articles of organization
- copy of your operating agreement
- certification of authority, or
- state certification form.

Let's look at each of these options.

Copy of Articles of Organization

In most states, your articles of organization list the *initial* members of your LLC and state whether the members will manage the LLC. If your LLC has adopted a manager-managed operating agreement, these individuals should be listed as managers in your articles of organization. To obtain certified copies of articles of organization (available for a small fee), contact your state LLC filing office—see your state sheet in Appendix A for the phone number and address.

Copy of Operating Agreement

If you need to certify the authority of a member or manager who assumed this role after your articles of organization were filed, you can provide a copy of the amended operating agreement signed by the new member or manager.

Certification of Authority

If you want to keep your operating agreement private, an alternative approach is to prepare a simple form to certify the authority of any members or managers. We include a Certification of Authority in Appendix B for this purpose. Below is a sample of this form, along with instructions.

 CD-ROM

The Certification of Authority form is included on the CD-ROM at the back of this book.

Special Instructions

❶ Here is a specific designation of authority you can fill in to underscore the member's or manager's authority to transact specific business for your LLC. In the blanks, describe the specific transaction for which the certification is being sought, such as:

- "the signing of a lease for the premises located at [*address*]"
- "entering into a contract with [*name of company or individual*] for [*specify product or services under consideration*]"
- if you don't want to limit the person's authority in any way, "any and all LLC business," or
- if you don't want to complete this blank, insert "N/A" instead.

Sample Certification of Authority

This LLC is managed by its ___["members" *or* "managers"]___ . The names and addresses of each of its current ___["members" *or* "managers"]___ as of ___[*date of certification*]___ are listed below. Each of these persons has managerial authority of the LLC and is empowered to transact business on its behalf.

Name of ___["Member" *or* "Manager"]___   Address

_____   _____

_____   _____

_____   _____

_____   _____

_____   _____

Further, each of the following ___["members" *or* "managers"]___ is specifically authorized to transact the following business on behalf of the LLC:

[*describe the specific business transaction*] ❶ _____ .

Date: [*date of signing—on or after certification date shown above*]

Name of LLC: [*name of LLC*] _____

by: [*signature*] _____

Name: [*typed or printed name of signer*] _____

Title: [*LLC title or status*] _____ ❷

❷ You can have your LLC secretary, president, or another designated officer prepare and sign this form, or you can have it signed by all current LLC members or managers. These signing procedures are authorized under the standard provisions in the tear-out operating agreements included in this book. (See Chapter 5, Special Instruction ㊽.) Simply fill in the appropriate title, such as "Secretary," "President," "Member," or "Manager."

State Certification Form

Some states let you file a form with the state LLC filing office certifying the names and authority of your LLC members and/or managers. They do this because LLCs are a relatively new type of business and the state recognizes that an official form may look better than an internal certification form provided by the LLC. To find out if your state has a form of this type, check your state website or call your state LLC filing office.

Once filed with the state, file-stamped copies of the statement of authority form can be provided to outside businesses and individuals to let them know who is in charge and has authority to act on behalf of the LLC. Note that some state forms allow the LLC to specify limitations on the members' or managers' authority. Such a statement can come in handy if you want outsiders to know that they must deal with *all* LLC members to transact specific business.

Below is a sample state certification form. This particular form certifies the authority of LLC members and/or managers to transfer real property on behalf of the LLC. This is the typical language found in state-sponsored forms, needed for the typical case where such certification may be necessary—for example, to set up an escrow account or record a real property document on behalf of the LLC.

Sample State Certification Form

Filing Fee $20.00

**DOMESTIC
LIMITED LIABILITY COMPANY**

STATE OF MAINE

_____
Deputy Secretary of State

**STATEMENT OF LIMITED LIABILITY
COMPANY AUTHORITY**

A True Copy When Attested By Signature

_____
Deputy Secretary of State

_____
(Name of Limited Liability Company)

Pursuant to 31 MRSA §626.1., the undersigned limited liability company executes and delivers for filing this statement of limited liability company authority:

FIRST: The street address of its principal place of business:

_____
(physical location - street (not P.O. Box), city, state and zip code)

_____
(mailing address if different from above)

SECOND: The street address of an office in this State: (if no office, so indicate)

_____
(physical location - street (not P.O. Box), city, state and zip code)

_____
(mailing address if different from above)

THIRD: ("X" one box only)

☐ A.   The names of the members or, if management is vested in a manager or managers, the names of the managers, authorized to execute an instrument transferring real property held in the name of the limited liability company are:

_____   _____
(name and capacity)   (mailing address)

_____   _____
(name and capacity)   (mailing address)

_____   _____
(name and capacity)   (mailing address)

☐ Names of additional members/managers with such authority are attached hereto as Exhibit _____, and made a part hereof.

☐ B.   The name of an agent maintaining a list of the names and mailing addresses of members or managers, authorized to execute an instrument transferring real property held in the name of the limited liability company is:

_____   _____
(name)   (mailing address)

Lawyers, Tax Specialists, and Legal Research

Much of the work involved in organizing and running an LLC (or other small business) is routine. One good way to learn more about tax matters and legal issues is to read up on them yourself. You've already taken a big step in this direction by using this book.

But there's no way around it—from time to time, you need help from outside sources. Quite likely, you will want to supplement your understanding of the legal and tax consequences of forming an LLC by asking a lawyer or tax professional to double check your decisions and review your paperwork or advise you on complex areas of law or taxation. At times, you may want to run important business decisions by an experienced adviser who has a mix of business, tax, and legal savvy.

Throughout this book, we have flagged instances where a lawyer or tax adviser can provide valuable assistance, such as to:

- review the legal options in your operating agreement
- add special provisions to satisfy the IRS if you will split profits and losses among members disproportionately to capital contributions, or
- customize buy-sell, or buyout, provisions.

In the sections below, we provide a few tips to help you locate a competent expert. Finally, if you want to do your own research, you'll find valuable suggestions on how to get started.

TIP

Consider joining one or more trade groups related to your business. These groups often track legislation in particular areas of business—such as LLC legal and tax developments—and provide sample contracts and other useful legal forms. Some also retain law firms for trade association purposes, which may be able to refer you to competent local lawyers.

Finding the Right Tax Adviser

You know that forming an LLC involves understanding and choosing among various tax options. Among these technical issues is finding out if it makes sense to elect corporate tax treatment with the IRS.

Other LLC business decisions involve tax issues and advice as well: understanding how your state treats LLCs for state income tax purposes; selecting a tax year and accounting period; setting up financial books and bookkeeping procedures; withholding and reporting payroll taxes; and preparing tax returns and schedules that allocate profits, losses, credits, and deductions among LLC members. To make informed decisions in these and other tax areas, you may need help from a tax adviser. Depending on the issue, this adviser may be a certified public accountant, financial or investment adviser, loan officer at a bank, pension plan specialist, or bookkeeper trained in employment tax reporting and return requirements.

The best way to find a knowledgeable and helpful tax adviser is to shop around for someone recommended by small business people whose judgment you trust. Your tax person should be available over the phone to answer routine questions and by mail or fax to handle paperwork and correspondence. It is likely that you will spend much more time dealing with your tax adviser than your legal adviser (discussed below), so be particularly attentive to the personal side of this relationship.

Tax issues are often cloudy and subject to a range of interpretations and strategies, particularly in the newish LLC legal arena, so it is absolutely essential that you discuss and agree to the level of tax aggressiveness you expect from your adviser. Some LLC owners want to live on the edge, saving every possible tax dollar. Others are content to forego contestable tax deductions to gain an extra measure of peace of mind. Whatever your tax strategy, make sure you find a tax adviser who feels the same way you do or is willing to defer to your more liberal or conservative tax tendencies.

It pays to spend some time learning about LLC and employment taxation. Not only will you have to buy less help from tax professionals, but you'll be in a good position to make good financial and tax planning decisions. IRS publications, business and law library materials, trade groups, and countless other sources provide a growing body of LLC tax information. Your accountant or other tax adviser should be able to help you get your hands on good LLC materials. (See the accompanying sidebar, "Resources for Tax and Financial Information.")

Resources for Tax and Financial Information

The Small Business Administration can be an ideal source of financial and tax information and resources (as well as financing, in some cases).

If you want to get copies of free IRS publications, you can find them online at www.irs.gov or at your local IRS office, or you can order them by phone (call the toll-free IRS forms and publications request telephone number at 1-800-TAX-FORM).

- Start by obtaining IRS Publication 509, *Tax Calendars*, prior to the beginning of each year. This pamphlet contains tax calendars showing the dates for business and employer filings during the year.

- You can find further information on withholding, depositing, reporting, and paying federal employment taxes in IRS Publication 15, *Circular E, Employer's Tax Guide*, and the Publication 15 *Supplement*. Also helpful is IRS Publication 334, *Tax Guide for Small Business*.

- IRS Publication 538, *Accounting Periods and Methods*, and IRS Publication 583, *Starting a Business and Keeping Records*, provide helpful information on accounting methods and bookkeeping procedures.

How to Find the Right Lawyer

Most small businesses can't afford to put a lawyer on retainer. Even when consulted on an issue-by-issue basis, lawyer's fees mount up fast—usually way too fast for all but the most pressing legal issues. Just as with individuals, more small businesses are trying to at least partially close this legal affordability gap by doing as much of their own legal research and form preparation as possible. This is one of the reasons we refer to various sections of your state's LLC act throughout the book—by spending a few minutes reading a section of your state's LLC act from time to time, you can save yourself lawyers' fees. Other times, it makes sense to consult briefly with a lawyer at an interim stage, or have your paperwork or conclusions reviewed, particularly for decisions that are complex or have significant legal consequences.

The "Legal Coach" Arrangement

Most readers will not want a lawyer who is programmed to take over all legal decision making and form drafting—this builds up billable hours that few can afford. Instead, we suggest you find someone we call a "legal coach": a professional who is willing to work with you—not just for you—in establishing your LLC and helping with ongoing legal formalities. Under this model, the lawyer helps you take care of many routine legal matters yourself, also being available to consult on more complicated legal issues as the need arises.

Not all lawyers will be comfortable with you taking an active role in your LLC's legal life, so you may need to interview several people before finding a compatible legal adviser. When you call a lawyer, announce your intentions in advance—that you are looking for someone who is willing to review your LLC operating agreement or to handle ongoing legal work from time to time. Mention that you are looking for someone who is flexible, points you in the right direction as the need arises, serves as a legal adviser as circumstances dictate, and tackles particular legal problems if necessary. In exchange for this, let the lawyer know you are willing to pay promptly and fairly.

Some lawyers may find a legal coach model unappealing—for example, they may not feel comfortable reviewing documents you have drafted using self-help materials. If so, thank the person for being frank and keep interviewing other lawyers, unless you are willing and able to pay to have a lawyer do all the work for you.

When you find a lawyer who seems agreeable to the arrangement you've proposed, ask to come in to meet for a half hour or so. Expect to pay for this initial consultation. At the in-person interview, reemphasize that you are looking for a legal coach relationship. You'll also want to discuss other important issues in this meeting, such as the lawyer's customary charges for services, as explained further below. Pay particular attention to the rapport between you and your lawyer. Remember, you are looking for a legal adviser who will work with you. Trust your instincts and seek a lawyer whose personality and business sense are compatible with your own.

> **TIP**
>
> **Look elsewhere for tax advice.** When it comes to special tax questions, such as when and if you should elect corporate tax treatment with the IRS, we think a tax adviser with LLC experience is the best person to ask for help. For other tax and financial decisions, such as the best tax year, accounting period, or employee benefit plan for your LLC, you'll find that accountants, financial planners, pension plan specialists, and bank officers often have a better grasp of the issues than lawyers. And an added bonus is that although tax advice doesn't come cheap, it usually costs less than legal advice.

Why To Hire a Small Business Lawyer

In your quest for a lawyer, remember:

- **You don't need a big-time business lawyer.** Look for a lawyer with some small business experience, preferably in your field or area of operations. For the most part, you don't want a lawyer who works with big businesses (publicly held corporations, large limited partnerships, or investment pools, and the like). Not only will this person deal with issues that are far from your concerns, but he or she is almost sure to charge too much.

- **You don't need a legal specialist.** What if you have a very technical legal question? Should you start by seeking out a legal specialist in an area such as insurance, banking, or securities law? For starters, the answer is probably no. First, find a good small business lawyer to act as your coach. Then rely on this person to suggest specialized materials or experts as the need arises. Again, finding a lawyer with LLC experience is helpful, but specialized legal involvement in narrower realms of business practice can wait until you actually need advice on a particular legal issue or problem.

How to Find a Lawyer

When you're ready to look for a lawyer, talk to people in your community who own or operate businesses of comparable size and scope. Try to get a personal recommendation of a knowledgeable and helpful lawyer. If possible, ask someone who has successfully formed an LLC for the name of the lawyer who helped get the LLC started and what he or she thinks of that person's work.

If you talk to half a dozen business people, chances are you'll come away with several good leads. Other people, such as your banker, accountant, insurance agent, or real estate broker, may also be able to provide the names of lawyers they trust to help them with business matters.

How shouldn't you search for a lawyer? Don't conduct a random search of phone books, legal directories, or advertisements. Lawyer referral services operated by bar associations are usually equally unhelpful. Often, these simply supply the names of lawyers who have signed onto the service, often accepting the lawyer's word for what types of skills he or she has.

> **CAUTION**
>
> **Don't wait until a legal problem arises before seeking out a lawyer.** Even if you have all your LLC formation work covered, it's not too early to find a lawyer to use later for ongoing business consultations. Once enmeshed in a crisis, you may not have time to hire a lawyer at affordable rates. Chances are you'll wind up settling for the first person available at a moment's notice—almost a guarantee you'll pay too much for possibly poor service.

Set the Extent and Cost of Services in Advance

When you hire a lawyer, get a clear understanding about how fees will be computed. For example, if you call the lawyer from time to time for general advice or to be steered to a good information source, how will you be billed? Some lawyers bill a flat amount for a call or a conference; others bill to the nearest 6-, 10- or 20-minute interval. Whatever the lawyer's system, you need to understand it.

Especially at the beginning of your relationship, when you bring a big job to a lawyer, ask specifically about what it will cost. If you feel it's too much, don't hesitate to negotiate; perhaps you can do some of the routine work yourself, thus reducing the fee.

It's a good idea to get all fee arrangements in writing—especially those for good-sized jobs, such as reviewing your operating agreement. In several states, fee agreements between lawyers and clients must be in writing only if the expected fee is $1,000 or more or is contingent on the outcome of a lawsuit. But whether required or not, it's always a good idea to get a written agreement.

TIP

Use nonlawyer professionals to cut down on legal costs. Often, nonlawyer professionals perform some tasks better and at less cost than lawyers. For example, look to management consultants for strategic business planning, real estate brokers or appraisers for valuation of properties, financial planners for investment advice, accountants for preparation of financial proposals, insurance agents for advice on insurance protection, independent paralegals for routine legal form

How Lawyers Charge for Legal Services

You can expect your lawyer to bill you in one of these ways:

- **By the hour.** In most parts of the United States, you can get competent services for your small business for $200 to $300 an hour, and often less. Newer attorneys still in the process of building a practice may be available for paperwork review, legal research, and other types of legal work at lower rates. However, they may take longer to complete these tasks, as well.

- **Flat fee for a specific job.** Under this arrangement, you pay an agreed-upon amount for a given project, regardless of how much time the lawyer spends. Particularly when you begin working with a lawyer and are worried about hourly costs getting out of control, it can make sense to negotiate a flat fee for a specific job, such as doing a prefiling review of your LLC paperwork. For example, the lawyer may review your articles of organization and operating agreement for $300, or prepare special buy-sell, or buyout, provisions to control the transfer of LLC interests for $500.

- **Retainer.** Some businesses can afford to pay relatively modest amounts, perhaps $1,000

to $2,000 a year, to keep a business lawyer "on retainer" for ongoing phone or in-person consultations or routine business matters during the year. Of course, your retainer won't cover a full-blown legal crisis, but it may take care of routine contract and other legal paperwork preparation and reviews.

- **Contingent fee based upon settlement amounts or winnings.** This type of fee typically occurs in personal injury, products liability, fraud, or employment discrimination disputes, where a lawsuit will likely be filed. The lawyer gets a percentage of the recovery (often 33% to 40%) if you win and nothing if you lose. (Of course, if your business is the defendant, not the plaintiff, expect to pay an hourly rate to defend the case or settle the dispute.)

Since most small business legal needs involve advice and help drafting paperwork, a contingency fee approach doesn't normally make sense. However, if you are seeking an award based upon a personal injury claim or lawsuit involving fraud, unfair competition, or the infringement of a patent or copyright, you may want to explore a contingency fee approach.

drafting, and CPAs for the preparation of tax returns. Each of these matters is likely to have a legal aspect, and you may eventually want to consult your lawyer, but normally you can wait until you've gathered information on your own from these nonlawyer professionals.

Confront Problems Head-On

If you have any questions about a lawyer's bill or the quality of services, speak up. Buying legal help should be just like purchasing any other consumer service. If you are dissatisfied, seek a reduction in your bill or make it clear that the work needs to be redone properly (a more comprehensive lease, a better contract). If the lawyer runs a decent business, he or she will promptly and positively deal with your concerns. If you don't get an acceptable response, find another lawyer pronto. If you switch lawyers, you are entitled to get your important documents back from the first lawyer.

Even if you fire your lawyer, you may still feel unjustly wronged. If you can't get satisfaction from the lawyer, write to the client grievance office of your state bar association (with a copy to the lawyer). Often, a phone call from this office to your lawyer will bring the desired results.

How to Do Your Own Legal Research

Law is information, not magic. If you can look up necessary information yourself, you need not purchase it from a lawyer—although if it involves important issues, you may wish to check your conclusions with a lawyer or use one as a sounding board for your intended course of action.

Much of the research necessary to understand your state's LLC law can be done without a lawyer by spending some time online or in a local law or business library browsing your state's LLC act. Even if you need to go to a lawyer for help preparing an LLC legal form or to discuss the legal implications of a proposed business transaction, you can give yourself a leg up by reading practice manuals prepared for lawyers and law students.

In doing legal research online or in a law library, there are a number of sources for legal rules, procedures, and issues that you may wish to examine. Here are a few:

- **State limited liability company statutes.** These state laws should be your primary focus for finding the rules for organizing and operating your LLC.

- **Other state laws, such as the Corporations, Partnerships, Securities, Commercial, Civil, Labor, and Revenue Codes.** These and other laws govern the operation of specific business transactions; the content, approval, and enforcement of commercial contracts; employment practices and procedures; employment tax requirements; and other aspects of doing business in your state. Depending on the type of business operations you engage in, you also may want to research statutes and regulations dealing with legal topics such as environmental law, products liability, real estate, copyrights, and so on.

- **Federal laws.** These include the tax laws and procedures found in the Internal Revenue Code; Treasury Regulations implementing these code sections; regulations dealing with advertising, warranties, and other consumer matters adopted by the Federal Trade Commission; and equal opportunity statutes such as Title VII of the Civil Rights

Act administered by the Justice Department and Equal Employment Opportunities Commission.

- **Administrative rules and regulations (issued by federal and state administrative agencies charged with implementing statutes).** State and federal statutes are often supplemented with regulations that clarify specific statutes and contain rules for an agency to follow in implementing and enforcing them. For example, most states have enacted special administrative regulations under their securities statutes that provide exemptions for businesses registering the offer and sale of business interests to others within the state.

- **Case law.** This consists of decisions of federal and state courts interpreting statutes—and sometimes making law, known as "common law," if the subject isn't covered by a statute. Annotated state legal codes contain not only the statutes, but also references to court cases interpreting and implementing specific provisions of the states' legal provisions.

- **Secondary sources.** Also important in researching business law are sources that provide background information on particular areas of law. One example is this book. Others are commonly found in the business, legal, or reference section of your local library or bookstore.

> **TIP**
>
> **How to locate state statutes online.** Go to Nolo's website at www.nolo.com. On the state laws page at www.nolo.com/statute/state.cfm, you'll find links to the statutes of each state.

Nolo Resources

Below are a few titles published by Nolo that we believe offer valuable business information for LLCs and can be ordered or downloaded from Nolo's website (www.nolo.com).

- *LLC or Corporation: How to Choose the Right Form for Your Business,* by Anthony Mancuso. This book explains in depth the legal and tax differences between an LLC and a corporation. It's filled with examples of how each type of entity works for new and growing businesses.

- *LLC Maker.* An interactive Windows program that produces the articles to form an LLC in each state.

- *Your Limited Liability Company: An Operating Manual,* by Anthony Mancuso. This book with CD-ROM provides ready-to-use minutes forms for holding formal LLC meetings; it also contains forms and information for formally approving legal, tax, and other important business decisions that arise in the course of operating an LLC.

- *Legal Guide for Starting & Running a Small Business,* by Fred S. Steingold. This book is an essential resource for every small business owner, whether just starting out or already established. Find out the basics about forming a business, negotiating a favorable lease, hiring and firing employees, writing contracts, and resolving business disputes.

Nolo Resources (cont'd.)

- *Tax Savvy for Small Business,* by Frederick W. Daily. This book gives business owners information about federal taxes and explains how to make the best tax decisions for business, maximize profits, and stay out of trouble with the IRS.

- *The Employer's Legal Handbook,* by Fred Steingold. Here's a comprehensive resource that compiles all the basics of employment law in one place. It covers safe hiring practices, wages, hours, tips and commissions, employee benefits, taxes and liability, insurance, discrimination, sexual harassment, and termination.

- *How to Write a Business Plan,* by Mike McKeever. If you're thinking of starting a business or raising money to expand an existing one, this book will show you how to write the business plan and loan package necessary to finance your business and make it work.

- *Quicken Legal Business Pro.* This software program contains over 140 business contracts, forms, letters, and checklists. It also contains five searchable Nolo business bestsellers, including *Tax Savvy for Small Business, Legal Guide for Starting & Running a Small Business,* and *The Manager's Legal Handbook,* as well as a downloadable version of *Deduct It! Lower Your Small Business Taxes.*

Small business owners often find that they need to learn more about intellectual property issues (patent, copyright, trademark, and trade secret law). Whether you're a do-it-yourselfer or simply wish to expand your knowledge of intellectual property law, here are some helpful resources:

- *Patent, Copyright and Trademark: An Intellectual Property Desk Reference,* by Richard Stim. Written for anyone who needs to understand the terminology of intellectual property law, this book provides overviews and straightforward explanations of the protections offered by patent, copyright, trademark, and trade secret laws.

- *Trademark: Legal Care for Your Business & Product Name,* by Stephen Elias. This book shows small business owners how to choose, use, and protect the names and symbols that identify their services and products. Provides step-by-step instructions and all the official forms necessary to register a trademark with the U.S. Patent and Trademark Office.

- *Patent It Yourself,* by David Pressman. This state-of-the-art guide is a must for any inventor who wants to get a patent—from the patent search to the actual application. Patent attorney and former patent examiner David Pressman covers use and licensing, successful marketing, and infringement. This best-selling book is also available in software (system requirements: mouse and hard disk, 4 MB RAM, Windows 3.1 or higher, VGA or higher monitor).

- *The Copyright Handbook: What Every Writer Needs to Know,* by Stephen Fishman. Provides fill-in-the-blanks forms and detailed instructions for protecting all types of written expression under U.S. and international copyright law. It also explains copyright infringement, fair use, works for hire, and transfers of copyright ownership.

State Sheets

The state sheets in this appendix provide the essential, state-specific information necessary to comply with state requirements to form an LLC.

Locate the material in this appendix for the state in which you plan to form your LLC (the states are listed alphabetically). You'll refer to this information as you prepare your LLC forms according to the instructions in Chapters 4 through 6 of this book.

Note that your state sheet is divided into four main headings, which we summarize just below:

- LLC Filing Office
- Articles of Organization (or Certificate of Formation)
- State Tax Status, and
- Operating Rules.

LLC Filing Office

Here you'll find the current Web address, physical address, and phone number of the state office that deals with LLCs and other business entities. As discussed in Chapter 4, you'll go online or contact the LLC filing office to download or request state-supplied LLC forms and information. The Secretary of State, Corporations Division, is the office that generally handles LLC forms and filings, but some states have a different name for this office.

- **Forms and Statutes:** In this section, we indicate whether your state's LLC filing office or website provides a sample or ready-to-use articles of organization form or publish guidelines for preparing your own form. We also provide the link to your state's LLC act online.

CAUTION

Get up-to-date state information. State-specific information changes frequently and may not always be current on all points in every state. To get the latest forms and instructions plus related LLC initial and ongoing legal and tax requirements, check your state's filing and tax office websites, and browse your state's LLC act. We provide the web links for each of these resources in your state sheet.

Articles of Organization (or Certificate of Formation)

This section contains information you'll need to complete fill-in-the-blanks articles of organization or to prepare your own articles. When you file this form with the state LLC filing office, your LLC begins its legal existence. (See Chapter 4.) The Articles of Organization section has several subheadings:

- **Name Requirements.** Each state requires certain words to be included in an LLC's formal name—typically "Limited Liability Company," "Ltd. Liability Co.," "LLC" or "L.L.C." We also indicate the fee and time period for which you may reserve an available LLC name prior to filing your articles. Typically, the state LLC office supplies a form you may use to apply for a name reservation, but a simple written name reservation request will normally work just as well. (We cover name reservations in Chapter 4.)

- **Filing Fee.** We list the fee you'll need to pay to file your LLC articles, plus, if applicable, any special rules for computing and paying the filing fee.

- **Annual Fees.** In some states, we add this section to cover any special (unusually costly) annual fee requirements. For example, in a few states, annual fees in excess of $100 must be paid to the LLC filing office to maintain your LLC's legal status. (See Chapter 7.)

- **Special Instructions and Filing Requirements.** This section tells you how many copies of the articles to send to your state LLC office for filing. It also covers any additional forms that must be filed along with your articles, as well as any special requirements for preparing and filing articles of organization in your state. If you form an LLC in a state that does not provide a printed or sample articles form, you'll find the statutory requirements for the contents of articles. In states such as these, we give sample wording if the required information seems particularly tricky or technical. (See Chapter 4 for more on preparing articles from scratch.)

State Tax Status

This is a short heading with two tax-related items:

- **State Tax Treatment of LLCs.** We fill you in on how your state treats LLCs for state tax purposes. Most states follow the federal tax scheme, and will treat your LLC the way the IRS does—as a partnership for a multi-member LLC; as a sole proprietorship for a one-member LLC; or as a corporation if your LLC has filed IRS Form 8832 and elected to be taxed by the IRS as a corporation. For further information on state and federal tax treatment of LLCs, see Chapter 3.

- **State Tax Office.** We list the city location and Web address of your state's revenue and taxation (or similar) main office. Note that some states also maintain branch offices in addition to the main tax office. We recommend you go to the state tax office website or call the tax office early in the LLC formation process, and obtain tax forms and other tax materials relevant to forming and operating an LLC in your state.

Operating Rules

Each state sheet covers several important statutory requirements:

- **Default Transfer Rule and Default Continuation Rule.** We address each state's rules for how members must vote to approve the transfer of membership to a new member or to continue the legal life of the LLC after a member is dissociated (leaves, dies, is expelled, or otherwise loses a membership interest). We summarize each state's limited liability company act provisions that govern these technical LLC operating options. In most cases, the rules shown are "default" rules—that is, they apply only if you do not come up with a different voting or approval rule in your LLC operating agreement. In some states, however, the state rules for these options are mandatory—and we point out when this is the case. Generally, the information given in these sections is important only if you wish to lower the unanimous-vote rule that we supply for each of these options in our operating agreements. (See Chapters 5 and 6.)

Even if your state is listed as requiring a vote to admit new members or to continue the LLC after a member leaves, the state may have repealed or changed the listed vote requirement, or be on the brink of doing so, by the time a member is admitted to or leaves your LLC. The best way to check is to look up these provisions in your state's LLC act (using the state LLC act link listed in your state sheet) to see if it still requires a vote or if it has been changed or repealed.

- **Special Statutory Rules.** We list uncharacteristic legal operating rules found in state LLC acts that caught our eye (those that vary significantly from LLC operating rules found in most other states).

Alabama

LLC Filing Office

Secretary of State
Corporate Section
P.O. Box 5616
Montgomery, AL 36103
Telephone: 334-242-5324

www.sos.state.al.us/business/corporations.aspx

Forms and Statutes: Alabama Secretary of State provides an "Articles of Organization Guidelines" PDF form.

Internet Forms: Guidelines for Alabama articles, LLC report forms, and other statutory forms can be downloaded from the state website. Additional links let you browse the state LLC act and other Alabama laws.

The Alabama LLC Act is contained in Title 10, Chapter 12 of the Alabama statutes, and is browsable from the following Web page (select Title 10, then Chapter 12):

www.legislature.state.al.us/CodeofAlabama/1975/coatoc.htm

Articles of Organization

Name Requirements: Must contain the words "Limited Liability Company" or the abbreviation "LLC" or "L.L.C." The Alabama LLC filing office currently does not reserve LLC names.

Filing Fee: $40, payable to "Secretary of State" plus a separate check for $35 for "Probate Court Judge," who receives and records the original articles. (See "Special Instructions and Filing Requirements" below.)

Special Instructions and Filing Requirements: Have initial member(s) sign the articles. Submit an original plus two copies of completed and signed articles to the nearest Probate Court judge (check local governmental telephone listing and call for address). The judge will record the original articles of organization and forward a copy with fees to the Secretary of State.

After filing articles of organization, fill in the "Domestic LLC Company Report" form and send the original plus two copies of the completed form, together with a check for $5, to the Secretary of State.

Tax Status

State Tax Treatment of LLCs: Follows IRS classification.

State Tax Office: Department of Revenue, Montgomery.

www.ador.state.al.us

Operating Rules

Default Transfer Rule: Unless otherwise provided in operating agreement, by unanimous written consent of all nontransferring members.

Default Continuation Rule: Vote to continue LLC after dissociation of member not required.

Special Statutory Rules: Unless provided otherwise in operating agreement, managers, if chosen, must be appointed or removed by a vote of at least one-half the number of members.

Alaska

LLC Filing Office

State of Alaska
Corporations Section
P.O. Box 110808
Juneau, AK 99811
Telephone: 907-465-2530
www.commerce.state.ak.us/occ/home.htm

Forms and Statutes: State provides fill-in-the-blanks articles of organization with instructions, plus an information booklet with requirements for organizing and operating an Alaska LLC.

Internet Forms: Alaska LLC articles and other statutory forms can be downloaded from the state website. Current Alaska LLC Act provisions and the status of pending LLC bills may be searched on the Alaska website. The state LLC filing office provides an online LLC formation service.

The Alaska LLC Act is contained in Title 10, Chapter 10.50 of the Alaska statutes, starting at Section 10.50.010, and is browseable online. Go to the Web page listed below (the corporations section home page), select the link to "Alaska Statutes and Regulations," then select "The Current Alaska Statutes." Expand the Title 10 heading and select "Chapter 10.50" to view the LLC Act.

www.commerce.state.ak.us/occ/home.htm

Articles of Organization

Name Requirements: Must contain the words "Limited Liability Company" or the abbreviations "LLC" or "L.L.C." The word ""Limited" may be abbreviated as "Ltd." and the word "Company" as "Co." The name may not contain the words "city" or "borough" or otherwise imply that the company is a municipality. An LLC name may be reserved for 120 days for $25. A proposed LLC name may be registered (kept on the rolls of the LLC filing office) by paying an annual fee of $25.

Filing Fee: $250 fee (includes $100 biennial license fee—due every two years), payable to "State of Alaska."

Special Instructions and Filing Requirements: Articles need not state a limit on the duration of the LLC—just check the box in Article 4 to give your LLC a perpetual duration.

You also must fill in the "Disclosure of Company" page that is included as the last page of the standard articles form. Select and insert in the box provided on this page the NAICS code that most clearly describes the initial activities of your LLC. A list of NAICS codes is provided online on the state filing office website.

If you are filing by mail, file the original and one copy of articles of organization.

If you are converting an existing partnership to an LLC, prepare and attach to your LLC articles Form 08-431, Application for Certificate of Conversion. This is a simple form, available for downloading from the state LLC office website, that contains general information on the prior partnership.

Tax Status

State Tax Treatment of LLCs: Follows IRS classification.

State Tax Office: Department of Revenue, Juneau. www.revenue.state.ak.us

Operating Rules

Default Transfer Rule: Unless otherwise provided in agreement, by unanimous consent of nontransferring members

Default Continuation Rule: After the loss of a member, the LLC continues—a vote to continue the LLC is not required.

Special Statutory Rules: Memberships can be issued to persons in exchange for a promissory note or promise to contribute property or services in the future only if the person has also paid in some property or services to the LLC.

Arizona

LLC Filing Office

Arizona Corporation Commission
Corporation Filing Section
1300 West Washington
Phoenix, AZ 85007- 2929
Telephone: 602-542-3026
Tucson Branch Office: 520-628-6560 (accepts LLC filings)
www.cc.state.az.us/corp/index.htm

Forms and Statutes: State provides fill-in-the-blank articles of organization.

Internet Forms: The latest Arizona LLC Articles of Organization with instructions, plus other Arizona LLC statutory forms (Notice of Filing, Application for Reservation of LLC Name, and others) can be downloaded from the state LLC filing office website. General instructions for forming an LLC plus a checklist of steps to take to form an Arizona LLC also are available for downloading.

The Arizona LLC Act is contained in Title 29, Chapter 4 of the Arizona statutes, starting at Section 29.601, and is browseable from the following Web page (scroll down to Chapter 4 to begin browsing the LLC Act):

www.azleg.state.az.us/ArizonaRevisedStatutes.asp?Title=29

Articles of Organization

Name Requirements: "LLC," "LC," "L.L.C.," or "L.C" in uppercase or lowercase letters. If you hold a trademark in your LLC name, attach a "Declaration of Trademark Holder" (available from the state LLC filing office or its website) to your articles.

Professional LLC names must include the words "Professional Limited Liability Company" or the abbreviations "P.L.L.C.," "P.L.C.," "PLLC," or "PLC" in uppercase or lowercase letters.

You can check the availability of a proposed LLC name and reserve it for 120 days online at the state filing office website for $45.00 ($10 filing fee plus $35 expedite fee). If you prefer, you can check name availability online then mail in a name reservation request to reserve your name for the standard fee of $10.00.

Filing Fee: $50, payable to "Arizona Corporation Commission."

Special Instructions and Filing Requirements: The address of the LLC's statutory agent stated in the articles must be a street address, and the statutory agent must sign the articles in the space provided to indicate acceptance of this position. Providing a specific date on which the LLC will dissolve is optional—most LLCs will select a perpetual existence instead. Submit the original of the articles for filing. Fill in and include with your articles the official cover sheet form provided on the state filing office website—see Form CFCVLR, Cover Sheet for Corporate Filings.

Within 60 days after filing your articles, you must publish a "Notice of Filing" form (Form LL0001, available on the state filing office website) three times in a newspaper of general circulation that publishes legal notices in the county where the LLC has its place of business (approved newspapers of general circulation are listed on the state LLC filing office website). The information supplied in the Notice can be copied from your articles. Within 90 days after you file your articles, an Affidavit of Publication, supplied by the newspaper, must be filed with the Corporation Commission (there is no fee for this filing). The newspaper will handle this second filing requirement.

Tax Status

State Tax Treatment of LLCs: Follows IRS classification.

State Tax Office: Department of Revenue, Phoenix.
www.revenue.state.az.us

Operating Rules

Default Transfer Rule: Unless otherwise provided in operating agreement, admission of transferee as a member must be approved by consent of all nontransferring members.

Default Continuation Rule: Vote to continue LLC after dissociation of member not required.

Arkansas

LLC Filing Office

Arkansas Secretary of State
Corporations Division
State Capitol
Little Rock, Arkansas 72201-1094
Telephone: 888-233-0325 (toll free)
or 501-682-3409
www.sosweb.state.ar.us/corp_ucc.html

Forms and Statutes: State provides fill-in-the-blanks articles of organization (Form LL-01) with instructions.

Internet Forms: The latest LLC articles of organization with instructions, plus other Arkansas LLC statutory forms ("Application for Reservation of LLC Name" and others) can be downloaded from the state LLC filing office website. You can prepare and file your articles as well as file a name reservation online for reduced filing fees (see below).

The Arkansas LLC Act (called the "Small Business Entity Tax Pass Through Act"), is located in Title 4 (Business and Commercial Law), Subtitle 3 (Corporations and Associations), Chapter 32, starting with Section 4-32-101, and is browseable from the following Web page (when you get there, click Arkansas Code, then select Title 4, then Subtitle 3, then Chapter 32):
www.arkleg.state.ar.us/Siteindex.asp?

Articles of Organization

Name Requirements: Must contain the words "Limited Liability Company," "Limited Company," or the abbreviation "L.L.C.," "L.C.," "LLC," or "LC." LLCs that perform professional services must have the words "Professional Limited Liability Company," "Professional Limited Company," or the abbreviations "P.L.L.C.," "P.L.C.," "PLLC," or "PLC" in their name. In any of these name variations, the word "Limited" may be abbreviated as "Ltd." and the word "Company" may be abbreviated as "Co." An LLC name may be reserved for 120 days for $25. You can check name availability online from the state filing office website. Also, you can prepare and file a name reservation for an available name online instead of preparing and mailing a paper name reservation form. The fee to file a name reservation online is a reduced fee of $22.50.

Filing Fee: $50 fee, payable to the "Arkansas Secretary of State." The fee is $45.00 if you prepare and file your articles online. Most organizers will use the online filing service since it's fast, easy, and less expensive than preparing and mailing paper articles to the state.

Note: Arkansas LLCs pay a minimum annual franchise tax of $150.

Special Instructions and Filing Requirements: The initial registered agent must accept the designation by signing on the signature line provided in the third article of the fill-in-the-blanks form. Send an original and one copy of completed articles for filing. A file-stamped copy will be returned to you.

Note: If you are converting an existing partnership into an LLC, obtain the Form for Conversion of Partnership to an LLC, available for downloading from the state website. Complete and attach it to your completed articles.

Tax Status

State Tax Treatment of LLCs: An LLC with two or more members will be treated as a partnership for state tax purposes. An LLC with only one member will be treated as a sole proprietorship. This state classification conforms to federal default classification rules for LLCs. Presumably, an Arkansas LLC that elects corporate tax treatment with the IRS will be treated as a corporation for state tax purposes as well.

State Tax Office: Department of Finance & Administration, Revenue Division, Little Rock. www.ark.org/dfa

Operating Rules

Default Transfer Rule: Unless otherwise stated in operating agreement, by unanimous consent of nontransferring members.

Default Continuation Rule: After a member withdraws, the LLC continues—a vote to continue the LLC is not required.

Special Statutory Rules: Default membership approval rule is by a vote of one-half or more of the number of members; operating agreement may change this requirement, and special statutory rules may require a greater vote in some matters (unanimous membership is the default rule to amend the operating agreement).

California

LLC Filing Office

California Secretary of State
Document Filing Support Unit
P.O. Box 944228
Sacramento, CA 94244-2280
Telephone: 916-657-5448
www.ss.ca.gov/business/business.htm

Branch offices of the Secretary of State are located in Fresno, Los Angeles, San Diego, and San Francisco. Currently, branch offices provide LLC forms over the counter only, and do not accept LLC filings.

Forms and Statutes: State provides fill-in-the-blanks articles of organization (Form LLC-1) with instructions, plus a summary of the California LLC Act (called the Beverly-Killea LLC Act). The basic articles form is all that is legally needed, although you may attach extra provisions to the state-provided form if you wish. The LLC filing office also provides an annual "LLC Statement of Information" form, which must be filed within 90 days of forming the LLC.

Internet Forms: The latest California LLC Articles of Organization with instructions, plus other California LLC statutory forms (Reservation of LLC Name and others) can be downloaded from the Secretary of State's website.

The California Beverly-Killea Limited Liability Company Act is contained in the California Corporations Code, Title 2.5 (Limited Liability Companies), starting with Section 17000, and is browseable from the following Web page (check the "Corporations Code" box, then click the search button at the bottom of the page; then scroll down to Section 17000 to find the LLC Act Sections): www.leginfo.ca.gov/calaw.html

Note for Professionals: The California Attorney General has said that only businesses that render services under nonprofessional, occupational licenses can form an LLC in California. Generally, professionals such as doctors, lawyers, accountants, and others that must meet educational, experience, and examination requirements to obtain a license cannot form an LLC in the state. If you provide any type of licensed service that may be considered a licensed professional service, contact your state licensing board and ask if you are allowed to form an LLC in California before starting the process.

Articles of Organization

Name Requirements: Must contain the words "Limited Liability Company" or the abbreviation "LLC" or "L.L.C." The word "Limited" may be abbreviated as "Ltd." and the word "Company" as "Co." The LLC name may contain the names of one or more members, but may not include the words "Bank," "Insurance," "Trust," "Trustee," "Incorporated," or "Corporation," or the abbreviations "Inc." or "Corp."

An available LLC name may be reserved for 60 days for a $10 fee. Name availability cannot be checked by phone unless you have set up a prepaid account with the LLC office. The best way to secure a name is to reserve it by mail with the LLC filing office (list one or more alternate names in case your first choice for a corporate name is not available for reservation).

Filing Fee: $70 filing fee, payable to "Secretary of State."

Annual Fees: California charges LLCs (as well as C corporations, S corporations and limited partnerships) a minimum annual tax of $800, payable to the Franchise Tax Board (but corporations do not have to pay the minimum tax the first tax year). You must pay this minimum amount within three months after forming your LLC. (If LLC elects corporate tax treatment, this minimum payment is made to the Secretary of State when articles are filed.) LLCs with total annual incomes of $250,000 or more ("total

income" includes the cost of goods sold for many businesses) must also estimate and pay the following additional annual amounts (check the California Tax Office website for the latest LLC tax information—see Tax Office Web address, below):

Annual Total Income Reportable to California	Additional Annual LLC Fee
$250,000–$499,99:	$900
$500,000–$999,99:	$2,500
$1,000,000–$4,999,99:	$6,000
$5,000,000 or more:	$11,790

Special Instructions and Filing Requirements: Send original articles of organization to the LLC office in Sacramento, together with a check for the filing fee. You will receive a certified copy from the LLC filing office.

Tax Status

State Tax Treatment of LLCs: Follows IRS classification rules.

State Tax Office: Franchise Tax Board, Sacramento. www.ftb.ca.gov

Operating Rules

Default Transfer Rule: Except as otherwise provided in articles or operating agreement, by consent of majority in interest nontransferring members.

Default Continuation Rule: After a member withdraws, the LLC continues—a vote to continue the LLC is not required.

Colorado

LLC Filing Office

Secretary of State
1560 Broadway, Suite 200
Denver, CO 80290
Telephone: 303-894-2200
www.sos.state.co.us/pubs/business/
main.htm

Forms and Statutes: Provides fill-in-the-blanks articles of organization with instructions for new businesses. Provides special articles of organization to convert existing general or limited partnership to a Colorado LLC.

Internet Forms: The latest LLC articles of organization, plus other Colorado LLC statutory forms (Reservation of LLC Name and others) can be downloaded from the state LLC filing office website. Colorado provides an online articles of organization filing service as an alternative to having to prepare and mail paper articles. Online form preparation takes just a few minutes and costs less than filing standard paper articles (see below).

The Colorado LLC Act is contained in Title 7, Chapter 80 of the Colorado Statutes, starting with Section 7-80-101, and is browseable from the following Web page (select "Colorado Statutes" in the left pane, then select Title 7 "Corporations and Associations," then "Limited Liability Companies"):
http://198.187.128.12/colorado/lpext.
dll?f=templates&fn=fs-main.htm&2.0

Articles of Organization

Name Requirements: Name must include the words "Limited Liability Company" or the abbreviation "LLC" or "L.L.C." The word "Limited" may be abbreviated as "Ltd." and the word "Company" as "Co." For name availability, call the LLC filing office. Go online to the state filing office to perform a name availability search.

You can search for an available name, then reserve it for 120 days online for $25 (the fee is $125 if you mail a name reservation request form instead of reserving the name online).

Filing Fee: If filed online, $25, payable to "Secretary of State." If you prepare and mail paper articles, the filing fee is $125.

Special Instructions and Filing Requirements: If you prepare and mail paper articles, type or print the information in the blanks on the state-provided form and supply a stamped, self-addressed envelope for the return of file-stamped articles to you. File the original and one copy of articles of organization.

Tax Status

State Tax Treatment of LLCs: Follows IRS classification.

State Tax Office: Revenue Department, Denver. www.revenue.state.co.us/main/home.asp

Operating Rules

Default Transfer Rule: By written consent of all nontransferring members; provision does not seem to allow this rule to be varied in the operating agreement. If unanimous consent is not obtained, transferee gets only an economic interest in the LLC (rights to profits and losses and return of capital contribution of transferring member), but no voting or management rights.

Default Continuation Rule: Vote to continue LLC not required.

Special Statutory Rules: LLC Act provides for annual meetings of members; if managers are chosen, they are elected or reelected by majority vote of the number of members at each annual meeting of members. In the absence of a provision in the operating agreement, profits and losses and distributions of capital are allocated and distributed to members according to the value of each member's capital contribution.

Connecticut

LLC Filing Office

Connecticut Secretary of State
ATTN: Commercial Recording Division
P.O. Box 150470
Hartford, CT 06115-0470
Telephone: 860-509-6002
www.sots.ct.gov/CommercialRecording/Crdindex.html

Forms and Statutes: Provides fill-in-the-blanks articles of organization, Domestic Limited Liability Company. Cannot form an LLC for a bank, trust, insurance, building and loan, utility (except telephone), or cemetery company.

Internet Forms: The latest LLC articles of organization with instructions, plus other Connecticut LLC statutory forms (Reservation of LLC Name and others) can be downloaded from the state LLC filing office website. The state's C.O.N.C.O.R.D. site at www.concord-sots .ct.gov/CONCORD/index.jsp may soon provide interactive LLC Articles and other forms that can be filled in online, then printed from your browser. The site may also allow online filing of the completed interactive forms—check the site for more information.

The Connecticut LLC Act is contained in Title 34, Chapter 613 of the Connecticut Statutes, starting with Section 34-100, and is browseable from the following Web page (when you get there, click "Browse Statutes," then select "Title 34," then "Chapter 613"):
www.cga.ct.gov/asp/menu/Statutes.asp

Articles of Organization

Name Requirements: Must contain the words "Limited Liability Company" or the abbreviations "LLC" or "L.L.C." The word "Limited" may be abbreviated as "Ltd." and the word "Company" as "Co." You can check name availability online by using the "Business and UCC Inquiries" link on the state filing office website (select "Search By Name" under "Business Inquiries") or by calling the state filing office at 860-509-6002. You can reserve an available LLC name for 120 days for a $30 fee.

Filing Fee: $60, payable to "Secretary of State."

Special Instructions and Filing Requirements: You only need to send the original articles. The Secretary of State will return a mailing receipt to you.

Tax Status

State Tax Treatment of LLCs: Follows IRS classification.

State Tax Office: Department of Revenue Services, Hartford.
www.ct.gov/drs/site/default.asp

Operating Rules

Default Transfer Rule: Unless otherwise provided in the operating agreement, by approval of a "majority in interest" of the members, not counting the interests of the transferring member. The term "majority in interest" is not defined in the Connecticut LLC Act, but probably follows the definition found in IRS Revenue Procedure 95-10, namely the vote of remaining members holding a majority of both the capital and profits interests in the LLC.

Default Continuation Rule: Vote to continue LLC after dissociation of member not required.

Special Statutory Rules: Profits and losses are allocated to members according to the value of their capital contributions, unless otherwise stated in the operating agreement.

Delaware

LLC Filing Office

Department of State
Division of Corporations
P.O. Box 898
Dover, DE 19903
Telephone: 302-739-3073

www.state.de.us/corp/default.shtml

Forms and Statutes: When you ask for LLC information, Delaware will send you its corporate formation package. Included in this package is a fill-in-the-blanks "Certificate of Formation" (Delaware's version of articles of organization).

Internet Forms: The latest "LLC Certificate of Formation," plus other LLC statutory forms (Reservation of LLC Name and others) can be downloaded from the state LLC filing office website (as part of the complete online forms package).

The Delaware LLC Act is contained in Title 6 (Commerce and Trade), Chapter 18 of the Delaware Statutes, starting with Section 18-101, and is browseable from the following Web page (when you get there, click "Title 6, Chapter 18, Limited Liability Company Act"):

www.state.de.us/corp/DElaw.shtml

Certificate of Formation

Name Requirements: Must contain the words "Limited Liability Company" or the abbreviation "L.L.C." or "LLC." May contain the words "Club," "Foundation," "Fund," "Institute," "Society," "Union," "Syndicate," or "Trust." Name availability can be checked online from the state filing office website. Name availability also may be checked by calling the state filing office.

An available name may be reserved for 120 days and the $75 fee paid from the state filing office website. An LLC name also may be reserved by sending two copies of an "Application for Reservation of Name" together with the fee to the Delaware Division of Corporations.

Filing Fee: $90, payable to "Delaware Department of State." The Department of State, Division of Corporations, also accepts major credit cards.

Annual Fees: A Delaware LLC must pay a flat annual franchise tax of $200. Contact the Franchise Tax Office of the Division of Corporations for more information and for annual franchise tax forms.

Special Instructions and Filing Requirements: Send the Department of State an original plus one copy, and request that the copy be certified and returned to you. Use letter-sized paper only and black ink printer ribbon or pen to fill in forms. Sign all forms with black ink pen. You may leave the third article of the state-provided Limited Liability Company Certificate of Formation blank; you do not have to specify a dissolution date for your LLC.

Tax Status

State Tax Treatment of LLCs: Follows IRS classification.

State Tax Office: Delaware Division of Revenue, Dover.

www.state.de.us/revenue/default.shtml

Operating Rules

Default Transfer Rule: In addition to any rule stated in the operating agreement, by vote of all nontransferring members of the LLC.

Default Continuation Rule: Vote to continue LLC after dissociation of member not required.

Special Statutory Rules: Unless otherwise stated in the operating agreement, members are vested with management power according to their percentage interests in the LLC, and are given voting power equal to these interests. A vote of more than 50% of the membership interests is the default rule to approve members' decisions. Profits and losses, and distributions of cash, are allocated to members according to the value of their respective capital contributions, unless otherwise stated in the operating agreement.

District of Columbia

LLC Filing Office

Department of Consumer & Regulatory Affairs
Corporations Division
P.O. Box 92300
Washington, DC 20090
Telephone: 202-442-4432

http://mblr.dc.gov/corp/index.shtm

Forms and Statutes: Provides guidelines and sample form for articles of organization. Use this information to type your own articles document according to the instructions.

Internet Forms: The latest District of Columbia LLC forms and information are available for viewing and downloading at the LLC filing office website.

The DC LLC Act is contained in Title 29 (Corporations), Chapter 10 of the DC Code, starting with Section 29-1001, and is browseable from the following Web page (select "District of Columbia," "District of Columbia Code," then "Division 5," then "Title 29," then "Chapter 10"): www.michie.com

Articles of Organization

Name Requirements: Must contain the words "Limited Liability Company" or the abbreviation "LLC" or "L.L.C." If a professional practice is being organized, the name must include the words "Professional Limited Liability Company" or the abbreviation "PLLC" or "P.L.L.C." You can check business names already in use online from the state filing office website or by calling the LLC filing office. Available LLC names may be reserved for 60 days for $35.

Filing Fee: $150, payable to "D.C. Treasurer."

Special Instructions and Filing Requirements: Type articles of organization on letter- or legal-sized paper. Submit two originally signed copies (sign each form with a pen) and attach a consent of the registered agent—a fill-in-the-blanks consent form is available on the state filing office website. Don't be confused by instructions to the articles that discuss your LLC operating agreement; you do not have to submit a copy of this agreement when you file articles of organization.

Tax Status

State Tax Treatment of LLCs: Follows IRS classification. Also note that DC LLCs are subject to 9.975% tax on income earned in DC.

State Tax Office: Office of Tax and Revenue.

http://cfo.dc.gov/otr/site/default.asp

Operating Rules

Default Transfer Rule: Unless otherwise restricted by the articles or operating agreement (see LLC Act for rules on permissible restrictions), with consent of nontransferring members holding a majority of the interests in profits of the LLC.

Default Continuation Rule: Vote to continue LLC after dissociation of member not required.

Special Statutory Rules: Unless otherwise stated in articles or the operating agreement, members vote according to their interests in the profits of the LLC, with the vote of a majority of the profits interests required to approve a membership decision.

A majority of the profits interests of members is also the default vote requirement for filling a vacant manager position. The default rule for allocating profits and losses, and distributing cash of LLC, is according to the value of each member's capital contribution to the LLC.

Florida

LLC Filing Office

Florida Department of State

Division of Corporations

P.O. Box 6327

Tallahassee, FL 32314

Telephone: 850-245-6051

www.dos.state.fl.us/doc/index.html

Forms and Statutes: Provides fill-in-the-blanks articles of organization with instructions.

Internet Forms: LLC forms, including articles and other statutory forms, are available for downloading from the Division of Corporation's website. The state provides an online filing service that allows you to fill in and file your articles online.

The Florida LLC Act is contained in Title XXXVI (Business Organizations), Chapter 608 of the Florida Statutes, starting with Section 608.401, and is browseable from the following Web page (click "Statutes, Constitution, and Laws of Florida," then "Florida Statutes," then select "Title XXXVI," then "Chapter 608" from the index):

www.leg.state.fl.us/Welcome/index.cfm

Articles of Organization

Name Requirements: Must end with the words "Limited Company" or the abbreviation "LLC," "LC," "L.L.C.," or "L.C." Names for use by LLCs (and other business entities) cannot be reserved. A preliminary name availability request can be handled over the phone by calling the state LLC filing office. You can also search name availability at the Division's website. Once you have determined that a name is available, quickly submit your proposed articles for filing. If the name is not available, you will be notified by the filing office.

Filing Fee: $100 for filing articles, plus $25 for designation of registered agent (included in articles) for a total of $125, payable to "Florida Department of State." The department will send you a letter of acknowledgment upon filing. You can add $30 to receive a certified copy of your articles from the LLC filing office, and/or add $5 for a "Certificate of Status" certifying that your LLC is an active Florida LLC as of its filing date. These extra copies and fees are optional.

Special Instructions and Filing Requirements: If you file articles by mail (instead of filing articles online), submit the signed original and one copy of articles of organization to the LLC filing office.

If you are converting an existing partnership to an LLC, complete and attach a "Certificate of Conversion," Form INHS11, to your articles. Also include an additional $25 in your filing fee check. This form can be downloaded from the state filing office website.

Tax Status

State Tax Treatment of LLCs: Generally, follows IRS classification. Florida has no personal income tax. LLCs are not subject to Florida's corporate income tax unless they elect corporate tax treatment with the IRS (or one of their owners is a corporation). If the LLC is taxed as a corporation, it must file an annual Corporate Income/Franchise Tax Return and make estimated tax payments if the expected annual tax exceeds specified limits. If the LLC is taxed as a partnership and one of the owners is a corporation, the LLC must file a Florida Partnership return, Form F-1065 (and the corporate owner must file a Florida corporate tax return).

State Tax Office: Revenue Department, Tallahassee.

http://sun6.dms.state.fl.us/dor

Operating Rules

Default Transfer Rule: Unless otherwise stated in the articles, by unanimous consent of nontransferring members.

Default Continuation Rule: Except as may be provided in the articles, vote to continue the LLC after dissociation of a member (cessation or termination of a membership interest) not required.

Special Statutory Rules: In manager-managed LLCs, managers must be elected annually.

Georgia

LLC Filing Office

Secretary of State
Corporations Division
Suite 315, West Tower
2 Martin Luther King Jr. Drive
Atlanta, GA 30334
Telephone: 404-656-2817
www.sos.state.ga.us/corporations/

Forms and Statutes: Provides sample articles of organization. Type or word-process articles on letter-sized paper following the format and content of the sample form. This short format produces minimal, though legally sufficient, articles of organization to form a Georgia LLC.

Internet Forms: LLC forms, including sample articles, "Transmittal of Articles" form (BR231), and other statutory forms, are available for downloading from the state LLC filing office website. An LLC can be formed online from the state filing office website.

The Georgia LLC Act starts with Section 14-11-100 of the Georgia Code, and is browseable from the following Web page (when you get there, expand "Title 14," then "Chapter 11" to start browsing the LLC Act—you may first be asked to acknowledge that you understand the terms of use before being granted free access to the Georgia Code, which is provided by the state of Georgia and LexisNexis):

http://w3.lexis-nexis.com/hottopics/gacode/Default.asp

Articles of Organization

Name Requirements: Must contain the words "Limited Liability Company" or "Limited Company" or one of the following abbreviations: "L.L.C.," "LLC," "L.C.," or "LC." The word "Limited" may be abbreviated as "Ltd." and the word "Company" may be abbreviated as "Co." The name must not exceed 80 characters, including spaces and punctuation.

An available LLC name may be reserved before filing articles. An LLC name reservation for 30 days costs $25 (if your first choice for a name is not available, you are allowed to select up to two more names to check—the first name of the three submitted will be reserved for your use). You can check name availability and reserve an available name from the state filing office website. Once a name is reserved, the office will email a name reservation number to you. If you prepare and file articles online, the availability of your name will be checked as the first step in preparing the online form.

Filing Fee: $100, payable to "Secretary of State." Attach check to completed Transmittal Form (see below).

Special Instructions and Filing Requirements:
The state provides an online filing service that allows you to fill in and file your articles online. If you file by mail, send original and one copy of articles of organization. Include the original name reservation certificate with your papers. Also include a completed Transmittal Form, with a check for the filing fee attached. The Transmittal Form should be completed to show the name of your LLC and your name reservation number if you reserved your name. If your papers are in order, the LLC filing office will attach a "Certificate of Organization" to the file copy of your articles and mail them to you.

Tax Status

State Tax Treatment of LLCs: Follows IRS classification.

State Tax Office: Department of Revenue, Atlanta. www.etax.dor.ga.gov/index.html

Operating Rules

Default Transfer Rule: Except as otherwise stated in articles or operating agreement, by unanimous consent of nontransferring members.

Default Continuation Rule: Except as may be provided in the articles, vote to continue the LLC after dissociation of a member (cessation or termination of a membership interest) not required.

Hawaii

LLC Filing Office

Dept. of Commerce and Consumer Affairs
Business Registration Division
P.O. Box 40
Honolulu, HI 96810
Telephone: 808-586-2744
www.hawaii.gov/dcca/areas/breg

Forms and Statutes: Provides fill-in articles of organization with instructions.

Internet Forms: LLC forms, including sample articles with separate instructions, are available for downloading from the state LLC filing office website. The state provides an online filing service that allows you to fill in and file your articles online. If you prefer to mail articles for filing, the site provides a form you can complete online, print with your browser, and mail to the state LLC filing office.

The Hawaii LLC Act is contained in Chapter 428 of the Hawaii Statutes, starting with Section 428-101, and is browseable from the following Web page (when you get there, select "Legal Information" at the right of the page, then select "Legal Information," then "Statutes," then "Hawaii Revised Statutes," then "HRS Chapter 428—Uniform Limited Liability Company Act"): www.businessregistrations.com

Articles of Organization

Name Requirements: The name must contain the words "Limited Liability Company" or the abbreviation "LLC" or "L.L.C." The word "Limited" may be abbreviated as "Ltd." and the word "Company" may be abbreviated as "Co." You can search to see if your proposed name is already in use by doing a business name search from the state filing office website. An available LLC name may be reserved for 120 days for $10.

Filing Fee: $50 fee, payable to "Department of Commerce and Consumer Affairs."

Special Instructions and Filing Requirements: The state provides an online filing service that allows you to fill in and file your articles online. If you prefer to mail articles for filing, the site provides a form you can fill in online, print with your browser and mail to the state LLC filing office. Mailed articles instructions: Only one person is required to sign the articles as the LLC's organizer. Submit original articles, plus the number of copies you want file-stamped and returned to you (one copy is sufficient). In Article V, most organizers will check the "at-will" box to give their LLC an unlimited duration. Of course, you will want to check the box under Article VII that specifies your members are not liable for the debts, obligations, and liabilities of your LLC.

Tax Status

State Tax Treatment of LLCs: Follows IRS classification.

State Tax Office: Hawaii Tax Department, Honolulu. www.state.hi.us/tax/tax.html

Operating Rules

Default Transfer Rule: Except as otherwise stated in operating agreement, by unanimous consent of nontransferring members.

Default Continuation Rule: Vote to continue LLC after dissociation (withdrawal or loss) of a member not required.

Idaho

LLC Filing Office

Idaho Secretary of State
Corporations Division
700 West Jefferson
P.O. Box 83720
Boise, ID 83720-0080
Telephone: 208-334-2301
www.idsos.state.id.us/corp/corindex.htm

Forms and Statutes: State provides fill-in-the-blanks articles of organization with instructions.

Note for Professionals: State also provides articles for organizing a professional limited liability company. This special professional form applies to LLCs formed to render licensed professional services in the fields of architecture, chiropractic, dentistry, engineering, landscape architecture, law, medicine, nursing, occupational therapy, optometry, physical therapy, podiatry, professional geology, psychology, certified or licensed public accountancy, social work, surveying, and veterinary medicine.

Internet Forms: LLC forms, including articles and other statutory forms, are available for downloading from the state LLC filing office website.

The Idaho LLC Act is contained in Title 53 (Partnership), Chapter 6 of the Idaho Statutes, starting with Section 53-601, and is browseable from the following Web page:
http://www3.state.id.us/idstat/TOC/53006KTOC.html

Articles of Organization

Name Requirements: The name must contain the words "Limited Liability Company" or "Limited Company" or the abbreviation "L.L.C." or "L.C." The word "Limited" may be abbreviated as "Ltd." and the word "Company" may be abbreviated as "Co." A professional services limited liability company name must end with the words "Professional Company" or the abbreviation "P.L.L.C." You can search the business entity name database from the state filing office website. An available LLC name may be reserved for four months for $20.

Filing Fee: $100 fee, payable to "Idaho Secretary of State." If the Articles are not typed, if attachments are included, or if expedited filing is requested, the filing fee is $120.

Special Instructions and Filing Requirements: Submit the original and two copies for filing to the Corporations Division. The filing fee is increased to $120 if articles of organization are not typed or if they include attachments. (To save money, type your responses on the fill-in-the-blanks articles form.)

Tax Status

State Tax Treatment of LLCs: Follows IRS classification.

State Tax Office: State Tax Commission, Boise. http://tax.idaho.gov

Operating Rules

Default Transfer Rule: Unless otherwise stated in the operating agreement, by unanimous written consent of nontransferring members.

Default Continuation Rule: Unless otherwise stated in the operating agreement, by unanimous consent of remaining members within 90 days of the dissociation (loss of membership rights) of a member.

Illinois

LLC Filing Office

Illinois Secretary of State
Department of Business Services
Limited Liability Company Division
Michael J. Howlett Bldg.
501 S. 2nd St., Rm 328
Springfield, IL 62756
Telephone: 800-252-8980

Branch Office: Chicago, telephone 312-793-3380 (for questions and info only; not LLC filings).

www.cyberdriveillinois.com/departments/ business_services/home.html

Forms and Statutes: State provides fill-in-the-blanks articles of organization.

Internet Forms: The latest Illinois LLC articles of organization (Form LLC-5.5), plus other Illinois LLC statutory forms (Reservation of LLC Name and others) can be downloaded from the state LLC office website.

The Illinois LLC Act is contained in Chapter 805 (Business Organizations), starting with section 180/1-1, and is browseable from the following Web page (when you get there, select "Chapter 805," then select "805 ILCS 180/ Limited Liability Company Act").

www.ilga.gov/legislation/ilcs/ilcs.asp

Articles of Organization

Name Requirements: Must contain the words "Limited Liability Company" or the abbreviation "LLC" or "L.L.C." The abbreviations "Ltd." and "Co." are not allowed in Illinois LLC names. You can check name availability online, by email, or by calling the state filing office.

An available LLC name may be reserved for 90 days for a whopping $300! A corporate name may be reserved for $25 in Illinois, so why so much for an LLC name reservation? We don't know, but this is what the statute currently requires. Perhaps this fee will be lowered to a more modest amount by future LLC legislation, but for now, you may want to skip reserving your name; just check name availability online or by calling the state filing office, then take your chances by promptly filing articles with your proposed name.

Filing Fee: $500, payable to the "Secretary of State." Payment must be made by certified check, cashier's check, money order, or Illinois attorney's or CPA's check (don't send a personal check).

Annual Fees: LLCs do not pay state franchise taxes, but must pay an annual LLC report fee of $250.

Special Instructions and Filing Requirements: Submit the original and one copy of the signed articles of organization form. The fill-in-the-blanks articles form must be completed with a typewriter.

- Article 1: Attach Form LLC-1.20, available from the state filing office website, to your articles if you will do business under a name other than the one stated in the articles (under an assumed business name).

- Article 6: Leave Article 6 blank to give your LLC a perpetual existence.

If you are converting an existing general or limited Illinois partnership to an LLC, read the requirements listed on the state filing office website. Follow these additional requirements if you wish to convert a partnership to an LLC in Illinois. You will need to include an attachment page with your articles and pay $100 extra for the conversion.

Tax Status

State Tax Treatment of LLCs: Follows IRS classification.

State Tax Office: Department of Revenue, Springfield.

www.revenue.state.il.us

Operating Rules

Default Transfer Rule: Unless otherwise stated in the operating agreement, by unanimous consent of nontransferring members

Default Continuation Rule: Vote to continue LLC after dissociation of member not required.

Indiana

LLC Filing Office

Indiana Secretary of State
Corporations Division
302 W. Washington, Room E018
Indianapolis, IN 46204
Telephone: 317-232-6576
www.in.gov/sos/business/corporations.html

Forms and Statutes: Provides articles and other statutory forms.

Internet Forms: Articles of organization and other standard statutory forms, such as a request to reserve a name, are downloadable from the state LLC filing office website.

The Indiana LLC Act (also called the "Indiana Business Flexibility Act") is contained in Title 23 (Business and Other Associations), Article 18 of the Indiana Code, starting with Section 23-18-1-1, and is browseable from the following Web page (select Title 23, then Article 18):

www.in.gov/legislative/ic/code

Articles of Organization

Name Requirements: Must include "Limited Liability Company" or abbreviations "L.L.C." or "LLC."

You can check name availability online at the state filing office website or by telephone. It costs $20 to reserve an available name for 120 days.

Filing Fee: $90, payable to "Secretary of State" (staple check to articles).

Special Instructions and Filing Requirements: File original and one copy of articles; file-stamped copy will be returned to you.

Tax Status

State Tax Treatment of LLCs: Follows IRS classification.

State Tax Office: Department of Revenue, Indianapolis.

www.state.in.us/dor

Operating Rules

Default Transfer Rule: Unless otherwise stated in operating agreement, by unanimous written consent of nontransferring members.

Default Continuation Rule: A membership vote to continue the LLC after dissociation of a member (cessation or termination of a membership interest) is not required.

Iowa

LLC Filing Office

Iowa Secretary of State
Corporations Division
Lucas Building, 1st Floor
321 E. 12th St.
Des Moines, IA 50319
Telephone: 515-281-5204
www.sos.state.ia.us/business/index.html

Forms and Statutes: Does not provide fill-in-the-blanks articles of organization.

Internet Forms: Section 490A.303 of the Iowa LLC law, which lists the required contents of articles, is posted online (see "Special Instructions and Filing Requirements," below). The Secretary of State provides reservation of name and other statutory forms on its website.

The Iowa LLC Act is contained in Title XII (Business Entities), Chapter 490A of the Iowa Code, starting with section 490A.100, and is browseable from the following Web page (when you get there, click "Tables and Index to the Code of Iowa" under the "2007 Iowa Code" heading, then click "Skeleton Index," then open the "2007 Iowa Code" folder in the left pane, then "Statutes," then "2007 IOWA Code," then select "Title XII Business Entities," then open the folder for "Subtitle 2," then open the folder for "Chapter 490A Limited Liability Companies"):

www.legis.state.ia.us/IowaLaw.html

Articles of Organization

Name Requirements: Must contain the words "Limited Liability Company" or "Limited Company" or the abbreviation "L.L.C." or "L.C." You can search the name database online from the state filing office website to see if your proposed name is already in use by business entity. An available LLC name may be reserved for 120 days for $10.

Filing Fee: $50, payable to the "Iowa Secretary of State."

Special Instructions and Filing Requirements: Type or word-process articles in black ink. You need to file the original articles only. The Secretary will return the document, endorsed as filed, to you together with a receipt for payment of the filing fee.

Below is a summary of the requirements for the contents of Iowa articles of organization, taken from the Iowa LLC Act. (See Chapter 4 for an example of how to draft your own articles based upon similar state statutory requirements.)

Section 490A.303.

1. The articles of organization must set forth all of the following:

   a. A name that satisfies the requirements of Section 490A.401 (see "Name Requirements," above).

   b. The street address of the LLC's initial registered office and the name of its initial registered agent at that office.

   c. The street address of the principal office of the LLC, which may be the same as the registered office, but need not be within the state.

   d. The period of the LLC's duration, which may be perpetual.

Additional information must be provided in articles if you are converting an existing partnership to an LLC. See the state website or call the state LLC filing office for instructions on adding this additional information to your articles.

Tax Status

State Tax Treatment of LLCs: Follows IRS classification.

State Tax Office: Department of Revenue & Finance, Des Moines.

www.state.ia.us/tax/index.html

Operating Rules

Default Transfer Rule: Unless otherwise stated in articles or operating agreement, by unanimous written consent or vote at meeting of nontransferring members.

Default Continuation Rule: Vote to continue LLC after dissociation of member not required.

Kansas

LLC Filing Office

Kansas Secretary of State
Corporation Division
First Floor, Memorial Hall
120 S.W. 10th Ave.
Topeka, KS 66612
Telephone: 785-296-4564
www.kssos.org/main.html

Forms and Statutes: Provides articles plus other statutory forms.

Internet forms: Kansas LLC articles (Form DL), instructions for articles, plus other forms can be downloaded from the LLC office website.

Note: Kansas provides an online articles of organization preparation and filing service at KS Business Center at https://www.accesskansas .org/businesscenter/index.html. Online form preparation and filing takes just a few minutes and costs less than filing paper articles, so we recommend you use the online service rather than preparing and filing paper articles.

The Kansas LLC Act is contained in Chapter 17 of the Kansas Statutes, Article 76, starting with Section 17-7662 (ignore Sections 17-7601 to 17-7661; this is the prior LLC Act), and is browseable from the Web page listed below. Use the arrow keys to highlight "Chapter 17, Corporations," in the center box, then press "Get Articles in Chapter." Then use the arrow keys to highlight "Article 76, Limited Liability Companies," and press "List Statutes in Article" to see a list of the LLC Act statutes.

www.kslegislature.org/legsrv-statutes/index.do

Articles of Organization

Name Requirements: Must contain the words "Limited Liability Company" or "Limited Company" or the abbreviation "LLC," "L.L.C.," "LC" or "L.C."

You can check name availability by searching the business entity database online or by calling the state filing office. It costs $35 to reserve an available name for 120 days by preparing and filing a paper name reservation request. An online name reservation costs $27.00, which costs less and is much easier and quicker to do. To check name availability and obtain an online name reservation, go to the KS Business Center at https://www.accesskansas.org/businesscenter/ index.html. An easy way to get there is to go to the state corporate filing office website by clicking the "State Web Site" button from the LLC Maker State Info window. Then select the Quick link at the bottom of the page labeled "File Formation Documents Online." This brings you to the Business Center. Enter the name you wish to reserve in the "Is the Name Available?" box, then press "Search." If the name is available, you can proceed by following the instructions that appear to reserve your name online.

Important: Under the Kansas LLC Act, the omission of a required LLC designator in an LLC name may subject an LLC member to personal liability for claims made against the LLC.

Filing Fee: $165 fee, payable to "Kansas Secretary of State." The fee is reduced to $160 if you file your articles online.

Special Instructions and Filing Requirements: If you are filing by mail, submit original signed articles.

Tax Status

State Tax Treatment of LLCs: Follows IRS classification. *But note:* Kansas LLCs are subject to a state franchise tax.

State Tax Office: Department of Revenue, Topeka. www.ksrevenue.org

Operating Rules

Default Transfer Rule: Unless otherwise provided in the operating agreement, the admission of a transferee as a member must be approved by majority of nontransferring members.

Default Continuation Rule: Vote to continue LLC after dissociation of member not required (but members can vote to dissolve the LLC, if they wish, within 90 days of the dissociation of a member).

Kentucky

LLC Filing Office

Kentucky Secretary of State

Business Filings

P.O. Box 718

Frankfort, KY 40601

Telephone: 502-564-2848

http://sos.ky.gov/business

Forms and Statutes: Secretary of State articles (SOS LAOO) with instructions and other statutory forms for LLCs ("Amendment of Articles," "Change of Registered Agent or Office," "Certificate of Existence or Authorization," "Articles of Dissolution").

Internet Forms: Kentucky articles plus other statutory LLC forms can be downloaded from the state LLC Office website.

The Kentucky LLC Act is contained in Title XXIII (Private Corporations and Associations), Chapter 275 of the Kentucky Statutes, starting with Section 275.001, and is browseable from the following Web page:

http://162.114.4.13/krs/275-00/CHAPTER.HTM

Articles of Organization

Name Requirements: Must contain the words "Limited Liability Company" or "Limited Company" or the abbreviation "LLC" or "LC." Professional LLCs must contain the words "Professional Limited Liability Company" or "Professional Limited Company" or "PLLC" or "PLC." The word "Limited" may be abbreviated as "Ltd." and the word "Company" may be abbreviated as "Co." in any limited liability company name.

You can search for available names online at the state filing office website or by calling the filing office. An available LLC name can be reserved for 120 days for $15. Professional LLCs are those whose members will practice one of the following professions: certified public or public accountant, architect or landscape architect, attorney, chiropractor, dentist, engineer, nurse, occupational therapist, optometrist, osteopath, pharmacist, physical therapist, physician, podiatrist, psychologist, or veterinarian.

Filing Fee: $40, payable to the "Kentucky State Treasurer."

Special Instructions and Filing Requirements: Type or print articles in black ink. Form can be signed by one or more members or managers or by an organizer of the LLC. Submit signed original plus two copies for filing. After filing, make sure to file a copy of the file-stamped articles with the county clerk of the county where your LLC's registered office is located.

Note for Professionals: If you are forming a professional Kentucky LLC, use Form SOS PLLC, available for downloading from the state LLC filing office website, to form your LLC.

Tax Status

State Tax Treatment of LLCs: Follows IRS classification.

State Tax Office: Kentucky Revenue Cabinet, Frankfort.

http://revenue.ky.gov

Operating Rules

Default Transfer Rule: Unless otherwise provided in the operating agreement, admission of transferee as a member must be approved by written consent of a majority-in-interest of members (unless otherwise provided in articles or operating agreement, this means members who have contributed a majority of the capital to the LLC).

Default Continuation Rule: Vote to continue LLC after dissociation of member not required.

Louisiana

LLC Filing Office

Louisiana Secretary of State
Corporations Division
P.O. Box 94125
Baton Rouge, LA 70804
Telephone: 225-925-4704

www.sec.state.la.us/comm/corp/corp-index
.htm

Forms and Statutes: State provides a fill-in-the-blanks articles of organization (Form 365) with instructions, as well as a "Limited Liability Company Initial Report," which must be filed with the articles.

Internet Forms: The above forms, plus other statutory forms, such as a Reservation of LLC Name form, can be downloaded from the state LLC office website.

The Louisiana LLC Law is contained in Chapter 22, Title 12 of the Louisiana Statutes, starting with Section 12:1301. See the following Web page to browse the Law (click "Louisiana Laws" in the left panel, then select the "RS" check box to search the Revised Statutes, then insert in the search box the section number you wish to view—currently, the law must be browsed section by section):
www.legis.state.la.us

Articles of Organization

Name Requirements: Must contain the words "Limited Liability Company" or the abbreviation "L.L.C." or "L.C." You can check LLC name availability online or by calling the state filing office website. An available LLC name may be reserved for 60 days for $25.

Filing Fee: $75, payable to "Secretary of State."

Special Instructions and Filing Requirements: Have one of your initial members (or managers) sign the articles in the presence of a notary. The "Transmittal Information" cover page, which

is included as the first page of the articles form provided online, also must be included with your articles. Also, a separate "Limited Liability Company Initial Report," available online, must accompany your articles when submitted for filing. This form must be signed by each person who signs your articles, and by a person whom you designate to act as your LLC's registered agent. Sign this form in the presence of a notary (have your articles notarized at the same time).

Mail the completed initial report plus your original signed and notarized articles and transmittal page, with any additional copies of articles you wish certified (for an additional $10 charge per copy), to the LLC filing office.

Note: If your articles are filed within five working days of the date of notarization of the initial report form, which is submitted with your articles, the legal date of existence begins on the date of notarization (prior to the actual date the articles are filed).

Tax Status

State Tax Treatment of LLCs: Follows IRS classification.

State Tax Office: Department of Revenue & Taxation, Baton Rouge.

www.rev.state.la.us

Operating Rules

Default Transfer Rule: Unless otherwise stated in articles or operating agreement, by unanimous written consent of nontransferring members.

Default Continuation Rule: Vote to continue LLC after dissociation of member not required.

Maine

LLC Filing Office

Secretary of State
Corporate Examining Section
101 State House Station
Augusta, ME 04333-0101
Telephone: 207-624-7740

www.state.me.us/sos/cec/cec.htm

Forms and Statutes: State provides fill-in-the-blanks forms for most LLC statutory filings, including articles of organization.

Internet Forms: The latest LLC articles of organization with instructions, plus other LLC statutory forms (Reservation of LLC Name and others) can be downloaded from the state's website.

The Maine LLC Act is contained in Title 31 (Partnerships and Associations), Chapter 13 of the Maine Statutes, starting with Section 601, and is browseable from the following Web page: http://janus.state.me.us/legis/statutes/31/title31sec601.html

Articles of Organization

Name Requirements: Must contain the words "Limited Liability Company" or the abbreviation "LLC" or "L.L.C." If a professional LLC, must contain the word(s) "Chartered," "Professional Association" or abbreviation "P.A." You can search for available names online at the state filing office website. Use the state-furnished LLC Application for Reservation of Name form and include $20 fee to reserve an LLC name for 120 days.

Filing Fee: $175, payable to the "Secretary of State."

Special Instructions and Filing Requirements: If you are forming a professional service LLC, check the box at the beginning of the fill-in-the-blanks articles of organization and insert the type of professional services to be rendered. Have the initial registered agent named in the articles date and sign in the space provided on the articles form.

Tax Status

State Tax Treatment of LLCs: Follows IRS classification.

State Tax Office: Bureau of Taxation, Augusta. www.state.me.us/revenue

Operating Rules

Default Transfer Rule: By unanimous written consent of nontransferring members or as may otherwise be provided in articles or operating agreement.

Default Continuation Rule: A vote to continue the LLC after withdrawal of a member is not required.

Maryland

LLC Filing Office

Maryland Department of Assessments & Taxation
Corporate Charter Division
301 West Preston Street, Room 801
Baltimore, MD 21201
Telephone: 410-767-1340
Outside the Baltimore Metro Area: 888-246-5941

www.dat.state.md.us/sdatweb/charter.html

Forms and Statutes: State provides articles and instructions.

Internet Forms: The latest Maryland LLC articles of organization and guidelines for preparing this form plus other Maryland LLC statutory forms (such as Reservation of LLC Name) can be downloaded from the state filing office website. The state also maintains a website at www.blis.state.md.us that contains specific licensing and business start-up information for various types of businesses.

The Maryland LLC Act is contained in the Corporations and Associations heading, Title 4A, starting with Section 4A-101, and is browseable from the following Web page (when you get there, click "Maryland," then "Maryland Code," then "Corporations and Associations," then select "Title 4A" to begin browsing the LLC Act): http://198.187.128.12

Articles of Organization

Name Requirements: Must contain the words "Limited Liability Company" or one of the following abbreviations: "LLC," "LC," "L.L.C.," or "L.C." You can check to see if your proposed name is already in use by searching the corporate database from the state filing office website or by calling the state filing office. An available name may be reserved for 30 days for a $25 fee.

Filing Fee: $100, payable to "SDAT" (this is the acronym for the State Department of Assessments & Taxation).

Special Instructions and Filing Requirements: Blanks in articles must be typed or printed, not handwritten. Submit the signed original for filing.

Tax Status

State Tax Treatment of LLCs: Follows IRS classification.

State Tax Office: Department of Assessments & Taxation, Baltimore.
www.comp.state.md.us/default.asp

Operating Rules

Default Transfer Rule: By unanimous written consent of nontransferring members or as may otherwise be specified in the operating agreement.

Default Continuation Rule: Vote to continue LLC after dissociation of member not required.

Massachusetts

LLC Filing Office

Commonwealth of Massachusetts
Corporations Division
One Ashburton Place, 17th Floor
Boston, MA 02108
Telephone: 617-727-9640
www.sec.state.ma.us/cor/coridx.htm

Forms and Statutes: The name of the document filed in Massachusetts to form an LLC is the "Certificate of Organization." Massachusetts does not provide a form, but does allow you to prepare and file the Certificate of Organization online from the filing office website. If you wish to prepare and mail a Certificate for filing, below we explain the statutory requirements for forming and operating a Massachusetts LLC (contained in Section 112.03 of the Massachusetts LLC regulations) (see "Special Instructions and Filing Requirements").

Note for Professionals: Existing Massachusetts professional practice general partnerships can register as Registered Limited Liability Partnership instead of converting their general partnerships to LLCs (the registration process is simple and provides limited liability protection to the LLP partners). For more information, see the Massachusetts Secretary of the Commonwealth LLP regulations, available upon request.

Internet Forms: Massachusetts does not provide a form, but does allow you to prepare and file the Certificate of Organization online from the filing office website. The required contents for the LLC Certificate of Organization also are posted on the state website.

The Massachusetts LLC Act is contained in Title XXII (Corporations), Chapter 156C of the Massachusetts General Laws, starting with Section 1, and is browseable from the following Web page (when you get there, scroll down to and select "Chapter 156C" to begin browsing the LLC Act): www.mass.gov/legis/laws/mgl/gl-pt1-toc.htm

Certificate of Organization

Name Requirements: Must contain the words "Limited Liability Company," "Limited Company," or the abbreviation "LLC," "LC," "L.L.C.," or "L.C." To check on the availability online, search the name database (for names in use by existing business entities) and the name reservation database (for names currently on reserve) on the state filing office website. Available LLC names may be reserved for 30 days for $15.

Filing Fee: $500 fee, payable to "Commonwealth of Massachusetts."

Annual Fees: You must file an annual report and pay a fee of $500 per year.

Special Instructions and Filing Requirements: Massachusetts does not provide a form, but does allow you to prepare and file the Certificate of Organization online from the filing office website. If you wish to prepare and mail a Certificate, prepare and submit an original and one copy of a completed, signed Certificate of Organization (the Massachusetts name for articles of organization). Type or print on only one side of 8½" x 11" paper.

If you do prepare your Certificate form, here is a list of the required contents of the Certificate of Organization for Massachusetts LLCs (see Chapter 4 for an example of how to draft your own articles based upon similar state statutory requirements):

1. Federal employer identification number (EIN), if available. To apply for an EIN online, go to the IRS website (www.irs.gov). If you have not yet received your federal EIN, just state in this paragraph of your articles: "The federal employer identification number of this limited liability company has been applied for, but has not yet been assigned."

2. The name of the LLC. (See "Name Requirements," above.)

3. The street address in Massachusetts where LLC records will be maintained. (Normally, this is the principal business office of the LLC.)

4. The general nature of the LLC's business. A statement that you plan to engage in any and all lawful business allowed LLCs under state law is not enough. You must indicate the nature of the LLC's actual business—for example, "The general nature of the business of this LLC is real estate sales" or "securities investments."

If your LLC plans to render licensed professional services, such as law, medicine, or accounting, you must include the following information: (1) the service to be rendered; (2) the names and addresses of each member or manager who will render the service; and (3) a statement that "The limited liability company will abide by and be subject to any conditions or limitations established by any applicable regulating board, including the provisions of liability insurance required under state law." A professional service LLC also must obtain a certificate from the state board that regulates the profession, which states that each member or manager who will render a professional service is duly licensed. Your state professional board should be able to provide this statement and help you prepare a Certificate of Organization for your professional LLC if you have any questions about these requirements.

5. The date the LLC will dissolve, if applicable. If your LLC wishes to have a perpetual existence (to dissolve only when the members or managers decide), simply don't include this statement in your Certificate.

6. The name and business address of the agent for service of process of the LLC. (If an individual, the agent must be a Massachusetts resident.)

7. If the LLC is manager-managed, the name and the business address of each LLC manager

(member-managed LLCs should ignore this item). The business address of a manager may be omitted if it is identical to the LLC's address.

8. The names and business addresses (again, only non-LLC business office addresses are required) of any nonmanagers who are authorized to execute documents on behalf of the LLC for filing with the Corporations Division of the Secretary of the Commonwealth. If you have a member-managed LLC, you must list at least one person here. Normally, member-managed LLCs will show the name of the member who prepares and files the Certificate of Organization—for example, "The name and business address of the person who is authorized to execute documents to be filed with the Corporations Division of the Secretary of the Commonwealth is [*name and address of member who is preparing the Certificate*]."

9. If desired, the name and business address (again, if different from the LLC business address) of any person specifically authorized to execute, acknowledge, deliver, and record any recordable instrument purporting to affect an interest in real property. Include this optional statement if your LLC may engage in real property transactions. (The LLC filing office will, for a fee, prepare a Certificate of Good Standing, which shows the names of persons listed in this clause as persons authorized to sign real property papers for your LLC.) You may use wording such as: "The names and addresses of persons who are authorized to execute, acknowledge, deliver, and record any recordable instrument affecting an interest in real property are: [*names and business addresses of one or more managers and/or members*]."

10. The Certificate can contain any additional information you wish to include—for example, the names and addresses of the initial members of your LLC.

The Certificate of Organization may be signed by any manager (if the LLC is manager-managed), any other person authorized to file papers for the LLC with the Corporations Division (see Item 8 above) or the organizer of the LLC (the person who is forming the LLC, whether or not listed in the Certificate). Generally, member-managed LLCs will list one of the members under Item 8 in the Certificate as a person who may make filings with the Division, and this member will sign the Certificate immediately after an execution paragraph included at the end of the Certificate:

Dated: _____

Signed: _____

Printed Name: _____

[*show capacity as* "Manager," "Member," *or* "Organizer"]

(Pursuant to Section 15(c) of the Massachusetts Limited Liability Company Act, the execution of this certificate by the above person constitutes an affirmation, under penalties of perjury, that the facts stated in this certificate are true.)

Tax Status

State Tax Treatment of LLCs: Follows IRS classification.

State Tax Office: Department of Revenue, Boston. www.dor.state.ma.us/Dorpg.htm

Operating Rules

Default Transfer Rule: By unanimous consent of nontransferring members or as provided in operating agreement.

Default Continuation Rule: The consent of members to continue the LLC after removal or withdrawal of a member is not required.

Michigan

LLC Filing Office

Bureau of Commercial Services
Corporation Division
P.O. Box 30054
Lansing, MI 48909
Telephone: 517-241-6470
www.michigan.gov/cis

Forms and Statutes: State provides fill-in-the-blanks articles of organization (Form 700) with instructions. Use Form 753 instead if converting a partnership to an LLC. Use Form 701 instead to file articles for an LLC rendering licensed professional services of public accountant, dentist, osteopathic physician, physician, surgeon, doctor of divinity or other clergy, or attorney, or use Form 753p instead if converting a professional partnership in one of these professions to an LLC. The latest versions of all of these forms, plus instructions and the state's guidelines for approving each form, are contained on the department's website.

Internet Forms: The latest versions of all of Michigan LLC forms, plus instructions and the state's guidelines for approving each form, are contained on the bureau's website. Note that articles can be filed by email through the state's FILEOnline service.

The Michigan LLC Act is contained in Chapter 450 (Corporations) of the Michigan Compiled Laws, Act 23 of 1993, starting with Section 450.4101, and is browseable from the following Web page (select "Chapter Index" under "Michigan Compiled Laws Information," then select "Chapter 450," then select "Act 23 of 1993" at the bottom of the page, which is the LLC Act): www.michiganlegislature.org

Articles of Organization

Name Requirements: Must contain the words "Limited Liability Company" or the abbreviation "LLC," "LC," "L.L.C.," or "L.C." A professional limited liability company (see list of professions above who must use Form 701 or 753p) name must, instead, include the words "Professional Limited Liability Company" or the abbreviation "PLLC," "PLC," "P.L.L.C.," or "P.L.C." Check preliminary name availability online by doing a business entity name search from the state filing office website, then call the state filing office at 517-241-6470 to confirm the availability of your proposed name. It costs $25 to reserve an available LLC name for six months.

Filing Fee: $50 nonrefundable fee, payable to "State of Michigan."

Special Instructions and Filing Requirements: You are only required to submit original articles. This document will be returned to you after it is copied and stored in the bureau's LLC database.

Use Form C & S 753 instead of standard C & S Form 700 if converting a partnership to an LLC. Use Form C & S 701 to file articles for an LLC rendering licensed professional services of public accountant, dentist, osteopathic physician, physician, surgeon, doctor of divinity or other clergy, or attorney, or use Form C & S 753p instead if converting a professional partnership in one of these professions to an LLC.

Tax Status

State Tax Treatment of LLCs: Follows IRS classification.

State Tax Office: Department of Treasury, Lansing. www.michigan.gov/treasury

Operating Rules

Default Transfer Rule: By unanimous consent of voting members.

Default Continuation Rule: Vote to continue LLC after dissociation of member not required.

Minnesota

LLC Filing Office

Minnesota Secretary of State

Business Services Division

180 State Office Building

100 Rev. Dr. Martin Luther King Jr. Blvd.

St. Paul, MN 55155-1299

Telephone: 651-296-2803 (toll free: 1-877-551-6767)

www.sos.state.mn.us/home/index.asp?page=3

Forms and Statutes: State provides fill-in-the-blanks articles of organization with instructions.

Internet Forms: Articles and other statutory forms are available for downloading from the state LLC filing office website. Subscribers to the online service can file documents online.

The Minnesota LLC Act is contained in Chapter 322B of the Minnesota Statutes, starting with Section 322B.01, and is browseable from the following Web page (select "Retrieve an entire chapter," then insert "322B" in the Chapter box, then click "Get Chapter"):

www.leg.state.mn.us/leg/statutes.asp

Articles of Organization

Name Requirements: Must contain the words "Limited Liability Company" or the abbreviation "LLC." Cannot include the words "incorporated" or "corporation" or their abbreviations. To find out whether your proposed name is available, search the names of existing business entities (including LLCs) online (or call the state filing office at 651-296-2803). You also can browse the name availability guidelines used by the corporate filing office online. It costs $35 to reserve an available name for 12 months.

Filing Fee: $135, payable to "Minnesota Secretary of State."

Special Instructions and Filing Requirements: Articles must be filled in with black ink only (use a black-ink pen or black-ribbon typewriter). The person who signs the articles must be at least 18 years of age. Send original of signed articles to the LLC filing office.

Here's how to address several particulars in the state articles form:

- Articles 2 and 3: Although you must specify a registered office in Article 2, designating a registered agent at this address in Article 3 is optional.

- Article 5: If you leave this article blank, the duration of the LLC will be presumed to be perpetual.

- Article 6: If your LLC will own or lease agricultural or farm land, look at Minnesota Statutes Section 500.24 to make sure you meet the legal requirements before checking the "Yes" box.

Tax Status

State Tax Treatment of LLCs: Follows IRS classification.

State Tax Office: Department of Revenue, St. Paul.

www.taxes.state.mn.us

Operating Rules

Default Transfer Rule: Unless otherwise stated in articles or operating agreement, by unanimous written consent of nontransferring members.

Default Continuation Rule: For LLCs formed on or after August 1, 1999, the LLC automatically dissolves upon the occurrence of an event that terminates the continued membership of an LLC member, but only if: (a) the articles of organization or a member control agreement specifically provide that the termination causes dissolution and in that event only as provided in the articles or member control agreement; or (b) the membership of the last or sole member terminates and the legal representative of that last or sole member does not cause the LLC to admit at least one member within 180 days after the termination.

Special Statutory Rules: The Minnesota LLC scheme presupposes management by a board of governors (management by governors is an anachronistic concept carried over from older nonprofit statutes still in force in some states). The LLC law specifies that LLCs must have one or more governors, elected by the members, who serve for an indefinite term of office. The Minnesota LLC Act, however, recognizes that LLCs may wish to adopt membership management. It says that the LLC members may act in the place of the governors as long as they make management decisions by unanimous vote; this is usually easy to achieve in smaller LLCs and we assume most smaller Minnesota LLCs will opt for membership management. To make sure you satisfy this vote requirement, you'll need to specify a unanimous membership vote requirement in Section B(5) of your member-managed LLC operating agreement.

To make matters more confusing, Minnesota law requires the appointment or election of one or two persons who function as the LLC president and treasurer, but who are called "managers" (the first position is called the "chief manager," the second is called the "treasurer." If you go through the Minnesota LLC Act, don't be confused by this nonstandard nomenclature. Simply decide which member(s) (or manager(s), in a manager-managed LLC) will be chief manager and treasurer).

You may instead decide to go along with the statutory scheme and opt for management by governors. Use the manager-managed operating agreement discussed in Chapter 6, but change all occurrences of the word "manager" to "governor" and "managers" to "board of governors." Although our general management provisions should work fine (in most cases, you can override the state law management rules with management rules of your own in your operating agreement), take a look at the Board of Governors sections in the Minnesota LLC Act to learn more about the default statutory management scheme.

Mississippi

LLC Filing Office

Mississippi Secretary of State
Corporate Division
P.O. Box 136
Jackson, MS 39205-0136
Telephone: 601-359-1633 (toll free: 1-800-256-3494)
www.sos.state.ms.us/busserv/corp/jer_corporations.asp

Forms and Statutes: The Mississippi Secretary of State provides a fill-in "Certificate of Formation" to use to create a Mississippi LLC. This is a special form designed to be scanned by a computer.

Internet Forms: You can fill in the Mississippi LLC Certificate of Formation (Form F100) online on the state filing office website.

The Mississippi LLC Act is contained in Title 79 (Corporations, Associations and Partnerships) of the Mississippi Code, Chapter 29, starting with Section 79-29-101, and is browseable from the following Web page (when you get there, select "Mississippi," then "Title 79," then "Chapter 29" to begin browsing the LLC Act):
www.michie.com

Certificate of Formation

Name Requirements: Must contain the words "Limited Liability Company" or the abbreviation "LLC" or "L.L.C." To see if your proposed name is already being used by another registered business entity, search the business entity database online from the filing office website or call the state filing office. You can reserve an available LLC name for 180 days for $25.

Filing Fee: $50, payable to the "Secretary of State."

Special Instructions and Filing Requirements: Make sure to fill in the fields in the scannable Certificate of Formation form according to the instructions on the website so that they fit in the fields and are in the correct format.

Tax Status

State Tax Treatment of LLCs: Follows IRS classification.

State Tax Office: Mississippi State Tax Commission, Jackson.

www.mstc.state.ms.us

Operating Rules

Default Transfer Rule: By unanimous consent of all nontransferring members or as provided in Certificate of Formation or operating agreement.

Default Continuation Rule: A membership vote to continue the LLC after dissociation of a member (cessation or termination of a membership interest) is not required.

Missouri

LLC Filing Office

Secretary of State
Corporation Division
P.O. Box 778
Jefferson City, MO 65102
Telephone: 573-751-4153 (toll free: 1-866-223-6535)

www.sos.mo.gov/business/corporations/Default. asp

Forms and Statutes: State provides fill-in-the-blanks articles of organization with instructions.

Internet Forms: The Missouri articles of organization form (LLC-1), plus other statutory forms, are available for downloading from the state LLC office website.

The Missouri LLC Act is contained in Title XXIII (Corporations, Associations and Partnerships) of the Missouri Statutes, Chapter 347, starting with Section 347.010, and is browseable from the following Web page: www.moga.state.mo.us/STATUTES/ C347.HTM

Articles of Organization

Name Requirements: Must contain the words "Limited Liability Company" or "Limited Company" or the abbreviation "LLC," "LC," "L.L.C.," or "L.C." It may not contain the abbreviation "Ltd." You can check the names of existing LLCs by following the link on the state filing office website to search the "Business Entity Database" or by calling the state corporate filing office. To reserve an available name for 60 days, submit an "Application for Reservation of Name" (available from the LLC filing office), together with a check for $25.

Filing Fee: $105, payable to "Secretary of State."

Special Instructions and Filing Requirements: Submit original of completed articles. Note this instruction for the Missouri articles:

- Article 5: You can insert "perpetual" in this blank to give your LLC an unlimited life.

Tax Status

State Tax Treatment of LLCs: Follows IRS classification.

State Tax Office: Department of Revenue, Jefferson City.

http://dor.state.mo.us/tax

Operating Rules

Default Transfer Rule: As provided in operating agreement.

Default Continuation Rule: A vote to continue the LLC after dissociation (cessation or termination of a membership interest) of a member is not required. But, except as provided in the operating agreement, a majority (in number) of the remaining members are allowed to vote to dissolve the LLC within 90 days of the dissociation.

Special Statutory Rules: A promise by a member to make a contribution to the LLC must be in writing to be enforceable. Therefore, make sure to execute a written promissory note or written contract to perform future services if a member promises to pay or perform future services as his or her capital contribution to your Missouri LLC.

Montana

LLC Filing Office

Montana Secretary of State
Corporation Bureau
P.O. Box 202801
Helena, MT 59620-2801
Telephone: 406-444-3665
http://sos.state.mt.us/BSB/index.asp

Forms and Statutes: State provides fill-in-the-blanks form for articles of organization.

Internet Forms: The latest version of the Montana LLC articles of organization (Form DLC-1), plus other statutory forms, can be downloaded from the state LLC filing office website.

The Montana LLC Act is contained in Title 35 (Corporations, Partnerships and Associations) of the Montana Code, Chapter 8, starting with Section 35-8-101, and is browseable from the following Web page (select Title 35, then Chapter 8):
http://data.opi.state.mt.us/bills/mca_toc/index.htm

Articles of Organization

Name Requirements: Must contain the words "Limited Liability Company" or "Limited Company" or the abbreviation "LLC," "LC," "L.L.C.," or "L.C." If you are forming a professional liability company, the LLC name must contain the words "Professional Limited Liability Company" or "Professional L.L.C." or the abbreviation "P.L.L.C." You can check available LLC names by calling the state filing office or by doing a business entity search from the link provided on the state filing office website. You can reserve an available LLC name for 120 days for $10.

Filing Fee: $70 fee, payable to "Montana Secretary of State."

Tax Status

State Tax Treatment of LLCs: Follows IRS classification.

State Tax Office: Department of Revenue, Helena.
http://mt.gov/revenue/default.asp

Operating Rules

Default Transfer Rule: Unless otherwise stated in operating agreement, by unanimous consent of nontransferring members.

Default Continuation Rule: A membership vote to continue the LLC after the dissociation of a member (cessation or termination of a membership interest) is not required.

Nebraska

LLC Filing Office

Nebraska Secretary of State
Corporate Division
P.O. Box 94608
Lincoln, NE 68509
Telephone: 402-471-4079
www.sos.state.ne.us/business/corp_serv

Forms and Statutes: State provides a fill-in-the-blanks form, "Articles of Organization—Limited Liability Company."

Internet Forms: The latest version of the Nebraska LLC articles of organization (Form 2606), plus other statutory LLC forms, can be downloaded from the state LLC filing office website.

The Nebraska LLC Act is contained in Chapter 21 (Corporations and Other Companies) of the Nebraska Statutes, starting with Section 21-2601. It is browseable from the Web page listed below (click the "Statutes" tab, select Chapter "21," then scroll down to Section 21-2601 to begin browsing the LLC Act): http://uniweb.legislature.ne.gov/legaldocs/search.php

Articles of Organization

Name Requirements: Must contain the words "Limited Liability Company" ("Limited" can be abbreviated as "Ltd." and "Company" as "Co.") or the abbreviation "LLC" or "L.L.C." You can check name availability online by using the corporate name search link on the state filing office website. You also can fax a name availability request to the state filing office with a list of names you wish to check. You can reserve an available corporate name for 120 days for $15.

Note: In Nebraska, you must identify your company as an LLC (by including the above words or abbreviation in your LLC name) on all correspondence, stationery, checks, invoices, and documents executed by the LLC. Failure to comply can result in personal liability for LLC members and managers (see Nebraska LLC Act, Section 21-2604).

Filing Fee: $100.00 plus $5.00 per page, plus an optional additional $10.00 to receive a certificate of organization from the Secretary of State after filing, payable to the "Secretary of State."

Special Instructions and Filing Requirements: Submit original and copy of signed articles for filing.

Following is specific information for filling in the state-provided form. If a particular item in the fill-in-the-blanks form does not apply, fill in "N/A" in the blank.

- **Period of Duration:** Insert "perpetual" to give your LLC an unlimited life.

- **Purpose:** Show the purpose of the LLC. You can simply indicate "to transact any or all lawful business for which limited liability companies may be organized in this state."

Professional LLCs: If you are providing a "professional service" (see below), fill in the name of the type of professional practice your LLC will engage in on the line provided under the standard purpose clause (the third blank on the form). Also note that the following also must be submitted with Articles of Organization for a professional LLC: Either a Certificate of Registration issued by the appropriate licensing board or, for health professions, an Application for Registration as a Professional Limited Liability Company (this additional form is provided on the state filing office website). Note that "professional service" means any type of personal service which requires obtaining a license and includes, but is not limited to: certified public accountant, public accountant, dentist, osteopathic physician, physician and surgeon, veterinarian, real estate broker, associate real estate broker, real estate salesperson, and attorney at law. Additional requirements apply to professional LLCs—see the state filing office website or call the filing office for additional information.

- **Contribution Information:** In the first blank, show the total amount of cash all initial members will contribute as capital to the LLC. (If no cash will be contributed, show "0"; if you are unsure whether all initial cash contributions will be reflected in the stated capital account in the LLC's books, ask your tax adviser.) In the second part of this article, describe any noncash capital contributions to be made by the initial members and state the fair market value of these noncash contributions.

- **Additional Contributions:** If LLC members will be required to make additional contributions after your LLC is formed (beyond the initial contributions listed above), list them in the blanks provided at the top of Page 2. Indicate the dates or circumstances when the additional contributions must be made.

- **Admission of Members:** If you adopt the standard language in our operating agreements, you may check the box that says members shall have the right to admit additional members. Then, you can use the following sentence to sum up the rights of members to admit additional members: "The existing members of this LLC must approve the admission of new members by a unanimous vote. Upon such approval, new members shall be accorded all rights associated with membership in this LLC."

Tax Status

State Tax Treatment of LLCs: Follows IRS classification.

State Tax Office: Department of Revenue, Lincoln. www.revenue.state.ne.us/index.html

Operating Rules

Default Transfer Rule: Unless otherwise provided in the articles or operating agreement, by consent of a majority in interest (presumably, a majority of capital and profits interests in the LLC) of nontransferring members.

Default Continuation Rule: Vote to continue LLC after dissociation of member not required.

Nevada

LLC Filing Office

Secretary of State
New Filings Section
206 North Carson Street
Carson City, NV 89701
Telephone: 775-684-5708

Filings may also be made at the Secretary of State satellite office in Las Vegas (702-486-2880).

http://sos.state.nv.us/comm_rec/index.htm

Forms and Statutes: State provides fill-in-the-blanks articles of organization with instructions.

Internet Forms: Provides downloadable articles of organization with instructions (either as a separate document or as part of a "Limited Liability Packet").

The Nevada LLC Act is contained in Title 7 (Business Associations; Securities; Commodities), Chapter 86 of the Nevada Statutes, starting with Section 86.011, and is browseable from the following Web page (select "Statutes and Regulations" then click on "NRS Chapter 86 - Limited Liability Companies").

http://sos.state.nv.us/comm_rec/index.htm

Articles of Organization

Name Requirements: Must contain the words "Limited Liability Company," "Limited Company," or "Limited" or the abbreviation "L.L.C.," "L.C.," "LLC," or "LC." The word "Company" may be abbreviated as "Co." You can check name availability from the state filing office website's corporate name database, which includes LLC names, or by calling the filing office. You can reserve an available name online by clicking the link on the home page to "Name Reservations." It costs $50 to reserve an available name for 90 days online. Alternatively, you can fill in and mail a paper name reservation form, available for download online, for a lesser filing fee of $25.00.

Filing Fee: $75, payable to "Secretary of State." Certified copies cost $30 extra each, and since the law requires you to keep one certified copy of the articles at the office of the resident agent, most organizers submit a filing fee check for $105 ($75 + $30 to certify the additional copy).

Additional Filing: In Nevada, your LLC must file an "Initial List of Managers or Members" form. Annual lists can be filed online from the state filing office website. The first initial list must be received by the Secretary of State by the close of business on the last day of the first month following the organization date (the date you file your LLC articles). The form includes a list of members (or, for manager-managed LLCs, managers) and the LLC's resident agent. The filing fee is $125. If you file late, you will be charged an additional $75 late fee.

Special Instructions and Filing Requirements: Your LLC's initial agent named in the articles must sign on the signature line provided at the bottom of the articles (in the certificate of acceptance section). The LLC organizer also signs in Article 6 on the first signature line. Submit an original and one copy of your articles (to be certified and returned to you for an additional $30 fee as explained above). Also make sure to complete and mail the state Customer Order Instructions form, available from the state website, with your mailed articles. There are two version of this customer order form—one for 2-hour processing, the other for regular and 24-hour filings.

Note that the right side of Article 1 contains a check box to indicate if you wish to form a series LLC. A series LLC is a special type of LLC authorized under Nevada law (and other cutting-edge business entity states like Delaware). It is used for special purposes, for example by real estate companies that hold title to multiple properties under the umbrella of a single LLC. Series LLCs are complicated, and you should consult an experienced lawyer if you wish to form one. The standard operating agreements included in this book are not appropriate for a series LLC.

Tax Status

State Tax Treatment of LLCs: Nevada does not have a state income tax scheme, and there is no special state entity tax levied on LLCs.

State Tax Office: Department of Taxation, Carson City.

http://tax.state.nv.us

Operating Rules

Default Transfer Rule: By unanimous written consent of majority in interest of (majority of profits interests held by) nontransferring members, unless otherwise provided in articles of operating agreement.

Default Continuation Rule: Unless required in the articles or operating agreement, vote to continue LLC after dissociation of member not required.

New Hampshire

LLC Filing Office

New Hampshire Secretary of State
Corporation Division
Department of State
107 North Main Street
Concord, NH 03301
Telephone: 603-271-3246
www.sos.nh.gov/corporate/

Forms and Statutes: State provides fill-in-the-blanks Certificate of Formation (Form LLC 1) with instructions, and Addendum to Business Organization and Registration Forms (Form SRA), which must be filed with the Certificate.

Internet Forms: The New Hampshire LLC Certificate of Formation, which includes the required SRA addendum to certificate, and other statutory forms are available on the state LLC filing office website.

The New Hampshire LLC Act is contained in Title XXVIII (Partnerships), Chapter 304C of the New Hampshire Statutes, starting with Section 304-C:1. It is browseable from the Web page listed below (when you get there, select "Title XXVIII Partnerships," then click "Chapter 304-C" to see a listing of the LLC Act sections): www.gencourt.state.nh.us/rsa/html/nhtoc.htm

Certificate of Formation

Name Requirements: Must contain the words "Limited Liability Company" or the abbreviation "LLC" or "L.L.C." The state specifically says that an additional space may be inserted between the letters or periods in each of these abbreviations. The name may contain the words "company," "association," "club," "foundation," "fund," "institute," "society," "union," "syndicate," "limited," or "trust" or abbreviations of these words. The name of a professional LLC in New Hampshire must end with the words "Professional Limited Liability Company" or the abbreviation "P.L.L.C." You can check on available names by calling the state filing office or by performing a business name lookup search from the state filing office website. It costs $15 to reserve an available LLC name for 120 days.

Filing Fee: $100, payable to the "Secretary of State." This fee includes $50 for filing an addendum form, discussed in "Special Instructions and Filing Requirements," which follows below.

Annual Fees: LLCs must pay an annual report fee of $100. The annual report can be filed online from the state filing office website.

Special Instructions and Filing Requirements:
When completing the fill-in-the-blanks Certificate of Formation, keep the following points in mind:

- **Second Article:** Be precise and state the nature of your LLC's specific business—for example, "real estate sales" or "automotive repair." You may add a general statement to your specific purposes if you wish: "and to engage in any lawful businesses permitted to limited liability companies under state law." New Hampshire LLCs may be formed for any lawful business purpose except banking, the construction or maintenance of railroads (unless a special permit is granted), the business of making contracts for the payment of money (loan agreements), or the business of a trust, surety, indemnity, or safe deposit company.

- **Fourth Article:** Insert the word "None" in this blank if, as is usually the case, you do not want to specify an automatic dissolution date for your LLC.

- **Fifth Article:** Most smaller LLCs—those without specially designated managers—will insert the words "is not" in the blank in this article.

You must include an "Addendum to Business Organization and Registration Form," which is included as part of the official state "Certificate of Formation" form. This form is designed to determine whether you are eligible to issue LLC membership interests under the New Hampshire securities laws. Most LLCs will be able to check box 1 in Part II, which indicates that the LLC qualifies to issue its initial membership interests under the New Hampshire small offering exemption for securities interests (contained in the New Hampshire Uniform Securities Act Section 421-B:17, II(k)). As explained in the instructions to Form SRA, under this exemption you do not have to register your sale of membership interests to your initial members if you sell these memberships, without advertising, to no more than ten people within 60 days after the date when you file your Certificate of Formation. Most New Hampshire LLCs with ten or fewer members should be eligible. For more information about this exemption, go to the New Hampshire Bureau of Securities Regulation website at www.sos. nh.gov/securities/. If you are not eligible for the New Hampshire small offering exemption, you must check one of the other boxes (2, 3, or 4) in Part II. In most cases, if you check a box other than box 1, you will need help to complete the SRA form and issue your membership interests in New Hampshire. Call the New Hampshire Division of Securities Regulation or ask a small business lawyer for further information. Also make sure to check Part III, Item 1 to show that your business is not a corporation or limited partnership. One or more LLC members or managers should sign the addendum form.

Tax Status

State Tax Treatment of LLCs: Follows IRS classification.

State Tax Office: Revenue Administration Department, Concord.

www.nh.gov/revenue

Operating Rules

Default Transfer Rule: Unless otherwise stated in operating agreement, by unanimous consent of nontransferring members.

Default Continuation Rule: Vote to continue LLC after dissociation of member not required.

New Jersey

LLC Filing Office

New Jersey Department of Treasury
Division of Revenue/Corporate Filing Unit
P.O. Box 308
Trenton, NJ 08646
Telephone: 609-292-9292

www.state.nj.us/njbgs

Forms and Statutes: New Jersey provides an online business formation service from its state filing office website. If you use the online service, you do not need to mail in forms to form your LLC. If you do not have an Internet connection or prefer to file paperwork to form your LLC, complete the "Public Record Filing for New Business Entity" portion of the New Jersey Business Registration Package (this package is available for download online). Complete this portion of the package and mail it together with your fees to the state filing office (see fee information below).

The New Jersey LLC Act is contained in Title 42 (Partnerships and Partnership Associations), Chapter 2B of the New Jersey Statutes, starting with Section 42:2B-1, and is browseable from the following Web page (when you get there, select "Statutes" under "Laws and Constitution" in the left panel, then keep expanding Title 42 until you can scroll to Section 42:2B-1, the beginning of the LLC Act):

www.njleg.state.nj.us

Certificate of Formation

Name Requirements: Must include "Limited Liability Company" or the abbreviation "L.L.C." You can check name availability and reserve a name online (name availability is automatically checked if you use the online business formation service). The fee for a separate online name availability check is $15; the fee for a name reservation is $50 (billed to your credit card). You can also check name availability online by comparing your proposed name to names already registered with the state. Click "browse business names for free" on the main page of the state filing office website. You also can check name availability by calling the state filing office.

Filing Fee: If you file and pay by mail, check or money order for $125, payable to "Secretary of State."

Special Instructions and Filing Requirements: See "Forms and Statutes," above

Tax Status

State Tax Treatment of LLCs: Follows IRS classification.

State Tax Office: Division of Taxation, Trenton.

www.state.nj.us/treasury/taxation

Operating Rules

Default Transfer Rule: By unanimous written consent of nontransferring members and by any other procedure provided in the operating agreement.

Default Continuation Rule: Vote to continue the LLC after termination of a membership not required.

New Mexico

LLC Filing Office

Public Regulation Commission
Corporations Bureau
Chartered Documents Division
P.O. Box 1269
Santa Fe, NM 87504

Telephone: 505-827-4511
toll free: 1-800-947-4722

www.nmprc.state.nm.us/cb.htm

Forms and Statutes: Provides fill-in-the-blanks articles of organization with instructions.

Internet Forms: LLC articles (Form NMSCC DLLC-CD) with instructions and a "Statement of Acceptance of Appointment of Registered Agent" (which must be completed and filed with the articles), plus other statutory forms, are available for downloading from the state LLC filing office website.

The New Mexico LLC Act is contained in Chapter 53 (Corporations), Article 19 of the New Mexico Statutes, starting with Section 53-19-1, and is browseable from the following Web page (when you get there, first select " Statutes" in the left panel, then in the left panel select the folder titled "New Mexico Statutes and Court Rules," select "Statutory Chapters in New Mexico Statutes Annotated 1978," then scroll down in the right panel and select "53. Corporations," then select "19. Limited Liability Companies, 53-19-1 through 53-19-74" to browse the sections of the act): http://legis.state.nm.us/lcs/default.asp

Articles of Organization

Name Requirements: Must contain the words "Limited Liability Company" or "Limited Company" or one of the following abbreviations: "LLC," "LC," "L.L.C.," or "L.C." The word "Limited" may be abbreviated as "Ltd." and the word "Company" may be abbreviated as "Co." You can check name availability online by comparing your proposed name to names already registered with the state. Click the "Corporation Information Inquiry" link on the state filing office website, then enter your proposed name in the search box to see if a similar name is already registered. You can also check name availability by calling the state filing office. It costs $20 to reserve an available name for 120 days.

Filing Fee: $50, payable to "New Mexico Public Regulation Commission" (or to "NMPRC").

Special Instructions and Filing Requirements: Submit the original and one copy of articles for filing.

A signed statement of the LLC's initial registered agent showing acceptance of the position must be included; this form is included with the articles form provided online.

Tax Status

State Tax Treatment of LLCs: Follows IRS classification.

State Tax Office: Taxation & Revenue Department, Santa Fe.

www.state.nm.us/tax

Operating Rules

Default Transfer Rule: Unless otherwise stated in articles or operating agreement, by unanimous written consent of nontransferring members.

Default Continuation Rule: No vote required to continue LLC after dissociation of a member.

New York

LLC Filing Office

Department of State
Division of Corporations
State Records and Uniform Commercial Code
41 State Street
Albany, NY 12231
Telephone: 518-473-2492

www.dos.state.ny.us/corp/corpwww.html

Forms and Statutes: State provides sample articles of organization (Form DOS-1336) with instructions.

Internet Forms: The New York Department of State (DOS) provides its statutory forms for downloading on its website, including standard LLC articles of organization (DOS-1336), articles of conversion of a partnership to an LLC and articles of organization for a professional service LLC.

If you wish to change a general or limited partnership to a New York LLC, the state provides a special "Certificate of Conversion" form (Form DOS-1363). Use this form instead of the standard LLC articles. (If converting a limited partnership, you must also file a certificate of cancellation for the limited partnership with the Department of State.)

Note for Professionals: Use the state-provided articles of organization for a professional service company (Form DOS-1374) instead of the standard New York LLC articles form if your LLC will perform licensed legal or medical professional services. Other licensed professionals, such as those licensed in the field of education, also need to use this special form. The state website provides a link to the list of professions that must use this special form to form a professional LLC.

The New York LLC Law is contained in Chapter 34 of the New York Consolidated Laws, starting with Section 101, and is browseable from the following Web page (when you get there, click "New York State Laws," then select "LLC - Limited Liability Company Law", from the list of titles): http://assembly.state.ny.us/leg

Articles of Organization

Name Requirements: Must contain the words "Limited Liability Company" or the abbreviation "LLC" or "L.L.C."

Certain words may not be contained in a New York LLC name unless special permission is obtained from the state. These prohibited or restricted words include the following: "community renewal," "tenant relocation," "urban development," "urban relocation," "acceptance," "guaranty," "annuity," "indemnity," "assurance," "insurance," "investment," "benefit," "loan," "bond," "mortgage," "casualty," "savings," "surety," "endowment," "title," "fidelity," "trust," "finance," and "underwriter." The names of professions, such as "doctor," "lawyer," and the like should not be used except with the permission of the state board that regulates the particular profession (also, see professional name rules below).

You can check name availability online by comparing your proposed name to names already registered with the state. Click the "Search the Corporation/Business Entity Database" link on the Division of Corporations homepage, then enter your proposed name in the search box to see if a similar name is already registered. As an alternative, you can call the state filing office 900-TEL-CORP (835-2677) information line to request a database search of up to five entity names during a single call. A fee of $4 (which will appear on your telephone bill) is charged for each call. Note that checking the database is an informal search—it does not tell you whether any names you find will be considered legally "distinguishable" from your proposed name. To get a definitive answer, you can mail, fax, or email a written request to the state filing office (see the website for addresses). The filing office will check up to five names for free, and charge $5 per name for each additional name you wish to check. It costs $20 to reserve an available name for 60 days.

Professional Service LLCs: If you are forming a professional LLC, your LLC name must, instead, end with the words "Professional Limited Liability Company" or "Limited Liability Company" or the abbreviation "P.L.L.C.," "PLLC," "LLC," or "L.L.C." Your LLC name may have to conform to additional rules enforced by the state board that regulates your profession.

Filing Fee: $200, payable to the "Department of State." Fee may be paid by check or money order. If a check is for an amount over $500, it must be a certified check.

Special Instructions and Filing Requirements:

When you mail your articles for filing, if you reserved your LLC name prior to filing your articles, include a copy of the certificate of name reservation you received from the Department of State. Also make sure to complete and include the official "backer" sheet provided as part of the official online articles form.

After filing, the state filing office sends a receipt of filing. Keep this receipt in your LLC records. Within 120 days of filing your articles, you must publish a copy of the information in your Articles in two newspapers (under Section 206 of the NY LLC Act). Your county clerk has a list of approved newspapers and journals—call and ask the county clerk where and how you should make these publications. After publication, a Certificate of Publication, with affidavits of publication (obtained from the newspapers) attached, must be submitted to the Department of State, with a $50 filing fee. A Certificate of Publication form is available for downloading from the state filing office website. The newspapers that handle the publication should be able to publish the notice and prepare the affidavits according to the latest requirements of Section 206.

Conversion of Limited Partnership: If you are converting an existing New York limited partnership to an LLC, the conversion does not become effective until a "Certificate of Cancellation" form (available from the Department of State) is filed for the limited partnership with the DOS. Make sure to use DOS Form 1363 instead of the standard LLC articles (DOS-1336) to form your LLC.

Note: There is a "Certificate of Conversion" form also posted on the state website. This is for use by LLCs that first file standard articles, then file a "Certificate of Conversion" (DOS Form 1364) that shows the date of filing of the original articles. We suggest you use Form 1363 instead, rather than using this alternate procedure. The two procedures are contained in Section 1006 of the NY LLC Act, which can be browsed through a link on the state LLC filing office website.

Formation of Professional Service LLC: If you are forming an LLC to engage in a licensed New York profession (including law, accounting, engineering, medicine, and the like—for a complete list, see the link to the Office of the Professions provided on the form download page of the state LLC filing office website), you must obtain a certificate from the New York licensing board that regulates your profession, which states that all LLC members and managers must hold valid licenses to practice the professional service rendered through the LLC. A copy of this certificate must be attached to your original articles filed with the Department of State. Also, a certified copy of the articles must be filed with the New York licensing board for the profession within 30 days after filing with the DOS. Make sure to use DOS Form 1374 to form your LLC instead of the standard LLC articles.

Tax Status

State Tax Treatment of LLCs: Follows IRS classification. State assesses a tax based upon the number of LLC members.

State Tax Office: Taxation & Finance Department, Albany. www.tax.state.ny.us

Operating Rules

Default Transfer Rule: Except as provided in the operating agreement, admission of transferee as a member must be approved by the vote or written consent of a majority in interest of nontransferring members (under Section 102(o)—this means nontransferring members with more than one-half shares of LLC profits unless otherwise provided in operating agreement).

Note: Notwithstanding anything to the contrary under applicable law, an operating agreement may provide that a membership interest may not be assigned prior to the dissolution and winding up of the LLC.

Default Continuation Rule: Membership vote to continue the LLC after dissociation of a member (cessation or termination of a membership interest) not required.

North Carolina

LLC Filing Office

North Carolina Department of the Secretary of State

Corporations Division

P.O. Box 29622

Raleigh, NC 27626-0622

Telephone: 919-807-2225

www.secretary.state.nc.us/corporations

Forms and Statutes: Provides fill-in-the-blanks articles of organization.

Internet Forms: North Carolina LLC articles with instructions, plus other statutory forms, are available for downloading from the state LLC filing office website. A guide to LLCs, which includes helpful name, trademark, and securities law information applicable to LLCs, plus state business and licensing office listings, is also available for downloading.

Note: An online forms filing service may soon be available. Check the state filing office website for details.

The North Carolina LLC Act is contained in Chapter 57C of the North Carolina Statutes, starting with Section 57C-1-01, and is browseable from the following Web page (when you get there, click "NC General Statutes" at the bottom of the page, then click "NC Statutes Table of Contents," then select "Chapter 57C, North Carolina Limited Liability Company Act"):

www.secstate.state.nc.us

Articles of Organization

Name Requirements: Must end with the words "Limited Liability Company" or the abbreviation "LLC" or "L.L.C." The words "Limited" and "Company" may be abbreviated to "Ltd." and "Co." If you are forming a professional LLC, your LLC name must, instead, end with the words "Professional Limited Liability Company" or the abbreviation "P.L.L.C." Your professional LLC name may have to conform to additional rules enforced by the state board that regulates your profession. You can check name availability online by comparing your proposed name to names already registered with the state. Click "Search By Corporate Name" on the state filing office home page (although the search page instructions only refer to corporate names, the database also includes the names of LLCs). You also can check name availability by calling the state filing office. It costs $30 to reserve an available corporate name for 120 days.

Filing Fee: $125, payable to "Secretary of State."

Annual Fees: LLCs must pay an annual report fee of $200.

Special Instructions and Filing Requirements: Submit original and one copy of state articles form (Form L-01).

A different articles form (Form PLLC-02), available from the state's website, should be used to form a professional LLC in North Carolina. Also, if you are converting an existing general or limited partnership to an LLC, use state articles Form L-01A instead of standard LLC articles.

Tax Status

State Tax Treatment of LLCs: Follows IRS classification.

State Tax Office: Department of Revenue, Raleigh. www.dor.state.nc.us

Operating Rules

Default Transfer Rule: Unless otherwise stated in articles or operating agreement, by unanimous agreement of members. The consent of a member may be evidenced in any manner specified in the operating agreement, but in the absence of such specification, consent shall be evidenced by a written instrument, dated and signed by the member, or evidenced by a vote taken at a meeting of members.

Default Continuation Rule: Membership vote to continue the LLC after dissociation of a member (cessation or termination of a membership interest) not required.

North Dakota

LLC Filing Office

North Dakota Secretary of State
Corporations Division
600 East Boulevard Avenue
Bismarck, ND 58505-0500

Telephone: 701-328-4284 (toll free: 800-352-0867 ext. 8-4284)

www.nd.gov/sos/businessserv

Forms and Statutes: The state provides sample articles of organization form that you can use to prepare your own form, along with a Registered Agent Consent to Serve form. LLCs formed to render licensed professional services should obtain and file articles of organization for a professional limited liability company; a sample form is available from the LLC filing office.

Internet Forms: Sample articles are available for downloading from the Secretary of State's website.

The North Dakota LLC Act is contained in Title 10-32 of the North Dakota Century Code, starting with Section 10-32-01, and is browseable from the Web page listed below (when you get there, select "ND Century Code" in the left panel, then click "10 Corporations," then select "Chapter 10-32" in the left-panel table of contents): www.legis.nd.gov/information/statutes/cent-code.html.

Articles of Organization

Name Requirements: Must contain the words "Limited Liability Company" or the abbreviation "LLC" or "L.L.C." Cannot contain the words "bank," "banker," or "banking." Check name availability by calling the state filing office or check your proposed name online by using the "Business Record Search" link on the state filing office website. You can reserve an available name for 12 months for $10.

Filing Fee: $135 ($125 for filing articles, plus $10 for filing Registered Agent Consent to Serve form), payable to the "Secretary of State."

Special Instructions and Filing Requirements: Follow the sample format provided by the Secretary of State's office when preparing articles (call the office for a copy of sample articles or follow the sample form available online from the state filing office website). Submit completed "Registered Agent Consent to Serve" form with the articles (a consent form, Form SFN 7974, is available from the office or online from the state filing office website).

Tax Status

State Tax Treatment of LLCs: Follows IRS classification.

State Tax Office: Office of State Tax Commission, Bismarck.
www.nd.gov/tax

Operating Rules

Default Transfer Rule: Except as otherwise provided in the articles or member-control agreement, by unanimous written consent of nontransferring members.

Default Continuation Rule: A vote to continue LLC after termination of a membership is not required unless and only to the extent provided in the articles or member-control agreement.

In the North Dakota LLC Act, the member-managers of an LLC are called the "board of governors." (The president and treasurer of the LLC—two positions that ND LLCs must fill (one person can serve in both capacities)—are called "managers" in the Act.) You can change the standard LLC operating agreements to reflect this nonstandard terminology, or you can simply decide that any reference in your agreement to managers of a manager-managed LLC is the same as a reference to your LLC's "board of governors." The most significant real-life difference to keep in mind is the following North Dakota rule (under Section 10-32-69 of the ND LLC Act): All members of a member-managed LLC must approve decisions that are specially assigned by the North Dakota statutes to the board of governors. In other words, if you run a member-managed North Dakota LLC, make sure to obtain and record the unanimous votes of all members regarding any important LLC decisions. This makes good business sense anyway, and should not be difficult to obtain for the average smaller-sized LLC.

Ohio

LLC Filing Office

Ohio Secretary of State
Business Services Division
P.O. Box 670
Columbus, OH 43216
Telephone: 614-466-3910
Toll free: 1-877-SOS-FILE (1-877-767-3453)
www.sos.state.oh.us/sos/businessservices/corp.aspx

Forms and Statutes: State provides fill-in-the-blanks articles of organization (Form 533) with instructions.

Internet Forms: Downloadable articles and other statutory forms are provided online at the state LLC filing office website.

The Ohio LLC Act is contained in Title XVII (Corporations-Partnerships), Chapter 1705 of the Ohio Statutes, starting with Section 1705.01, and is browseable from the following Web page (click "Revised Code," select "Title 17" in the left pane, click "Chapter 1705," then select each section of the Act you wish to view):

http://codes.ohio.gov.

Articles of Organization

Name Requirements: Must contain the words "Limited Liability Company" or "Limited" or the abbreviation "LLC," "L.L.C.," "Ltd," or "Ltd." Call the LLC filing office for name availability. You can check name availability online by comparing your proposed name to those already listed in the state filing office's business name database. You can also check name availability by calling the state filing office or emailing your name availability request to busserv@sos .state.oh.us. It costs $50 to reserve an available corporate name for 180 days—use the state's "Name Registration Form," Form 534, to reserve a name—the state requires customers to use the official state forms for all filings.

Filing Fee: $125 fee, payable to the "Ohio Secretary of State."

Special Instructions and Filing Requirements: You need to file original articles only (copies are not required).

Tax Status

State Tax Treatment of LLCs: Follows IRS classification.

State Tax Office: Taxation Department, Columbus.

http://tax.ohio.gov

Operating Rules

Default Transfer Rule: Unless otherwise stated in operating agreement, by unanimous consent of nontransferring members.

Default Continuation Rule: No consent required to continue LLC after withdrawal of member.

Oklahoma

LLC Filing Office

Oklahoma Secretary of State
Business Filing Department
2300 N. Lincoln Blvd., Room 101
Oklahoma City, OK 73105-4897
Telephone: 405-521-3912

www.sos.state.ok.us/business/business_filing.htm

Forms and Statutes: Provides sample articles of organization with instructions.

Internet Forms: LLC statutory forms, including articles of organization, are available for downloading from the state LLC filing office website. You can prepare and file articles and other business entity forms online using the SOONERAccess service.

Professional LLCs: Licensed professionals should use SOS Form 01, "Professional Articles of Organization," instead of the standard Oklahoma LLC articles to form their LLCs. A downloadable form is available from the state LLC filing office website.

The Oklahoma LLC Act is contained in Title 18 (Corporations) Oklahoma Statutes, Chapter 32, starting with Section 18-2000. It is browseable from the Web page listed below. When you get there, first click "Links to Statutes" in the left margin. Then click the "Expand" link for "Title 18, Corporations." Finally, scroll down the chapter index to Chapter 32, the Oklahoma LLC Act.

www.sos.state.ok.us/exec_legis/exec_leg_home.htm

Articles of Organization

Name Requirements: Must contain the words "Limited Liability Company" or "Limited Company" or the abbreviation "LLC," "LC," "L.L.C.," or "L.C." The word "Limited" may be abbreviated as "Ltd." and "Company" may be abbreviated as "Co." Call the state filing office to check name availability or use the online name availability search service on the state filing office website. It costs $10 to reserve an available LLC name for 60 days.

Filing Fee: $100, payable to "Secretary of State."

Special Instructions and Filing Requirements: If you file by mail, send one copy of the signed articles for filing.

Professional LLCs: Licensed professionals should use SOS Form 01, "Professional Articles of Organization," instead of the standard Oklahoma LLC articles to form their LLC. A downloadable form is available from the state LLC filing office website.

Tax Status

State Tax Treatment of LLCs: Follows IRS classification.

State Tax Office: Tax Commission, Oklahoma City.

www.oktax.state.ok.us

Operating Rules

Default Transfer Rule: Either as stated in operating agreement, or by consent of majority of capital interests in the LLC (not counting the capital interests being transferred to the new member).

Default Continuation Rule: Vote to continue LLC after dissociation of member not required.

Oregon

LLC Filing Office

Oregon Secretary of State
Corporation Division
Business Registry Section
Public Service Building
255 Capitol Street NE, Suite 151
Salem, OR 97310-1327
Telephone: 503-986-2200

www.filinginoregon.com

Forms and Statutes: State provides articles of organization (Form CR151) with instructions.

Internet Forms: Oregon LLC articles, plus other statutory forms, are available on the state LLC filing office website.

The Oregon LLC Act is contained in Chapter 63 of the Oregon Statutes, starting with Section 63.001, and is browseable from the following Web page: www.leg.state.or.us/ors/063.html.

Articles of Organization

Name Requirements: Must contain the words "Limited Liability Company" or the abbreviation "LLC" or "L.L.C." May not contain the words "Cooperative" or "Limited Partnership" or the abbreviation "L.P." To check name availability, call the state filing office or use the business name availability search service available on the state filing office website. It costs $50 to reserve an available LLC name for 120 days.

Filing Fee: $50, payable by check to the "Corporation Division."

Special Instructions and Filing Requirements: Most organizers will check the box in Article 2 that specifies a perpetual duration for the LLC.

If you are forming an LLC to practice one of a number of special professions (such as law, accounting, or medicine), Article 8 of your articles must specify the type of professional services your LLC will perform. The state licensing board that regulates your profession can tell you if your profession must comply with this requirement (and other requirements relating to Oregon professional LLCs).

Mail one signed original of the articles. If you submit one or more copies to be file stamped and returned to you, add $5 to your filing fee for each copy. If you want each copy to be certified, instead submit an additional $15 per certified copy. Articles also may be filed by fax (503-378-4381) after calling the Corporation Division and making fee payment arrangements.

Tax Status

State Tax Treatment of LLCs: Follows IRS classification.

State Tax Office: Department of Revenue, Salem. http://egov.oregon.gov/DOR

Operating Rules

Default Transfer Rule: Unless otherwise stated in articles or operating agreement, by consent of majority of nontransferring members.

Default Continuation Rule: Vote to continue LLC after dissociation of member not required.

Pennsylvania

LLC Filing Office

Commonwealth of Pennsylvania
Department of State
Corporation Bureau
P.O. Box 8722
Harrisburg, PA 17105-8722
Telephone: 717-787-1057 (toll free: 888-659-9962)
www.dos.state.pa.us/corps/site/default.asp

Forms and Statutes: State provides fill-in-the-blanks "Certificate of Organization—Domestic Limited Liability Company" with instructions, as well as an LLC office Docketing Statement.

Internet Forms: The "Certificate of Organization" with instructions, plus the Entity Docketing Statement and other statutory forms, are available for downloading from the state LLC filing office.

The Pennsylvania LLC Act is contained in Title 15 (Corporations and Business Associations), Chapter 89 of the Pennsylvania Statutes, starting with Section 8901. Chapter 89 (the LLC Act) is not posted on a state website as of the date of our research. Please check the state filing office Web page to see if the Pennsylvania LLC Act has been linked to the website. A copy of the LLC Act can be obtained upon request from The Agricultural

Law Research and Education Center website listed below (or call the Pennsylvania State Bookstore in Harrisburg—look under state of Pennsylvania listings in directory assistance—and ask about purchasing a copy of the Associations Code that contains the LLC Act): www.dsl.psu.edu/centers/aglawpubs/llc.html.

Certificate of Organization

Name Requirements: Must contain the words "Company," "Limited," or "Limited Liability Company," or an abbreviation of one of these three choices. The statute does not provide examples of acceptable abbreviations for these words—our guess is that "Ltd." and "Co." can be used, but not "Liab." You can check proposed names against those in the online business entity database or call the state filing office—two names can be checked by phone (mailing a written name availability request costs $15 for three names). It costs $70 to reserve an available name for 120 days. The state filing office does not provide a form for name reservation on its website so simply send a letter asking to reserve the available name together with your check for the reservation fee, made payable to the "Department of State."

Filing Fee: $125 fee, payable to the "Department of State."

Annual Fees: An annual LLC registration fee of at least $380, payable to the Department of State (call the Department to determine the current annual fee amount).

Special Instructions and Filing Requirements: Here's how most LLCs will complete these blanks on the state-provided form:

- **Article 4:** Smaller LLCs normally will not issue membership certificates and can strike out this language.

- **Article 5:** Most smaller LLCs will be managed by members and should strike out this language.

- **Article 6:** Insert "Not Applicable" in the blank unless you want the LLC office to file your certificate on a particular day after your articles are received by the office for filing. This would only be applicable if you want to start the legal life of your LLC on a particular day—for example, the first of the month.

- **Article 7:** Strike out the language of this article unless you are forming an LLC to render licensed professional services. In the latter case, you may need to submit written approval of the state professional board that oversees your profession with your articles. Such a requirement applies to the following types of practices: chiropractic, dentistry, law, medicine and surgery, optometry, osteopathic medicine and surgery, podiatric medicine, public accounting, psychology, and veterinarian medicine. It may also apply to others—so if you are forming an LLC to practice a licensed profession, check with your state board and make sure you can form a Pennsylvania LLC and how to deal with this article (whether to strike it out or fill it in). Also note that you may be required to pay the annual registration fee of $380 for each member in your professional LLC—call the Department of State to ask for the annual registration fee that will apply to your LLC.

Submit an original Certificate of Organization form and one copy of the state docketing statement (DCSB: 15-134A). Also enclose a stamped, self-addressed postcard (or envelope with an additional copy of the certificate enclosed) to obtain a receipt (or file-stamped copy of your certificate) from the LLC filing office.

Professional LLCs: If you are forming one of the special restricted professional LLCs, you may be required to attach a consent form to your certificate, which shows the approval from the board that regulates your profession of the formation of your LLC (the board first checks to make sure all members/managers are licensed). If a professional association is being converted to an LLC, a "Certificate of Election by Professional Association of Limited Liability Company," available for downloading from the state LLC filing office website, may be required to be filed. Check with the Corporation Bureau or your professional association board.

Tax Status

State Tax Treatment of LLCs: Follows the IRS classification.

State Tax Office: Department of Revenue, Harrisburg.

www.revenue.state.pa.us

Operating Rules

Default Transfer Rule: Unless otherwise stated in operating agreement, by unanimous written consent of nontransferring members.

Default Continuation Rule: Either as provided in the operating agreement or by unanimous consent of remaining members within 90 days of the dissociation event.

Rhode Island

LLC Filing Office

Rhode Island Secretary of State
Corporations Division
148 W. River Street
Providence, RI 02904-2615
Telephone: 401-277-3040
http://www3.sec.state.ri.us/divs/corps

Forms and Statutes: Provides fill-in-the-blanks form for articles of organization.

Internet Forms: LLC articles plus other statutory forms can be downloaded from the state LLC filing office website.

The Rhode Island LLC Act is contained in Title 7 (Corporations, Associations and Partnerships), Chapter 7-16 of the Rhode Island General Laws, starting with Section 7-16-1, and is browseable from the following Web page: www.rilin.state.ri.us/Statutes/TITLE7/7-16/INDEX.HTM.

Articles of Organization

Name Requirements: Must end with the words "Limited Liability Company" or the abbreviations "LLC" or "L.L.C." (upper or lower case is specifically permitted). Call the LLC filing office to check name availability. You can find out whether your proposed name is available by calling the state filing office or by searching the online corporation database linked to the state filing office website. It costs $50 to reserve an available name for 120 days.

Note: The Rhode Island LLC Act allows all professions listed under Section 7-5.1-2 of the Rhode Island General Laws (doctors, lawyers, CPAs, architects, engineers, and the like) to elect to organize as either a limited liability company or a limited liability partnership. Check with the state regulatory agency for your profession for information on the rules and regulations that apply to your profession if it operates as either an LLC or an LLP.

Filing Fee: $150, payable to "Secretary of State."

Special Instructions and Filing Requirements: File two original, signed articles forms. The Secretary will return a file-stamped copy to you, together with a Certificate of Organization.

Follow these guidelines when preparing your articles:

- **Article 3:** Most multi-member LLCs will check the box in Article 3 that indicates the LLC intends to be treated as a partnership for federal income tax purposes. If your LLC has just one member, you will want to change this selection, moving the "X" to the third box in this article, which reads "disregarded as an entity separate from its member" (this means that your LLC will be taxed as a sole proprietorship). If your single-member or multi-member LLC wishes to be taxed as a corporation (and plans to file a business entity classification election with IRS Form 8832 for this purpose), you will move the "X" to the second box (the corporation box) instead. For further guidance with selecting the best tax classification for your LLC, ask your tax adviser.

Tax Status

State Tax Treatment of LLCs: Follows IRS classification.

State Tax Office: Division of Taxation, Providence. www.tax.state.ri.us

Operating Rules

Default Transfer Rule: Unless otherwise stated in operating agreement, by unanimous consent of nontransferring members.

Default Continuation Rule: Vote to continue LLC after dissociation of member not required.

South Carolina

LLC Filing Office

South Carolina Secretary of State
Corporations Department
P.O. Box 11350
Columbia, SC 29211
Telephone: 803-734-2158
www.scsos.com/Corporations.htm

Forms and Statutes: State LLC office provides fill-in-the-blanks articles of organization, articles of organization for professional LLCs, and other LLC forms.

Internet Forms: LLC articles are available for downloading from the state LLC filing office website.

The South Carolina Uniform Limited Liability Company Act of 1996 is contained in Title 33 (Corporations, Partnerships and Associations), Chapter 44 of the South Carolina Code, starting with Section 33-44-101, and is browseable from the web page listed below (Click on "Title 33," then select the "Chapter 44" from the list—chapter numbers are referenced in the right margin; click on the leftmost "HTML" link to open the chapter as an html page in your browser). Note that the prior LLC Act (Chapter 43) also is available for downloading (repealed January 1, 2001): www.scstatehouse.net/code/statmast.htm.

Articles of Organization

Name Requirements: Must contain the words "Limited Liability Company" or "Limited Company" or the abbreviations "L.L.C.," "LLC," "LC," or "L.C." The word "Limited" may be abbreviated as "Ltd." and the word "Company" may be abbreviated as "Co." To find out whether your proposed name is available, call the state filing office or search the online business filings database linked to the state filing office website. An LLC name may be reserved for 120 days by filing two copies of an Application to Reserve an LLC Name along with a $25 fee.

Filing Fee: $110 fee, payable to "South Carolina Secretary of State."

Special Instructions and Filing Requirements: File original and one copy of articles. Most LLC organizers will not wish to limit the life of their LLC by specifying a term for its existence, and will therefore not check the box or fill in the blank in Article 5 of the state's official form. We assume no member of the LLC wishes to be personally liable for LLC debts, and therefore Box 7 and the lines in this article should be left blank.

Conversion of Partnership to LLC: If you are converting an existing partnership to an LLC, obtain a special articles form, "Conversion of

Partnership or Limited Partnership to Limited Liability Company Articles of Organization," instead of the standard LLC articles to form your LLC. This special articles form is available for downloading from the state LLC filing office website.

Tax Status

State Tax Treatment of LLCs: Follows IRS classification.

State Tax Office: Department of Revenue, Columbia.

www.sctax.org/default.htm

Operating Rules

Default Transfer Rule: By unanimous consent of nontransferring members, and as may be provided in the LLC operating agreement.

Default Continuation Rule: A membership vote to continue the LLC after dissociation of a member (cessation or termination of a membership interest) is not required.

South Dakota

LLC Filing Office

South Dakota Secretary of State
State Capitol
500 East Capitol Ave.
Pierre, SD 57501
Telephone: 605-773-4845
www.sdsos.gov/busineservices/corporations
.shtm

Forms and Statutes: State provides fill-in-the-blanks "Articles of Organization for Domestic Limited Liability Company" with instructions.

Internet Forms: LLC articles, plus other statutory forms, are available for downloading online at the state LLC filing office website.

The South Dakota LLC Act is contained in Title 47 (Corporations), Chapter 34 of the South Dakota Codified Laws, starting with Section 47-34-1, and is browseable from the following Web page (when you get there, choose "South Dakota," drill down through the folder headings in the left pane, as follows: "South Dakota Codified Laws," "Title 47," "Chapter 47-34"): www.michie.com.

Articles of Organization

Name Requirements: Must contain the words "Limited Liability Company" or "Limited Company" or the abbreviation "LLC," "LC," "L.L.C.," or "L.C." "Limited" may be abbreviated as "Ltd." and "Company" as "Co." You can check to see whether your proposed corporate name is available by calling the state filing office or by checking the online organization database linked to the state filing office website. It costs $20 to reserve an available corporate name for 120 days.

Filing Fee: $125, payable to the "Secretary of State."

Special Instructions and Filing Requirements: File the original and one copy of the articles.

You are required to complete and file an Annual Report (for a domestic LLC), available on the state website, which is delinquent if not filed by the end of the month following the month that you receive your Certificate of Organization. The filing fee for the annual report is $50.

Tax Status

State Tax Treatment of LLCs: South Dakota does not impose a state income tax.

State Tax Office: Department of Revenue, Pierre.

www.state.sd.us/drr2/revenue.html

Operating Rules

Default Transfer Rule: Unless otherwise provided in operating agreement, by consent of all members.

Default Continuation Rule: Vote to continue LLC after dissociation of member not required.

Tennessee

LLC Filing Office

Tennessee Department of State
Corporate Filings
312 Eighth Avenue North
6th Floor, Snodgrass Tower
Nashville, TN 37243
Telephone: 615-741- 2286
www.state.tn.us/sos/bus_svc/corporations
.htm

Forms and Statutes: State provides fill-in-the-blanks articles of organization with instructions.

Internet Forms: LLC articles with instructions, articles of conversion, and other statutory forms are available from the state LLC office website. A "Limited Liability Companies Filing Guide" is also available for downloading.

Note: You can ignore the "Certificate of Formation" form listed in the index to downloadable forms. It is an optional form that can be filed to show when the LLC began its legal existence.

The Tennessee Revised Limited Liability Company Act, effective January 1, 2006, is contained in Title 48 (Corporations and Associations), Chapter 249 of the Tennessee Code Annotated, starting with Section 48-249-101, and is browseable from the following web page (select the link to the Tennessee Revised Limited Liability Company Act at the bottom of the page): www.state.tn.us/sos/bus_svc/index
.htm.

Articles of Organization

Name Requirements: Must contain the words "Limited Liability Company" or the abbreviation "L.L.C." or "LLC." You can check to see whether your proposed name is available by calling the state corporate filing office or by using the business name availability search at the filing office's website. You can reserve an available corporate name for four months for $20.

Filing Fee: $50 per LLC member as of the date of filing, with a minimum fee of $300 (maximum fee is $3,000). Make check payable to the "Tennessee Secretary of State."

Special Instructions and Filing Requirements: Submit an original and one copy of the articles of organization. If you are converting an existing partnership to an LLC, use the special state-provided articles of conversion instead of the standard LLC articles to form your LLC (articles of conversion are available for downloading from the state LLC filing office website).

Here's how to complete specific articles:

• **Article 3:** Most organizers ignore the box in Article 3. It applies to a special type of Tennessee LLC management structure, called "director management." Instead, organizers check either the first or second box according to whether they have chosen standard member-management or manager-management. If you wish to learn more about the special type of director management in Tennessee, see Section 401(c) of the Tennessee Revised Limited Liability Company Act.

• **Article 7:** Leave this blank to give your LLC a perpetual existence. Insert a date or term of years in the blank only if you wish to limit the duration of your LLC.

• **Article 9:** We assume you will form a profit-making LLC and, therefore, will not check the box that applies to special Tennessee nonprofit LLCs.

Articles should be signed by a member or manager; show the person's title as member or manager in the line marked "signer's capacity."

Tax Status

State Tax Treatment of LLCs: Follows IRS classification.

State Tax Office: Department of Revenue, Nashville.

www.state.tn.us/revenue

Operating Rules

Default Transfer Rule: Generally, transfer of governance rights attached to a membership is effective only if all of the members, other than the member seeking to make the transfer, approve the transfer by unanimous consent (Section 508(b)(3)). Apparently, this restriction can be waived or altered in the LLC operating agreement (see Section 205 and check with a lawyer).

Default Continuation Rule: A vote to continue LLC after termination of a membership is not required.

Special Statutory Rules: Section 401(c) of the Tennessee Revised Limited Liability Company Act provides for a third type of LLC management in addition to the two standard types of member-management and manager-management. This third type is called "director management" and allows an LLC to be managed by an elected board of directors, much like a corporation. If you wish to learn more about the special type of director management in Tennessee, see Section 401(c) of the Tennessee Revised Limited Liability Company Act.

If the LLC documents do not provide for allocations of profits and losses, profits and losses shall be allocated among the members and holders of financial rights in equal shares.

Professional LLCs: See Section 1101 and following of the Tennessee Revised Limited Liability Company Act and the state filing office website and contact your state licensing board for information on the special requirements that apply to forming and operating a Tennessee professional LLC.

Texas

LLC Filing Office

Texas Secretary of State
Statutory Filings Division
Corporations Section
P.O. Box 13697
Austin, TX 78711-3697
Telephone: 512-463-5583
www.sos.state.tx.us/corp/index.shtml

Forms and Statutes: State provides "Certificate of Formation" (Form 205) plus other statutory forms.

Internet Forms: Texas provides an online certificate of formation preparation and filing service through the SOS Direct link on the corporate filing office website. Online certificate preparation and filing takes just a few minutes. If you prefer to prepare and mail paper forms, "Certificate of Formation" (Form 205) and other statutory forms are available for downloading from the state filing office website. The website also provides a helpful "Filing Guide."

The Texas Limited Liability Company Law, effective January 1, 2006, is contained in Title 3, Chapter 101 of the Texas Business Organizations Code (BOC). General provisions that apply to LLCs and other business entities are contained in Title 1 of the Code. The LLC Law can be browsed from the following web page (scroll down to Title 3, and expand the link to Chapter 101 to browse the LLC Law): http://tlo2.tlc.state.tx.us/statutes/bo.toc.htm

Certificate of Formation

Name Requirements: Must contain the words "Limited Liability Company" or "Limited Company" or the abbreviation "L.L.C.," "LLC," "LC," or "L.C." "Limited" may be abbreviated as "Ltd." or "LTD" and "Company" as "Co." You can check name availability online by using the SOSDirect name availability search service, over the phone by calling the state filing office, or by email to corpinfo@sos.state.tx.us. The SOSDirect name availability search fee is $1 per name searched, but the fee is not charged when the search is made when ordering copies/certificates or when making a document filing, such as a reservation of name through SOSDirect. You can reserve an available LLC name for 120 days for $40. If you reserve a name, you can do so online using the SOSDirect service linked to the corporate filing office website, but you can prepare and mail a name reservation request to the office if you prefer.

Filing Fee: $300, payable to "Secretary of State."

Special Instructions and Filing Requirements: If you mail a paper certificate of formation instead of using the online certificate filing service, submit an original and one copy of the certificate of formation. You will be mailed a file-stamped copy after the original is filed.

If you are converting a partnership to an LLC, see Form 642, Certificate of Conversion of a Limited Partnership Converting to a Limited Liability Company. This form as well as other conversion forms to use to convert different types of existing entities to and from an LLC are available on the state filing office website.

Tax Status

State Tax Treatment of LLCs: Texas imposes a franchise tax on LLCs as well as corporations. Texas has no personal income tax scheme.

State Tax Office: Comptroller of Public Accounts, Austin.

www.window.state.tx.us

Operating Rules

Default Transfer Rule: On the approval of all of the company's members.

Default Continuation Rule: A vote to continue LLC after termination of a membership is not required.

Utah

LLC Filing Office

Utah Division of Corporations & Commercial Code
Box 146705
Salt Lake City, UT 84114-6705
Telephone: 801-530-4849 (toll free: 877-526-3994)

http://corporations.utah.gov/index.html

Forms and Statutes: State provides sample articles of organization.

Internet Forms: LLC articles of organization plus other statutory forms are provided on the website.

The Utah LLC Act is contained in Title 48 (Partnership), Chapter 2c of the Utah Code, starting with Section 48-2c-101, and is browseable from the Web page listed below (when you get there, select "Utah Code/Constitution—Keyword Search," then expand the "Utah Code and Constitution" folder, "Title 48, Chapter 2c" to begin selecting and reading sections of the LLC Act): www.le.state.ut.us.

Articles of Organization

Name Requirements: Must contain the words "Limited Liability Company" or "Limited Company" or the abbreviation "LLC," "LC," "L.L.C.," or "L.C." You can check the availability of your proposed LLC name online at the state filing office website (use the business name availability search link) or by calling the filing office. You can reserve an available LLC name for 120 days for $22.

Filing Fee: $52, payable to "State of Utah."

Special Instructions and Filing Requirements: Submit a signed original and one photocopy of the articles along with a stamped, self-addressed envelope in which the filing office will return the file-stamped copy to you.

Tax Status

State Tax Treatment of LLCs: Follows IRS classification.

State Tax Office: Utah State Tax Commission, Salt Lake City.

http://tax.utah.gov

Operating Rules

Default Transfer Rule: Except as otherwise provided in the articles or operating agreement, admission of transferee as a member must be approved by consent of all members.

Default Continuation Rule: Vote to continue LLC after termination of a member is not required.

Special Statutory Rules: Note that Section 48-2c-803.1 of the LLC Act provides that for the purpose of determining compliance with a provision of the LLC Act that requires the votes of members holding a certain percentage of the company's profits interests, unless otherwise provided in the articles of organization or the operating agreement, each member's profits interest shall be determined based on the members' capital account balances on the date on which compliance is measured.

Vermont

LLC Filing Office

Vermont Secretary of State
Corporations Division
81 River Street, Drawer 09
Montpelier, VT 05609-1104
Telephone: 802-828-2386

www.sec.state.vt.us/corps/corpindex.htm

Forms and Statutes: Provides fill-in-the-blanks articles of organization with instructions and background information on the Vermont LLC Act and how it affects the formation and operation of Vermont LLCs.

Internet Forms: Vermont LLC statutory forms, including articles of organization, are available from the state LLC filing office website.

The Vermont LLC Act is contained in Title 11 (Corporations, Partnerships and Associations), Chapter 21 of the Vermont Statutes, starting with Section 3001, and is browseable from the following Web page (select the "Vermont Statutes Online" link in the left pane, then select "Title 11," then "Chapter 21"): www.leg.state.vt.us.

Articles of Organization

Name Requirements: Must contain the words "Limited Liability Company" or "Limited Company" or the abbreviation "LLC," "LC," "L.L.C.," or "L.C." "Limited" may be abbreviated as "Ltd." and "Company" as "Co." You can find out if your proposed LLC name is available by searching the online corporate database from the state filing office website (use the "Search Name Availability" link) or by calling the office. It costs $20 to reserve an available LLC name for 120 days.

Filing Fee: $75, payable to "Vermont Secretary of State."

Special Instructions and Filing Requirements: Mail an original and one copy of the articles to the Secretary of State.

The articles ask if the company will be a "term" company (one whose duration is limited to a definite term of years). If the LLC answers "No," its duration is perpetual, and it is called an "at-will" company under the Vermont LLC Act. Articles must also indicate if any members have agreed to assume personal liability for LLC debts and obligations (this assumption of liability is specifically allowed under Section 3043(b) of the Vermont LLC Act). Since one of the benefits of forming an LLC is immunity for all members from personal liability for LLC debts, the usual answer to this question is "No."

Tax Status

State Tax Treatment of LLCs: Follows IRS classification.

State Tax Office: Vermont Department of Taxes, Montpelier.

www.state.vt.us/tax/index.shtml

Operating Rules

Default Transfer Rule: By unanimous consent of nontransferring members; it appears the operating agreement can provide an alternate means of admission of transferees as new members (for example, by saying that any transferee who has been transferred an LLC interest together with all membership rights automatically becomes a new member). Most LLCs will want to stay with the default rule to allow existing members to affirmatively vote on the admission of future transferees.

Default Continuation Rule: By vote of a "majority in interest" of remaining members within 90 days of the dissociation (termination of membership rights) of a member (or a member-manager, if any, of a manager-managed LLC), or as may additionally be provided in the operating agreement. The dissociation events that trigger dissolution (or a vote to avoid dissolution) differ for at-will and term LLCs. *Note:* The vote of a "majority in interest" is not defined in the definitions section of the Act—our guess, by analogy to federal tax rules, is that this term means the vote of remaining members holding a majority of both the capital and profits interests in the LLC. *Also note:* The Act also says that the operating agreement can provide that the LLC automatically continues without a vote of the remaining members after the dissociation of a member or member-manager.

Virginia

LLC Filing Office

Clerk of the State Corporation Commission
P.O. Box 1197
First Floor
Richmond, VA 23218

Telephone: 804-371-9733 (toll free: 866-SCC-CLK1)

www.scc.virginia.gov/division/clk/index
.htm

Forms and Statutes: Provides fill-in-the-blanks "Articles of Organization," "Articles of Organization to Convert Existing Partnership to an LLC," and "Articles of Organization for a Professional LLC" with instructions for each form. Persons forming an LLC practice in medicine, law, dentistry, accounting, pharmacy, optometry, behavioral sciences, veterinary medicine, or insurance consulting form a professional LLC. All others should form a regular LLC.

Internet Forms: Virginia LLC statutory forms, including articles of organization (both regular LLCs—Form 1011—and professional LLCs—Form 1103, as well as Form 1010.1 for the conversion of a partnership into an LLC), are available for downloading from the state LLC office website in Microsoft Word and Adobe Acrobat (PDF) formats. A helpful "Business Registration Guide," which contains statutory forms plus tax, licensing, and other state information, also is available for downloading.

The Virginia LLC Act is contained in Title 13.1 (Corporations) of the Virginia Code, Chapter 12, starting with Section 13.1-1000, and is browseable from the following Web page (click "Code of Virginia,'" then click "Table of Contents" on the search page; select the "Title 13.1" heading, then click "Chapter 12, Virginia Limited Liability Company Act" to see a list of the sections in the LLC Act): http://legis.state
.va.us/codecomm/codehome.htm.

Articles of Organization

Name Requirements: Must contain the words "Limited Liability Company" or "Limited Company" or the abbreviation "LLC," "LC," "L.L.C.," or "L.C." You can check to see whether your proposed name is available by performing a business entity name search on the Clerk's Information System, which is linked to the state filing office website. You can also check name availability by calling the state filing office. It costs $10 to reserve an available LLC name for 120 days (the reservation can be renewed up to 30 days prior to the expiration of the reservation). Note that LLC names must be distinguishable from names in use by all other types of entities registered with the state, including corporations and others. So make sure to check your proposed name against names used by all other entities registered with the state (select "Name Search All Entities" when performing an online name search).

Filing Fee: $100, payable to "State Corporation Commission."

Special Instructions and Filing Requirements: You only need to send original articles for filing. Type or print in blanks of state form in black ink only.

To form a professional LLC, download and use Form 1103 from the state LLC office website. For the conversion of an existing partnership into a new LLC, use Form 1010.1 (also available from the state website).

Tax Status

State Tax Treatment of LLCs: Follows IRS classification.

State Tax Office: Department of Taxation, Richmond.

www.tax.virginia.gov

Operating Rules

Default Transfer Rule: Unless otherwise provided in the articles or operating agreement, by the consent of a majority of the member-managers (other than the assignor member) of a manager-managed limited liability company of which one or more members is a manager, or by a majority vote of the members (other than the assignor member) of any other limited liability company.

Default Continuation Rule: Vote to continue LLC after dissociation of member not required.

Washington

LLC Filing Office

Washington Secretary of State
Corporations Division
P.O. Box 40234
Olympia, WA 98504-0234
Telephone: 360-753-7115

www.secstate.wa.gov/corps

Forms and Statutes: State provides a fill-in-the-blank "Certificate of Formation" form.

Internet Forms: Washington LLC statutory forms, including the Certificate of Formation, are available for downloading from the state LLC office website. *Note:* Washington provides an online "Application to Form a Limited Liability Company," which you can prepare and file online from the state filing office website. Use this service instead of preparing, printing, and mailing a paper form to the state filing office. There is an additional $20 expedited processing fee to use the online service. Just click on the "Online Registration" link on the main page of the website, then fill in the screens as you follow the online instructions.

The Washington LLC Act is contained in Title 25.15 (Partnerships) of the Washington Code, starting with Section 25.15.005, and is browseable from the following Web page (insert "25.15" in the "Search Legislative Documents" box, check the "RCW & Dispositions" check box, then click "Search." You will see a listing of related links. Select the link that says "Chapter 25.15 RCW LIMITED LIABILITY COMPANIES," which will list the sections of the LLC Act): http://search.leg.wa.gov/pub/textsearch/default.asp.

Certificate of Formation

Name Requirements: Must contain the words "Limited Liability Company" or "Limited Liability Co." or the abbreviation "LLC" or "L.L.C." You can check to see whether your proposed LLC name is available online by clicking the "Corporations Search" link from the state filing office website. You can also check name availability by calling the filing office. It costs $30 to reserve an available LLC name for 180 days. *Note:* If you choose to file your certificate of formation online, you will automatically search for name availability as you step through the screens to prepare your application.

Filing Fee: $175, payable to "Secretary of State." If you file online, add $20 as an expedited processing fee for a total of $195.

Special Filing Instructions and Requirements: Most LLCs will specify "Not Applicable" in the "Date of Dissolution" box to give their LLC a perpetual existence. If you are preparing and mailing a paper "Certificate of Formation" for filing, make sure the registered agent signs the certificate in the space provided. Submit original and one copy to the LLC filing office.

Tax Status

State Tax Treatment of LLCs: The state applies a business and occupation tax (B&O), which is based on gross receipts, to LLCs (this tax also applies to corporations, partnerships, and sole proprietorships). The state has no personal income tax.

State Tax Office: Department of Revenue, Olympia.

http://dor.wa.gov

Operating Rules

Default Transfer Rule: Unless otherwise stated in operating agreement, by unanimous consent of nontransferring members.

Default Continuation Rule: Membership vote to continue the LLC after dissociation of a member (cessation or termination of a membership interest) not required.

West Virginia

LLC Filing Office

West Virginia Secretary of State
Corporations Division
Bldg. 1, Suite 157-K
1900 Kanawha Blvd. East
Charleston, WV 25305-0770
Telephone: 304-558-8000

www.wvsos.com

Forms and Statutes: Provides standard fill-in articles of organization (Form LLD-1).

Internet Forms: Articles (Form LLD-1) plus other statutory forms, such as an application to reserve an LLC name, are available for downloading from the state LLC filing office website. *Note:* West Virginia provides an online filing service, Business4WV, which you can use to form your LLC and register it with the state.

The West Virginia LLC Act is contained in Chapter 31B of the West Virginia Code, starting with Section 31B-1-101, and is browseable from the following Web page (when you get there, select "WV Code" at the top of the page, then select "Limited Liability Companies"): www.wvsos.com/business

Articles of Organization

Name Requirements: The name of a West Virginia LLC must contain the words "Limited Liability Company" or "Limited Company" or the abbreviation "L.L.C.," "LLC," "LC," or "L.C."

The word "Limited" may be abbreviated as "Ltd." and the word "Company" may be abbreviated as "Co." You can check name availability online using the Business Organizations Database at the state filing office website. Then, follow up by calling the state filing office to confirm availability. You can check the availability of up to three proposed names per phone call by calling the state filing office. It costs $15 to reserve an available LLC name for 120 days.

Professional Service LLCs: If you are forming a professional service LLC (for example, a law, accounting, or medical practice LLC) your LLC name must, instead, include the words "Professional Limited Liability Company" or the abbreviation "Professional L.L.C." or "P.L.L.C." A professional LLC must carry at least $1 million in professional liability insurance coverage. Call your state board to determine if a licensed profession is subject to these special professional service LLC requirements.

Filing Fee: $100, plus an "attorney-in-fact" charge (maximum $25) that is computed from a chart provided with the instructions to the online articles form, payable to the "Secretary of State."

Special Instructions and Filing Requirements: If you are filing by mail, submit one original copy of the articles, plus a manually signed copy, which will be date and time stamped and returned to you.

Note: We assume you will check "No" in Article 9 to show that no member is individually liable for LLC debts.

Article 2 contains a box to check if you are forming a professional LLC (for example, one engaged in the practice of accounting, architecture, law, chiropody, chiropractic, dentistry, osteopathy, medicine, podiatry, or veterinary medicine). As explained in the official instructions to the form provided on the state filing office website, articles for a professional LLC will not be filed until the LLC filing office receives a confirmation from the state licensing board that all LLC members have current licenses and have met the professional requirements of the board (the secretary determines how this confirmation is to be made; it is the responsibility of the organizer to obtain this confirmation).

If you are converting a general or limited partnership to an LLC, attach a completed Form LLD/F-6, "Statement of Conversion" (available from the LLC filing office), to your Form LLD-1.

Tax Status

State Tax Treatment of LLCs: Follows IRS classification.

State Tax Office: Department of Tax & Revenue, Charleston.

www.state.wv.us/taxdiv

Operating Rules

Default Transfer Rule: By unanimous consent of nontransferring members, and as may be provided in the LLC operating agreement.

Default Continuation Rule: By vote of members entitled to receive a majority of current or future distributions within 90 days of the dissociation of a member. This statutory majority-of-distributions voting rule to continue the LLC applies in manager-managed LLCs only when a member who is also a manager is dissociated— a vote is not required when a nonmanaging member's interest is terminated in a manager-managed LLC. Also note your operating agreement can provide that the LLC automatically continues without a vote after the dissociation of a member or member-manager. Special rules also apply depending on whether the LLC is a "term" company (has a dissolution date specified in its articles) or is an "at-will" company (has an indefinite duration).

Wisconsin

LLC Filing Office

Department of Financial Institutions
Division of Corporate and Consumer Services
Corporations Section, 3rd Floor
P.O. Box 7846
Madison, WI 53707-7846
Telephone: 608-261-7577
www.wdfi.org/corporations

Forms and Statutes: Provides fill-in-the-blanks articles of organization with instructions.

Internet Forms: Articles of organization plus other statutory forms are available from the state LLC office website. *Note:* You can prepare and file your LLC articles online with the Wisconsin Quickstart LLC service (see below).

The Wisconsin LLC Act is contained in Chapter 183 of the Wisconsin Statutes, starting with Section 183.0102, and is browseable from the following Web page (when you get there, click "Item 19 Statutes" in the main portion of the page, then continue expanding the chapter list by selecting "More" until Chapter 183 is visible and can be selected): http://folio.legis.state.wi.us.

Articles of Organization

Name Requirements: Must contain the words "Limited Liability Company" or "Limited Liability Co." or end with the abbreviation "LLC" or "L.L.C." You can check available names online from the state filing office website by clicking the CRIS (Corporate Registration Information System) link or by calling the state filing office. You can reserve an available LLC name for 120 days. If you reserve by telephone, it will cost $30; reserving by mail costs $15.

Filing Fee: $170, payable to "Department of Financial Institutions." *Note:* You pay a lower $130 fee to form your LLC online with the Wisconsin Quickstart LLC service.

Special Instructions and Filing Requirements: The state LLC filing office provides an online LLC formation service called Quickstart LLC. We recommend you use this online service to form your LLC instead of the state-provided paper articles from the state filing office because the online service costs less ($130 instead of the $170 charge for filing paper articles) and the online service is fast and easy to use.

If you file paper articles by mail, submit both pages of the state-provided articles form to the LLC filing office. Mail one signed original of the articles plus one copy for filing. A file-stamped copy will be returned to you.

Tax Status

State Tax Treatment of LLCs: Follows IRS classification.

State Tax Office: Department of Revenue, Madison.
www.dor.state.wi.us

Operating Rules

Default Transfer Rule: Unless otherwise stated in the operating agreement, by unanimous written consent of nontransferring members.

Default Continuation Rule: A vote to continue the LLC after the dissociation of a member is not required.

Wyoming

LLC Filing Office

Wyoming Secretary of State
Corporations Division
The Capitol Building, Room 110
200 W. 24th Street
Cheyenne, WY 82002-0020
Telephone: 307-777-7311
http://soswy.state.wy.us/corporat/corporat.htm

Forms and Statutes: State provides fill-in-the-blanks articles of organization.

Internet Forms: Articles of organization, as well as other statutory forms, are available from the state LLC filing office website.

The Wyoming LLC Act is contained in Title 17 of the Wyoming Statutes, Chapter 15, starting with Section 17-15-101, and is browseable from the following Web page (click the link to "Limited Liability Company Act," scroll down in the left panel and select "Title 17," then click on the "+" next to Title 17 to expand the list of chapters in the title, then scroll down and select "Chapter 15"): http://soswy.state.wy.us/corporat/statutes.htm.

Articles of Organization

Name Requirements: Must contain the words "Limited Liability Company" or "Limited Company" or the abbreviation "LLC," "L.L.C.," "LC," or "L.C." or one of the following combination forms: "Ltd. Liability Company," "Ltd. Liability Co.," or "Limited Liability Co." (Any of these nine forms is acceptable.) You can check name availability online by clicking the Corporation Database link from the state filing office website or by calling the state filing office. It costs $50 to reserve an available LLC name for 120 days.

Filing Fee: $100, payable to the "Secretary of State."

Annual Fees: Annual report license tax, which applies to business entities including LLCs, is $50 or two-tenths of one million on the dollar ($.0002) applied to the company's assets located and employed in Wyoming, whichever is greater. An entity with $250,000 or less in assets in Wyoming pays the minimum annual tax of $50.

Special Instructions and Filing Requirements: Submit an original plus one copy of articles for filing.

Here are instructions for some of the less straightforward articles:

- **Article 2:** State the period of duration of the LLC. Most organizers specify "perpetual" (to give their LLC an unlimited legal life). If you want to limit the duration of your LLC, specify a date, or a term of years, such as 50 or 75. If no response is provided in this blank, the law says your LLC's duration is 30 years from the date of filing.

- **Article 3:** Fill in the purpose(s) of your LLC. Rather than referring to the specific business of the LLC (for example, "real estate sales"), you can provide a general statement—but you must specifically exclude the banking and insurance businesses in such a statement. For example, the following general statement of purpose will work fine: "Any lawful business except the business of banking or insurance."

- **Article 6:** Specify the cash and value of property to be contributed to start up the LLC.

- **Article 7:** Indicate the amount or circumstances for any additional contributions required of members of your LLC.

- **Article 8:** If you adopt the standard language contained in our operating agreements, you can use the following sentence to sum up the rights of members to admit additional members, and the terms of such admission: "The existing members of this LLC must approve the admission of new members by a unanimous vote. Upon such approval, new members shall be accorded all rights associated with membership in this LLC."

- **Article 9:** If you adopt the standard language contained in our operating agreements, the following sentence will sum up the rights of remaining members to continue the LLC after dissociation of a member: "The unanimous approval of the remaining members is required to continue the business of this LLC upon the death, retirement, resignation, expulsion, bankruptcy, or dissolution of a member or the occurrence of any other event that terminates the continued membership of a member in this limited liability company."

If you wish to form a one-member LLC, you must retype the standard articles, and add an article (you can add it to the end of your articles and label it "Article 11"). In this article you must elect "flexible LLC" status (Wyoming flexible LLCs can say in their operating agreement that they will have just one member). See the specific instructions in "Special Statutory Rules," below.

The written consent of the registered agent to his or her appointment in this capacity must accompany the articles. Simply use the "Consent of Agent" form included as the last page of the articles in the downloadable form provided on the state filing office website.

Tax Status

State Tax Treatment of LLCs: No state income tax.

State Tax Office: Department of Revenue, Cheyenne.

http://revenue.state.wy.us

Operating Rules

Default Transfer Rule: By unanimous written consent of nontransferring members; this consent requirement appears mandatory (unless the LLC elects "flexible" LLC status—see "Special Statutory Rules" below).

Default Continuation Rule: By unanimous consent of remaining members; this right of remaining members to consent to continue the LLC after the dissociation of a member must be stated in the articles (see "Special Instructions and Filing Requirements," above, Article 8); this unanimous consent requirement and its inclusion in the articles is mandatory (unless the LLC elects "flexible" LLC status—see "Special Statutory Rules" below).

Special Statutory Rules: Section 17-15-144 of the Wyoming LLC Act allows the articles to contain a provision, which elects "flexible Limited Liability Company" status. This means that the LLC can have only one member (regular Wyoming LLCs must have at least two members). It also means that special provisions for the assignment of membership interests and for continuance of the LLC after a member is dissociated can be adopted by the LLC in its operating agreement; that is, the LLC can waive the otherwise mandatory default rules listed in the preceding two paragraphs. If you wish to form a flexible LLC, do the following:

1. Add a new Article 11 to the bottom of your articles just before the date and signature lines (you'll have to retype the last page of the state's fill-in article form), which reads as follows: "Article 11. Pursuant to W.S. 17-15-107(a)(x), this limited liability company elects to be a flexible limited liability company, and is thereby authorized to adopt provisions within its operating agreement as authorized by W.S. 17-15-144."

2. Next, use the following as your response in Article 8 (admission of new members) of your articles of organization (instead of the language given above in the "Special Instructions and Filing Requirements" section): "Except as may be permitted in the operating agreement of this limited liability company, the existing members of this LLC must approve the admission of new members by a unanimous vote. Upon such approval, new members shall be accorded all rights associated with membership in this LLC."

3. Finally, use the following as your response to Article 9 (continuance of the LLC): "Except as may be permitted in the operating agreement of this limited liability company, the unanimous approval

of the remaining members is required to continue the business of this LLC upon the death, retirement, resignation, expulsion, bankruptcy, or dissolution of a member or the occurrence of any other event that terminates the continued membership of a member in this limited liability company."

The result of making these changes to your articles is that you can have just one member and you are allowed to override the default transfer and continuation rules noted above—that is, you can provide in your operating agreement for the admission of new members (including those who have been transferred a membership from a prior member) and the continuance of the LLC after a member's interest is terminated by less than unanimous approval of nontransferring or remaining members. Again, we think going with the default unanimous rules makes the most sense—in small LLCs, obtaining full membership approval is usually best, but you can adopt these provisions and make up your own less-than-unanimous rules if you wish. ●

Tear-Out LLC Forms

IRS Form 8832, Entity Classification Election

LLC Filing Office Contact Letter

LLC Reservation of Name Letter

Articles of Organization

LLC Articles Filing Letter

Operating Agreement for Member-Managed Limited Liability Company

Limited Liability Company Management Operating Agreement

Minutes of Meeting

Certification of Authority

Form **8832**
(Rev. March 2007)
Department of the Treasury
Internal Revenue Service

Entity Classification Election

OMB No. 1545-1516

Type or Print	Name of eligible entity making election	Employer identification number
	Number, street, and room or suite no. If a P.O. box, see instructions.	
	City or town, state, and ZIP code. If a foreign address, enter city, province or state, postal code and country. Follow the country's practice for entering the postal code.	

▶ Check if: ☐ Address change

1 **Type of election** (see instructions):

a ☐ Initial classification by a newly-formed entity. Skip lines 2a and 2b and go to line 3.
b ☐ Change in current classification. Go to line 2a.

2a Has the eligible entity previously filed an entity election that had an effective date within the last 60 months?

☐ **Yes.** Go to line 2b.
☐ **No.** Skip line 2b and go to line 3.

2b Was the eligible entity's prior election for initial classification by a newly formed entity effective on the date of formation?

☐ **Yes.** Go to line 3.
☐ **No.** Stop here. You generally are not currently eligible to make the election (see instructions).

3 Does the eligible entity have more than one owner?

☐ **Yes.** You can elect to be classified as a partnership or an association taxable as a corporation. Skip line 4 and go to line 5.
☐ **No.** You can elect to be classified as an association taxable as a corporation or disregarded as a separate entity. Go to line 4.

4 If the eligible entity has only one owner, provide the following information:

a Name of owner ▶ --
b Identifying number of owner ▶ --

5 If the eligible entity is owned by one or more affiliated corporations that file a consolidated return, provide the name and employer identification number of the parent corporation:

a Name of parent corporation ▶ --
b Employer identification number ▶ ---

For Paperwork Reduction Act Notice, see instructions.   Cat. No. 22598R   Form **8832** (Rev. 3-2007)

6   **Type of entity** (see instructions):

a ☐ A domestic eligible entity electing to be classified as an association taxable as a corporation.

b ☐ A domestic eligible entity electing to be classified as a partnership.

c ☐ A domestic eligible entity with a single owner electing to be disregarded as a separate entity.

d ☐ A foreign eligible entity electing to be classified as an association taxable as a corporation.

e ☐ A foreign eligible entity electing to be classified as a partnership.

f ☐ A foreign eligible entity with a single owner electing to be disregarded as a separate entity.

7   If the eligible entity is created or organized in a foreign jurisdiction, provide the foreign country of organization ▶ --

8   Election is to be effective beginning (month, day, year) (see instructions) . . . . ▶ ___ / ___ / ___

9 Name and title of contact person whom the IRS may call for more information	**10** Contact person's telephone number
	( )

Consent Statement and Signature(s) (see instructions)

Under penalties of perjury, I (we) declare that I (we) consent to the election of the above-named entity to be classified as indicated above, and that I (we) have examined this consent statement, and to the best of my (our) knowledge and belief, it is true, correct, and complete. If I am an officer, manager, or member signing for all members of the entity, I further declare that I am authorized to execute this consent statement on their behalf.

Signature(s)	Date	Title

General Instructions

Section references are to the Internal Revenue Code unless otherwise noted.

What's New

This revision of the Form 8832 instructions reflects an update to the filing locations. Our previous revision (December 2006) stated that all entity classification elections were sent to the service center in Ogden, UT. *This is no longer the case.* Now the form is filed either in Cincinnati or Ogden depending upon your principal business location. See *Where To File* on page 4 for your filing location.

● You are not required to sign the copy of Form 8832 filed with your tax return. See *Consent statement and signature(s)* on page 6.

● New questions on lines 2a and 2b highlight the general rule which limits an eligible entity's ability to change its classification by election again during the 60 months after the effective date of making an earlier entity classification election.

● All single-owner eligible entities electing either corporate or disregarded entity status must provide the name and identifying number of their owner on lines 4a and 4b. Previously this requirement applied only to single-owner eligible entities electing disregarded entity status.

● All eligible entities owned by one or more affiliated corporations that file a consolidated return must provide the name and employer identification number (EIN) of their parent corporation on lines 5a and 5b. Previously this requirement applied only to single-owner eligible entities electing disregarded entity status.

● All foreign eligible entities making an entity classification election, including those also organized under domestic law, must provide the name of the foreign country in which they are organized on line 7. Previously this requirement applied only to single-owner foreign eligible entities electing disregarded entity status.

Purpose of Form

An eligible entity uses Form 8832 to elect how it will be classified for federal tax purposes, as a corporation, a partnership, or an entity disregarded as separate from its owner. An eligible entity is classified for federal tax purposes under the default rules described below unless it files Form 8832 or Form 2553, Election by a Small Business Corporation, to elect a classification or change its current classification. See *Who Must File* on page 4.

 A new eligible entity should not file Form 8832 if it will be using its default classification (see Default Rules below).

Eligible entity. An eligible entity is a business entity that is not included in items 1, or 3 through 9, under the definition of **corporation** provided under *Definitions.*

Eligible entities include limited liability companies (LLCs), partnerships, and any foreign entity that is not identified as a corporation under Regulations section 301.7701-2(b)(8) (see item 3 below).

Generally, corporations are not eligible entities. However, the following types of corporations are treated as eligible entities:

1. An eligible entity that previously elected to be an association taxable as a corporation by filing Form 8832. An entity that elects to be classified as a corporation by filing Form 8832 can make another election to change its classification (see the *60-month limitation rule* discussed below in the instructions for lines 2a and 2b).

2. A foreign eligible entity that became an association taxable as a corporation under the foreign default rule described below.

3. A foreign corporation that is not identified as a corporation under Regulations section 301.7701-2(b)(8). If a foreign corporation is not identified on the list included in these regulations, it qualifies as an eligible entity. See the list of *Foreign Entities Classified as Corporations for Federal Tax Purposes* under this regulation on page 6. Refer to the regulations for any changes to the list made after these instructions were printed.

The IRS will use the information entered on this form to establish the entity's filing and reporting requirements for federal tax purposes.

Default Rules

Existing entity default rule. Certain domestic and foreign entities that were in existence before January 1, 1997, and have an established federal tax classification generally do not need to make an election to continue that classification. If an existing entity decides to change its classification, it may do so subject to the 60-month limitation rule. See the instructions for lines 2a and 2b. See Regulations sections 301.7701-3(b)(3) and 301.7701-3(h)(2) for more details.

Domestic default rule. Unless an election is made on Form 8832, a domestic eligible entity is:

1. A partnership if it has two or more members.

2. Disregarded as an entity separate from its owner if it has a single owner.

A change in the number of members of an eligible entity classified as an **association** (defined below) does not affect the entity's classification. However, an eligible entity classified as a partnership will become a disregarded entity when the entity's membership is reduced to one member and a disregarded entity will be classified as a partnership when the entity has more than one member.

Foreign default rule. Unless an election is made on Form 8832, a foreign eligible entity is:

1. A partnership if it has two or more members and at least one member does not have limited liability.

2. An association taxable as a corporation if all members have limited liability.

3. Disregarded as an entity separate from its owner if it has a single owner that does not have limited liability.

Definitions

Association. For purposes of this form, an association is an eligible entity taxable as a corporation by election or, for foreign eligible entities, under the default rules (see Regulations section 301.7701-3).

Business entity. A business entity is any entity recognized for federal tax purposes that is not properly classified as a trust under Regulations section 301.7701-4 or otherwise subject to special treatment under the Code regarding the entity's classification. See Regulations section 301.7701-2(a).

Corporation. For federal tax purposes, a corporation is any of the following:

1. A business entity organized under a federal or state statute, or under a statute of a federally recognized Indian tribe, if the statute describes or refers to the entity as incorporated or as a corporation, body corporate, or body politic.

2. An association (as determined under Regulations section 301.7701-3).

3. A business entity organized under a state statute, if the statute describes or refers to the entity as a joint-stock company or joint-stock association.

4. An insurance company.

5. A state-chartered business entity conducting banking activities, if any of its deposits are insured under the Federal Deposit Insurance Act, as amended, 12 U.S.C. 1811 et seq., or a similar federal statute.

6. A business entity wholly owned by a state or any political subdivision thereof, or a business entity wholly owned by a foreign government or any other entity described in Regulations section 1.892-2T.

7. A business entity that is taxable as a corporation under a provision of the Code other than section 7701(a)(3).

8. A foreign business entity listed on page 6. See Regulations section 301.7701-2(b)(8) for any exceptions and inclusions to items on this list and for any revisions made to this list since these instructions were printed.

9. An entity created or organized under the laws of more than one jurisdiction (business entities with multiple charters) if the entity is treated as a corporation with respect to any one of the jurisdictions. See Regulations section 301.7701-2(b)(9) for examples.

Disregarded entity. A disregarded entity is an eligible entity that is treated as an entity not separate from its single owner. Its separate existence will be ignored for federal tax purposes unless it elects corporate tax treatment.

Limited liability. A member of a foreign eligible entity has limited liability if the member has no personal liability for any debts of or claims against the entity by reason of being a member. This determination is based solely on the statute or law under which the entity is organized (and, if relevant, the entity's organizational documents). A member has personal liability if the creditors of the entity may seek satisfaction of all or any part of the debts or claims against the entity from the member as such. A member has personal liability even if the member makes an agreement under which another person (whether or not a member of the entity) assumes that liability or agrees to indemnify that member for that liability.

Partnership. A partnership is a business entity that has at least two members and is not a corporation as defined on page 3 under *Corporation.*

Who Must File

File this form for an eligible entity that is one of the following:

● A domestic entity electing to be classified as an association taxable as a corporation.

● A domestic entity electing to change its current classification (even if it is currently classified under the default rule).

● A foreign entity that has more than one owner, all owners having limited liability, electing to be classified as a partnership.

● A foreign entity that has at least one owner that does not have limited liability, electing to be classified as an association taxable as a corporation.

● A foreign entity with a single owner having limited liability, electing to be an entity disregarded as an entity separate from its owner.

● A foreign entity electing to change its current classification (even if it is currently classified under the default rule).

Do not file this form for an eligible entity that is:

● Tax-exempt under section 501(a);

● A real estate investment trust (REIT), as defined in section 856; or

● Electing to be classified as an S corporation. An eligible entity that timely files Form 2553 to elect classification as an S corporation and meets all other requirements to qualify as an S corporation is deemed to have made an election under Regulations section 301.7701-3(c)(v) to be classified as an association taxable as a corporation.

All three of these entities are deemed to have made an election to be classified as an association.

Effect of Election

The federal tax treatment of elective changes in classification as described in Regulations section 301.7701-3(g)(1) is summarized as follows:

● If an eligible entity classified as a partnership elects to be classified as an association, it is deemed that the partnership contributes all of its assets and liabilities to the association in exchange for stock in the association, and immediately thereafter, the partnership liquidates by distributing the stock of the association to its partners.

● If an eligible entity classified as an association elects to be classified as a partnership, it is deemed that the association distributes all of its assets and liabilities to its shareholders in liquidation of the association, and immediately thereafter, the shareholders contribute all of the distributed assets and liabilities to a newly formed partnership.

● If an eligible entity classified as an association elects to be disregarded as an entity separate from its owner, it is deemed that the association distributes all of its assets and liabilities to its single owner in liquidation of the association.

● If an eligible entity that is disregarded as an entity separate from its owner elects to be classified as an association, the owner of the eligible entity is deemed to have contributed all of the assets and liabilities of the entity to the association in exchange for the stock of the association.

Note. For information on the federal tax consequences of elective changes in classification, see Regulations section 301.7701-3(g).

When To File

An election specifying an eligible entity's classification cannot take effect more than 75 days prior to the date the election is filed, nor can it take effect later than 12 months after the date the election is filed.

Late election relief. A newly formed entity may be eligible for late election relief under Rev. Proc. 2002-59, 2002-39 I.R.B. 615 if:

● The entity failed to obtain its desired classification solely because Form 8832 was not timely filed,

● The due date for the entity's desired classification tax return (excluding extensions) for the tax year beginning with the entity's formation date has not passed, and

● The entity has reasonable cause for its failure to make a timely election.

To obtain relief, a newly formed entity must file Form 8832 on or before the due date of the first federal tax return (excluding extensions) of the entity's desired classification. The entity must also write "FILED PURSUANT TO REV. PROC. 2002-59" at the top of the form. The entity must attach a statement to the form explaining why it failed to file a timely election. If Rev. Proc. 2002-59 does not apply, an entity may seek relief for a late entity election by requesting a private letter ruling and paying a user fee in accordance with Rev. Proc. 2006-1, 2006-1 I.R.B. 1 (or its successor).

Where To File

File Form 8832 with the Internal Revenue Service Center for your state listed below.

Attach a copy of Form 8832 to the entity's federal tax return for the tax year of the election. If the entity is not required to file a return for that year, a copy of its Form 8832 must be attached to the federal tax returns of all direct or indirect owners of the entity for the tax year of the owner that includes the date on which the election took effect. Failure to attach a copy of Form 8832 will not invalidate an otherwise valid election, but penalties may be assessed against persons who are required to, but do not, attach Form 8832.

Each member of the entity is required to file their return consistent with the entity election. Penalties apply to returns filed inconsistent with the entity's election.

If the entity's principal business, office, or agency is located in:	Use the following Internal Revenue Service Center address:
Connecticut, Delaware, District of Columbia, Illinois, Indiana, Kentucky, Maine, Maryland, Massachusetts, Michigan, New Hampshire, New Jersey, New York, North Carolina, Ohio, Pennsylvania, Rhode Island, South Carolina, Vermont, Virginia, West Virginia, Wisconsin	Cincinnati, OH 45999

If the entity's principal business, office, or agency is located in:	Use the following Internal Revenue Service Center address:
Alabama, Alaska, Arizona, Arkansas, California, Colorado, Florida, Georgia, Hawaii, Idaho, Iowa, Kansas, Louisiana, Minnesota, Mississippi, Missouri, Montana, Nebraska, Nevada, New Mexico, North Dakota, Oklahoma, Oregon, South Dakota, Tennessee, Texas, Utah, Washington, Wyoming	Ogden, UT 84201
A foreign country or U.S. possession	Ogden, UT 84201-0023

Note. Also attach a copy to the entity's federal income tax return for the tax year of the election.

Acceptance or Nonacceptance of Election

The service center will notify the eligible entity at the address listed on Form 8832 if its election is accepted or not accepted. The entity should generally receive a determination on its election within 60 days after it has filed Form 8832.

Care should be exercised to ensure that the IRS receives the election. If the entity is not notified of acceptance or nonacceptance of its election within 60 days of the date of filing, take follow-up action by calling 1-800-829-0115, or by sending a letter to the service center to inquire about its status. Send any such letter by certified or registered mail via the U.S. Postal Service, or equivalent type of delivery by a designated private delivery service (see Notice 2004-83, 2004-52 I.R.B. 1030 (or its successor)).

If the IRS questions whether Form 8832 was filed, an acceptable proof of filing is:

● A certified or registered mail receipt (timely postmarked) from the U.S. Postal Service, or its equivalent from a designated private delivery service;

● Form 8832 with an accepted stamp;

● Form 8832 with a stamped IRS received date; or

● An IRS letter stating that Form 8832 has been accepted.

Specific Instructions

Name. Enter the name of the eligible entity electing to be classified.

Employer identification number (EIN). Show the EIN of the eligible entity electing to be classified.

Caution. Do not put "Applied For" on this line.

Note. Any entity that has an EIN will retain that EIN even if its federal tax classification changes under Regulations section 301.7701-3.

If a disregarded entity's classification changes so that it becomes recognized as a partnership or association for federal tax purposes, and that entity had an EIN, then the entity must continue to use that EIN. If the entity did not already have its own EIN, then the entity must apply for an EIN and not use the identifying number of the single owner.

A foreign person that makes an election under Regulations section 301.7701-3(c) and (d) must also use its own taxpayer identifying number. See sections 6721 through 6724 for penalties that may apply for failure to supply taxpayer identifying numbers.

If the entity electing to be classified using Form 8832 does not have an EIN, it must apply for one on Form SS-4, Application for Employer Identification Number. If the filing of Form 8832 is the only reason the entity is applying for an EIN, check the "Other" box on line 9 of Form SS-4 and enter "Form 8832" to the right of that box. The entity must have received an EIN by the time Form 8832 is filed in order for the form to be processed. An election will not be accepted if the eligible entity does not provide an EIN. **Caution.** Do not apply for a new EIN for an existing entity that is changing its classification if the entity already has an EIN.

Address. Enter the address of the entity electing a classification. All correspondence regarding the acceptance or nonacceptance of the election will be sent to this address. Include the suite, room, or other unit number after the street address. If the Post Office does not deliver mail to the street address and the entity has a P.O. box, show the box number instead of the street address. If the electing entity receives its mail in care of a third party (such as an accountant or an attorney), enter on the street address line "C/O" followed by the third party's name and street address or P.O. box.

Address change. If the eligible entity has changed its address since filing Form SS-4 or the entity's most recently-filed return (including a change to an "in care of" address), check the box for an address change.

Note. If a change of address occurs after the later of the filing of Form SS-4 or the most recently-filed return, use Form 8822, Change of Address, to notify the IRS of the new address. A new address shown on Form 8832 will not update the entity's address of record with the IRS.

Line 1. Check box 1a if the entity is choosing a classification for the first time (i.e., the entity does not want to be classified under the applicable default classification). Do not file this form if the

entity wants to be classified under the default rules.

Check box 1b if the entity is changing its current classification.

Lines 2a and 2b. 60-month limitation rule. Once an eligible entity makes an election to *change* its classification, the entity generally cannot change its classification by election again during the 60 months after the effective date of the election. However, the IRS may (by private letter ruling) permit the entity to change its classification by election within the 60-month period if more than 50% of the ownership interests in the entity, as of the effective date of the election, are owned by persons that did not own any interests in the entity on the effective date or the filing date of the entity's prior election.

Note. The 60-month limitation does not apply if the previous election was made by a *newly formed* eligible entity and was effective on the date of formation.

Line 4. If an eligible entity has only one owner, provide the name of its owner on line 4a and the owner's identifying number (social security number, or individual taxpayer identification number, or EIN) on line 4b. Enter "DE" if the owner is a disregarded entity that does not have an identifying number. If the owner is a foreign person or entity and does not have a U.S. identifying number, enter "none" on line 4b.

Line 5. If the eligible entity is owned by one or more members of an affiliated group of corporations that file a consolidated return, provide the name and EIN of the parent corporation.

Line 6. Check the appropriate box if you are changing a current classification (no matter how achieved), or are electing out of a default classification. Do not file this form if you fall within a default classification that is the desired classification for the new entity.

Line 7. If the entity making the election is created or organized in a foreign jurisdiction, enter the name of the foreign country in which it is organized. This information must be provided even if the entity is also organized under domestic law.

Line 8. Generally, the election will take effect on the date you enter on line 8 of this form, or on the date filed if no date is entered on line 8. An election specifying an entity's classification for federal tax purposes can take effect no more than 75 days prior to the date the election is filed, nor can it take effect later than 12 months after the date on which the election is filed. If line 8 shows a date more than 75 days prior to the date on which the election is filed, the election will default to 75 days before the date it is filed. If line 8 shows an effective date more than 12 months from the filing date, the election will take effect 12 months after the date the election is filed.

Consent statement and signature(s).
Form 8832 must be signed by:

1. Each member of the electing entity who is an owner at the time the election is filed; or

2. Any officer, manager, or member of the electing entity who is authorized (under local law or the organizational documents) to make the election. The elector represents to having such authorization under penalties of perjury.

If an election is to be effective for any period prior to the time it is filed, each person who was an owner between the date the election is to be effective and the date the election is filed, must sign.

If you need a continuation sheet or use a separate consent statement, attach it to Form 8832. The separate consent statement must contain the same information as shown on Form 8832.

Note. Do not sign the copy that is attached to your tax return.

Paperwork Reduction Act Notice

We ask for the information on this form to carry out the Internal Revenue laws of the United States. You are required to give us the information. We need it to ensure that you are complying with these laws and to allow us to figure and collect the right amount of tax.

You are not required to provide the information requested on a form that is subject to the Paperwork Reduction Act unless the form displays a valid OMB control number. Books or records relating to a form or its instructions must be retained as long as their contents may become material in the administration of any Internal Revenue law. Generally, tax returns and return information are confidential, as required by section 6103.

The time needed to complete and file this form will vary depending on individual circumstances. The estimated average time is:

Recordkeeping . . . . 1 hr., 49 min.

**Learning about the
law or the form** . . . . 2 hr., 7 min.

**Preparing and sending
the form to the IRS** . . . . . 23 min.

If you have comments concerning the accuracy of these time estimates or suggestions for making this form simpler, we would be happy to hear from you. You can write to the Internal Revenue Service, Tax Products Coordinating Committee, SE:W:CAR:MP:T:T:SP, 1111 Constitution Ave. NW, IR-6406, Washington, DC 20224. Do not send the form to this address. Instead, see *Where To File* on page 4.

Foreign Entities Classified as Corporations for Federal Tax Purposes:

American Samoa—Corporation
Argentina—Sociedad Anonima
Australia—Public Limited Company
Austria—Aktiengesellschaft
Barbados—Limited Company
Belgium—Societe Anonyme
Belize—Public Limited Company
Bolivia—Sociedad Anonima
Brazil—Sociedade Anonima
Canada—Corporation and Company
Chile—Sociedad Anonima
People's Republic of China—Gufen Youxian Gongsi
Republic of China (Taiwan)—Ku-fen Yu-hsien Kung-szu
Colombia—Sociedad Anonima
Costa Rica—Sociedad Anonima
Cyprus—Public Limited Company
Czech Republic—Akciova Spolecnost
Denmark—Aktieselskab
Ecuador—Sociedad Anonima or Compania Anonima
Egypt—Sharikat Al-Mossahamah
El Salvador—Sociedad Anonima
Estonia—Aktsiaselts
European Economic Area/European Union—Societas Europaea
Finland—Julkinen Osakeyhtio/Publikt Aktiebolag
France—Societe Anonyme
Germany—Aktiengesellschaft
Greece—Anonymos Etairia
Guam—Corporation
Guatemala—Sociedad Anonima
Guyana—Public Limited Company
Honduras—Sociedad Anonima
Hong Kong—Public Limited Company
Hungary—Reszvenytarsasag
Iceland—Hlutafelag
India—Public Limited Company
Indonesia—Perseroan Terbuka
Ireland—Public Limited Company
Israel—Public Limited Company
Italy—Societa per Azioni
Jamaica—Public Limited Company
Japan—Kabushiki Kaisha
Kazakstan—Ashyk Aktsionerlik Kogham
Republic of Korea—Chusik Hoesa
Latvia—Akciju Sabiedriba
Liberia—Corporation
Liechtenstein—Aktiengesellschaft
Lithuania—Akcine Bendroves
Luxembourg—Societe Anonyme

Malaysia—Berhad
Malta—Public Limited Company
Mexico—Sociedad Anonima
Morocco—Societe Anonyme
Netherlands—Naamloze Vennootschap
New Zealand—Limited Company
Nicaragua—Compania Anonima
Nigeria—Public Limited Company
Northern Mariana Islands—Corporation
Norway—Allment Aksjeselskap
Pakistan—Public Limited Company
Panama—Sociedad Anonima
Paraguay—Sociedad Anonima
Peru—Sociedad Anonima
Philippines—Stock Corporation
Poland—Spolka Akcyjna
Portugal—Sociedade Anonima
Puerto Rico—Corporation
Romania—Societe pe Actiuni
Russia—Otkrytoye Aktsionernoy Obshchestvo
Saudi Arabia—Sharikat Al-Mossahamah
Singapore—Public Limited Company
Slovak Republic—Akciova Spolocnost
Slovenia—Delniska Druzba
South Africa—Public Limited Company
Spain—Sociedad Anonima
Surinam—Naamloze Vennootschap
Sweden—Publika Aktiebolag
Switzerland—Aktiengesellschaft
Thailand—Borisat Chamkad (Mahachon)
Trinidad and Tobago—Limited Company
Tunisia—Societe Anonyme
Turkey—Anonim Sirket
Ukraine—Aktsionerne Tovaristvo Vidkritogo Tipu
United Kingdom—Public Limited Company
United States Virgin Islands—Corporation
Uruguay—Sociedad Anonima
Venezuela—Sociedad Anonima or Compania Anonima

 See Regulations section 301.7701-2(b)(8) for any exceptions and inclusions to items on this list and for any revisions made to this list since these instructions were printed.

LLC Filing Office Contact Letter

_____

_____

_____

_____

LLC Filings Office:

I am in the process of forming a domestic limited liability company (LLC). Please note:

☐ I am or ☐ I am not converting an existing _____ partnership to an LLC.

☐ I am or ☐ I am not forming an LLC to perform the professional services of
_____, which are licensed by the state.

Please send me the following forms, material, and other information:

1. printed, sample, or specimen LLC articles of organization, with instructions. If your office reviews articles of organization for correctness prior to filing, please advise me of the procedure I should follow to obtain this prefiling review;

2. the telephone number or address I can contact to determine if a proposed limited liability company name is available for my use, plus any forms necessary to reserve an LLC name;

3. a current schedule of fees for LLC filings;

4. other LLC forms and publications provided by your office (or a list of these) for forming, operating, and dissolving an LLC in this state; and

5. the name and price of a publication that contains the limited liability company statutes of this state. Please indicate whether it may be ordered from your office or, if applicable, another office or supplier.

If there is a fee for any of the above materials, please advise. Enclosed is a self-addressed, stamped envelope for your reply.

Thank you for your assistance,

_____

_____

_____

Enclosure: self-addressed, stamped envelope

LLC Reservation of Name Letter

_____

_____

_____

LLC Filings Office:

Please reserve the following proposed limited liability company name for my use for the allowable period specified under state law:

_____ .

☐ If the above name is not available, please reserve the first available name from the following list of alternative names:

Second Choice: _____

Third Choice: _____

I enclose a check in payment of the reservation fee. Please send a certificate, receipt for payment, or other acknowledgment or approval of my reservation request to me at my address shown below.

Thank you for your assistance,

_____

_____

_____

Enclosure: check reservation fee; stamped, self-addressed envelope

Articles of Organization
of

_____

The undersigned natural person(s), of the age of eighteen years or more, acting as organizers of a limited liability company under the State of _____ Limited Liability Company Act, adopt(s) the following Articles of Organization for such limited liability company.

Article 1. Name of Limited Liability Company. The name of this limited liability company is

_____.

Article 2. Registered Office and Registered Agent. The initial registered office of this limited liability company and the name of its initial registered agent at this address are:

_____

_____

_____.

Article 3. Statement of Purposes. The purposes for which this limited liability company is organized are:

_____

_____

_____

_____

_____

_____.

Article 4. Management and Names and Addresses of Initial _____. The management of this limited liability company is reserved to the _____. The names and addresses of its initial _____ are:

_____

_____

_____

_____

_____.

Article 5. Principal Place of Business of the Limited Liability Company. The principal place of business of the limited liability company shall be: _____

_____.

Article 6. Period of Duration of the Limited Liability Company. The period of duration of the limited liability company shall be: _____

_____.

    In Witness Whereof, the undersigned organizer(s) of this Limited Liability Company has (have) signed these articles of organization on the date indicated.

Date: _____

Signature(s): _____

_____   _____
Organizer   Typed or Printed Name

_____   _____
Organizer   Typed or Printed Name

_____   _____
Organizer   Typed or Printed Name

_____   _____
Organizer   Typed or Printed Name

_____   _____
Organizer   Typed or Printed Name

_____   _____
Organizer   Typed or Printed Name

Operating Agreement for
Member-Managed Limited Liability Company

I. Preliminary Provisions

(1) **Effective Date:** This operating agreement of _____

_____ ,

effective _____ , is adopted by the members

whose signatures appear at the end of this agreement.

(2) **Formation:** This limited liability company (LLC) was formed by filing articles of organization, a certificate of formation, or a similar organizational document with the LLC filing office of the state of

_____ on

_____ .

A copy of this organizational document has been placed in the LLC's records book.

(3) **Name:** The formal name of this LLC is as stated above. However, this LLC may do business under a different name by complying with the state's fictitious or assumed business name statutes and procedures.

(4) **Registered Office and Agent:** The registered office of this LLC and the registered agent at this address are as follows: _____

_____ .

The registered office and agent may be changed from time to time as the members may see fit, by filing a change of registered agent or office form with the state LLC filing office. It will not be necessary to amend this provision of the operating agreement if and when such a change is made.

(5) **Business Purposes:** The specific business purposes and activities contemplated by the founders of this LLC at the time of initial signing of this agreement consist of the following:

_____

_____

_____ .

It is understood that the foregoing statement of purposes shall not serve as a limitation on the powers or abilities of this LLC, which shall be permitted to engage in any and all lawful business activities. If this LLC intends to engage in business activities outside the state of its formation that require the qualification of the LLC in other states, it shall obtain such qualification before engaging in such out-of-state activities.

(6) **Duration of LLC:** The duration of this LLC shall be _____

_____ .

Further, this LLC shall terminate when a proposal to dissolve the LLC is adopted by the membership of this LLC or when this LLC is otherwise terminated in accordance with law.

II. Membership Provisions

(1) **Nonliability of Members:** No member of this LLC shall be personally liable for the expenses, debts, obligations, or liabilities of the LLC, or for claims made against it.

(2) Reimbursement for Organizational Costs: Members shall be reimbursed by the LLC for organizational expenses paid by the members. The LLC shall be authorized to elect to deduct and amortize organizational expenses and start-up expenditures as permitted by the Internal Revenue Code and as may be advised by the LLC's tax adviser.

(3) Management: This LLC shall be managed exclusively by all of its members.

(4) Members' Percentage Interests: A member's percentage interest in this LLC shall be computed as a fraction, the numerator of which is the total of a member's capital account and the denominator of which is the total of all capital accounts of all members. This fraction shall be expressed in this agreement as a percentage, which shall be called each member's "percentage interest" in this LLC.

(5) Membership Voting: Except as otherwise may be required by the articles of organization, certificate of formation, or a similar organizational document, by other provisions of this operating agreement, or under the laws of this state, each member shall vote on any matter submitted to the membership for approval in proportion to the member's percentage interest in this LLC. Further, unless defined otherwise for a particular provision of this operating agreement, the phrase "majority of members" means the vote of members whose combined votes equal more than 50% of the votes of all members in this LLC, and a majority of members, so defined, may approve any item of business brought before the membership for a vote unless a different vote is required under this operating agreement or state law.

(6) Compensation: Members shall not be paid as members of the LLC for performing any duties associated with such membership, including management of the LLC. Members may be paid, however, for any services rendered in any other capacity for the LLC, whether as officers, employees, independent contractors, or otherwise.

(7) Members' Meetings: The LLC shall not provide for regular members' meetings. However, any member may call a meeting by communicating his or her wish to schedule a meeting to all other members. Such notification may be in person or in writing, or by telephone, facsimile machine, or other form of electronic communication reasonably expected to be received by a member, and the other members shall then agree, either personally, in writing, or by telephone, facsimile machine, or other form of electronic communication to the member calling the meeting, to meet at a mutually acceptable time and place. Notice of the business to be transacted at the meeting need not be given to members by the member calling the meeting, and any business may be discussed and conducted at the meeting.

If all members cannot attend a meeting, it shall be postponed to a date and time when all members can attend, unless all members who do not attend have agreed in writing to the holding of the meeting without them. If a meeting is postponed, and the postponed meeting cannot be held either because all members do not attend the postponed meeting or the nonattending members have not signed a written consent to allow the postponed meeting to be held without them, a second postponed meeting may be held at a date and time announced at the first postponed meeting. The date and time of the second postponed meeting shall also be communicated to any members not attending the first postponed meeting. The second postponed meeting may be held without the attendance of all members as long as a majority of the percentage interests of the membership of this LLC is in attendance at the second postponed meeting. Written notice of the decisions or approvals made at this second postponed meeting shall be mailed or delivered to each nonattending member promptly after the holding of the second postponed meeting.

Written minutes of the discussions and proposals presented at a members' meeting, and the votes taken and matters approved at such meeting, shall be taken by one of the members or a person designated at the meeting. A copy of the minutes of the meeting shall be placed in the LLC's records book after the meeting.

(8) **Membership Certificates:** This LLC shall be authorized to obtain and issue certificates representing or certifying membership interests in this LLC. Each certificate shall show the name of the LLC and the name of the member, and state that the person named is a member of the LLC and is entitled to all the rights granted members of the LLC under the articles of organization, certificate of formation, or a similar organizational document; this operating agreement; and provisions of law. Each membership certificate shall be consecutively numbered and signed by one or more officers of this LLC. The certificates shall include any additional information considered appropriate for inclusion by the members on membership certificates.

In addition to the above information, all membership certificates shall bear a prominent legend on their face or reverse side stating, summarizing, or referring to any transfer restrictions that apply to memberships in this LLC under the articles of organization, certificate of formation, or a similar organizational document, and/or this operating agreement as well as the address where a member may obtain a copy of these restrictions upon request from this LLC.

The records book of this LLC shall contain a list of the names and addresses of all persons to whom certificates have been issued, show the date of issuance of each certificate, and record the date of all cancellations or transfers of membership certificates.

(9) **Other Business by Members:** Each member shall agree not to own an interest in, manage, or work for another business, enterprise, or endeavor, if such ownership or activities would compete with this LLC's business goals, mission, profitability, or productivity, or would diminish or impair the member's ability to provide maximum effort and performance in managing the business of this LLC.

III. Tax and Financial Provisions

(1) **Tax Classification of LLC:** The members of this LLC intend that this LLC be initially classified as a _____ for federal and, if applicable, state income tax purposes. It is understood that, subject to federal and state law requirements, all members may agree to change the tax treatment of this LLC by signing, or authorizing the signature of, IRS Form 8832, Entity Classification Election, and filing it with the IRS and, if applicable, the state tax department within the prescribed time limits.

(2) **Tax Year and Accounting Method:** The tax year of this LLC shall be _____ _____. The LLC shall use the _____ method of accounting. Both the tax year and the accounting period of the LLC may be changed with the consent of all members if the LLC qualifies for such change, and may be effected by the filing of appropriate forms with the IRS and state tax authorities.

(3) **Tax Matters Partner:** If this LLC is required under Internal Revenue Code provisions or regulations, it shall designate from among its members a "tax matters partner" in accordance with Internal Revenue Code Section 6231(a)(7) and corresponding regulations, who will fulfill this role by being the spokesperson for the LLC in dealings with the IRS as required under the Internal Revenue Code and Regulations, and who will report to the members on the progress and outcome of these dealings.

(4) Annual Income Tax Returns and Reports: Within 60 days after the end of each tax year of the LLC, a copy of the LLC's state and federal income tax returns for the preceding tax year shall be mailed or otherwise provided to each member of the LLC, together with any additional information and forms necessary for each member to complete his or her individual state and federal income tax returns. If this LLC is classified as a partnership for income tax purposes, this additional information shall include a federal (and, if applicable, state) Schedule K-1 (Form 1065, Partner's Share of Income, Deductions, Credits) or equivalent income tax reporting form. This additional information shall also include a financial report, which shall include a balance sheet and profit and loss statement for the prior tax year of the LLC.

(5) Bank Accounts: The LLC shall designate one or more banks or other institutions for the deposit of the funds of the LLC, and shall establish savings, checking, investment, and other such accounts as are reasonable and necessary for its business and investments. One or more members of the LLC shall be designated with the consent of all members to deposit and withdraw funds of the LLC, and to direct the investment of funds from, into, and among such accounts. The funds of the LLC, however and wherever deposited or invested, shall not be commingled with the personal funds of any members of the LLC.

(6) Title to Assets: All personal and real property of this LLC shall be held in the name of the LLC, not in the names of individual members.

IV. Capital Provisions

(1) Capital Contributions by Members: Members shall make the following contributions of cash, property, or services as shown next to each member's name below. Unless otherwise noted, cash and property described below shall be paid or delivered to the LLC on or by _____ _____ . The fair market values of items of property or services as agreed between the LLC and the contributing member are also shown below. The percentage interest in the LLC that each member shall receive in return for his or her capital contribution is also indicated for each member.

Name	Contribution	Fair Market Value	Percentage Interest in LLC
_____	_____	$_____	_____
_____	_____	$_____	_____
_____	_____	$_____	_____
_____	_____	$_____	_____
_____	_____	$_____	_____
_____	_____	$_____	_____

(2) Additional Contributions by Members: The members may agree, from time to time by unanimous vote, to require the payment of additional capital contributions by the members, on or by a mutually agreeable date.

(3) Failure to Make Contributions: If a member fails to make a required capital contribution within the time agreed for a member's contribution, the remaining members may, by unanimous vote, agree to reschedule the time for payment of the capital contribution by the late-paying member, setting any additional repayment terms, such as a late payment penalty, rate of interest to be applied to the unpaid balance, or other monetary amount to be paid by the delinquent member, as the remaining members decide. Alternatively, the remaining members may, by unanimous vote, agree to cancel the membership of the delinquent member, provided any prior partial payments of capital made by the delinquent member are refunded by the LLC to the member promptly after the decision is made to terminate the membership of the delinquent member.

(4) No Interest on Capital Contributions: No interest shall be paid on funds or property contributed as capital to this LLC, or on funds reflected in the capital accounts of the members.

(5) Capital Account Bookkeeping: A capital account shall be set up and maintained on the books of the LLC for each member. It shall reflect each member's capital contribution to the LLC, increased by each member's share of profits in the LLC, decreased by each member's share of losses and expenses of the LLC, and adjusted as required in accordance with applicable provisions of the Internal Revenue Code and corresponding income tax regulations.

(6) Consent to Capital Contribution Withdrawals and Distributions: Members shall not be allowed to withdraw any part of their capital contributions or to receive distributions, whether in property or cash, except as otherwise allowed by this agreement and, in any case, only if such withdrawal is made with the written consent of all members.

(7) Allocations of Profits and Losses: No member shall be given priority or preference with respect to other members in obtaining a return of capital contributions, distributions, or allocations of the income, gains, losses, deductions, credits, or other items of the LLC. The profits and losses of the LLC, and all items of its income, gain, loss, deduction, and credit shall be allocated to members according to each member's percentage interest in this LLC.

(8) Allocation and Distribution of Cash to Members: Cash from LLC business operations, as well as cash from a sale or other disposition of LLC capital assets, may be distributed from time to time to members in accordance with each member's percentage interest in the LLC, as may be decided by _____ of the members.

(9) Allocation of Noncash Distributions: If proceeds consist of property other than cash, the members shall decide the value of the property and allocate such value among the members in accordance with each member's percentage interest in the LLC. If such noncash proceeds are later reduced to cash, such cash may be distributed among the members as otherwise provided in this agreement.

(10) Allocation and Distribution of Liquidation Proceeds: Regardless of any other provision in this agreement, if there is a distribution in liquidation of this LLC, or when any member's interest is liquidated, all items of income and loss shall be allocated to the members' capital accounts, and all appropriate credits and deductions shall then be made to these capital accounts before any final distribution is made. A final distribution shall be made to members only to the extent of, and in proportion to, any positive balance in each member's capital account.

V. Membership Withdrawal and Transfer Provisions

(1) Withdrawal of Members: A member may withdraw from this LLC by giving written notice to all other members at least _____ days before the date the withdrawal is to be effective.

(2) Restrictions on the Transfer of Membership: A member shall not transfer his or her membership in the LLC unless all nontransferring members in the LLC first agree to approve the admission of the transferee into this LLC. Further, no member may encumber a part or all of his or her membership in the LLC by mortgage, pledge, granting of a security interest, lien, or otherwise, unless the encumbrance has first been approved in writing by all other members of the LLC.

Notwithstanding the above provision, any member shall be allowed to assign an economic interest in his or her membership to another person without the approval of the other members. Such an assignment shall not include a transfer of the member's voting or management rights in this LLC, and the assignee shall not become a member of the LLC.

VI. Dissolution Provisions

(1) Events That Trigger Dissolution of the LLC: The following events shall trigger a dissolution of the LLC, except as provided:

(a) the death, incapacity, bankruptcy, retirement, resignation, or expulsion of a member, except that within _____ of the happening of any of these events, all remaining members of the LLC may vote to continue the legal existence of the LLC, in which case the LLC shall not dissolve;

(b) the expiration of the term of existence of the LLC if such term is specified in the articles of organization, certificate of formation, or a similar organizational document, or this operating agreement;

(c) the written agreement of all members to dissolve the LLC;

(d) entry of a decree of dissolution of the LLC under state law.

VII. General Provisions

(1) Officers: The LLC may designate one or more officers, such as a president, vice president, secretary, and treasurer. Persons who fill these positions need not be members of the LLC. Such positions may be compensated or noncompensated according to the nature and extent of the services rendered for the LLC as a part of the duties of each office. Ministerial services only as a part of any officer position will normally not be compensated, such as the performance of officer duties specified in this agreement, but any officer may be reimbursed by the LLC for out-of-pocket expenses paid by the officer in carrying out the duties of his or her office.

(2) Records: The LLC shall keep at its principal business address a copy of all proceedings of membership meetings, as well as books of account of the LLC's financial transactions. A list of the names and addresses of the current membership of the LLC also shall be maintained at this address, with notations on any transfers of members' interests to nonmembers or persons being admitted into membership in the LLC.

Copies of the LLC's articles of organization, certificate of formation, or a similar organizational document; a signed copy of this operating agreement; and the LLC's tax returns for the preceding three tax years shall be kept at the principal business address of the LLC. A statement also shall be kept at this address containing any of the following information that is applicable to this LLC:

- the amount of cash or a description and value of property contributed or agreed to be contributed as capital to the LLC by each member;

- a schedule showing when any additional capital contributions are to be made by members to this LLC;

- a statement or schedule, if appropriate, showing the rights of members to receive distributions representing a return of part or all of members' capital contributions; and

- a description of, or date when, the legal existence of the LLC will terminate under provisions in the LLC's articles of organization, certificate of formation, or a similar organizational document, or this operating agreement.

If one or more of the above items is included or listed in this operating agreement, it will be sufficient to keep a copy of this agreement at the principal business address of the LLC without having to prepare and keep a separate record of such item or items at this address.

Any member may inspect any and all records maintained by the LLC upon reasonable notice to the LLC. Copying of the LLC's records by members is allowed, but copying costs shall be paid for by the requesting member.

(3) All Necessary Acts: The members and officers of this LLC are authorized to perform all acts necessary to perfect the organization of this LLC and to carry out its business operations expeditiously and efficiently. The secretary of the LLC, or other officers, or all members of the LLC, may certify to other businesses, financial institutions, and individuals as to the authority of one or more members or officers of this LLC to transact specific items of business on behalf of the LLC.

(4) Mediation and Arbitration of Disputes Among Members: In any dispute over the provisions of this operating agreement and in other disputes among the members, if the members cannot resolve the dispute to their mutual satisfaction, the matter shall be submitted to mediation. The terms and procedure for mediation shall be arranged by the parties to the dispute.

If good-faith mediation of a dispute proves impossible or if an agreed-upon mediation outcome cannot be obtained by the members who are parties to the dispute, the dispute may be submitted to arbitration in accordance with the rules of the American Arbitration Association. Any party may commence arbitration of the dispute by sending a written request for arbitration to all other parties to the dispute. The request shall state the nature of the dispute to be resolved by arbitration, and, if all parties to the dispute agree to arbitration, arbitration shall be commenced as soon as practical after such parties receive a copy of the written request.

All parties shall initially share the cost of arbitration, but the prevailing party or parties may be awarded attorney fees, costs, and other expenses of arbitration. All arbitration decisions shall be final, binding, and conclusive on all the parties to arbitration, and legal judgment may be entered based upon such decision in accordance with applicable law in any court having jurisdiction to do so.

(5) Entire Agreement: This operating agreement represents the entire agreement among the members of this LLC, and it shall not be amended, modified, or replaced except by a written instrument executed by all the parties to this agreement who are current members of this LLC as well as any and all additional parties who became members of this LLC after the adoption of this agreement. This agreement replaces and supersedes all prior written and oral agreements among any and all members of this LLC.

(6) Severability: If any provision of this agreement is determined by a court or arbitrator to be invalid, unenforceable, or otherwise ineffective, that provision shall be severed from the rest of this agreement, and the remaining provisions shall remain in effect and enforceable.

VIII. Signatures of Members and Spouses

(1) Execution of Agreement: In witness whereof, the members of this LLC sign and adopt this agreement as the operating agreement of this LLC.

Date:_____

Signature: _____

Printed Name:_____ , Member

Date:_____

Signature: _____

Printed Name:_____ , Member

Date:_____

Signature: _____

Printed Name:_____ , Member

Date:_____

Signature: _____

Printed Name:_____ , Member

Date:_____

Signature: _____

Printed Name:_____ , Member

Date:_____

Signature: _____

Printed Name:_____ , Member

(2) Consent of Spouses: The undersigned are spouses of the members of this LLC who have signed this operating agreement in the preceding provision. These spouses have read this agreement and agree to be bound by its terms in any matter in which they have a financial interest, including restrictions on the transfer of memberships and the terms under which memberships in this LLC may be sold or otherwise transferred.

Date: _____

Signature: _____

Printed Name: _____

Spouse of: _____

Date: _____

Signature: _____

Printed Name: _____

Spouse of: _____

Date: _____

Signature: _____

Printed Name: _____

Spouse of: _____

Date: _____

Signature: _____

Printed Name: _____

Spouse of: _____

Date: _____

Signature: _____

Printed Name: _____

Spouse of: _____

Date: _____

Signature: _____

Printed Name: _____

Spouse of: _____

Limited Liability Company
Management Operating Agreement

I. Preliminary Provisions

(1) **Effective Date:** This operating agreement of _____

_____,

effective _____ , is adopted

by the members whose signatures appear at the end of this agreement.

(2) **Formation:** This limited liability company (LLC) was formed by filing articles of organization, certificate of formation, or a similar organizational document with the LLC filing office of the state of _____ on _____.
A copy of this organizational document has been placed in the LLC's records book.

(3) **Name:** The formal name of this LLC is as stated above. However, this LLC may do business under a different name by complying with the state's fictitious or assumed business name statutes and procedures.

(4) **Registered Office and Agent:** The registered office of this LLC and the registered agent at this address are as follows: _____

_____.

The registered office and agent may be changed from time to time as the members or managers may see fit, by filing a change of registered agent or office form with the state LLC filing office. It will not be necessary to amend this provision of the operating agreement if and when such a change is made.

(5) **Business Purposes:** The specific business purposes and activities contemplated by the founders of this LLC at the time of initial signing of this agreement consist of the following:

_____

_____

_____.

It is understood that the foregoing statement of purposes shall not serve as a limitation on the powers or abilities of this LLC, which shall be permitted to engage in any and all lawful business activities. If this LLC intends to engage in business activities outside the state of its formation that require the qualification of the LLC in other states, it shall obtain such qualification before engaging in such out-of-state activities.

(6) **Duration of LLC:** The duration of this LLC shall be_____

_____.

Further, this LLC shall terminate when a proposal to dissolve the LLC is adopted by the membership of this LLC or when this LLC is otherwise terminated in accordance with law.

II. Management Provisions

(1) **Management by Managers:** This LLC will be managed by the managers listed below. All managers who are also members of this LLC are designated as "members"; nonmember managers are designated as "nonmembers."

Name: _____ ☐ Member ☐ Nonmember

Address: _____

Name: _____ ☐ Member ☐ Nonmember

Address: _____

Name: _____ ☐ Member ☐ Nonmember

Address: _____

Name: _____ ☐ Member ☐ Nonmember

Address: _____

Name: _____ ☐ Member ☐ Nonmember

Address: _____

Name: _____ ☐ Member ☐ Nonmember

Address: _____

(2) **Nonliability of Managers:** No manager of this LLC shall be personally liable for the expenses, debts, obligations, or liabilities of the LLC, or for claims made against it.

(3) **Authority and Votes of Managers:** Except as otherwise set forth in this agreement, the articles of organization, certificate of organization, or similar organizational document, or as may be provided under state law, all management decisions relating to this LLC's business shall be made by its managers. Management decisions shall be approved by _____ of the current managers of the LLC, with each manager entitled to cast one vote for or against any matter submitted to the managers for a decision.

(4) **Term of Managers:** Each manager shall serve until the earlier of the following events:

(a) the manager becomes disabled, dies, retires, or otherwise withdraws from management;

(b) the manager is removed from office; or

(c) the manager's term expires, if a term has been designated in other provisions of this agreement.

Upon the happening of any of these events, a new manager may be appointed to replace the departing manager by _____.

(5) **Management Meetings:** Managers shall be able to discuss and approve LLC business informally, and may, at their discretion, call and hold formal management meetings according to the rules set forth in the following provisions of this operating agreement.

Regularly scheduled formal management meetings need not be held, but any manager may call such a meeting by communicating his or her request for a formal meeting to the other managers, noting the purpose or purposes for which the meeting is called. Only the business stated or summarized in the notice for the meeting shall be discussed and voted upon at the meeting.

The meeting shall be held within a reasonable time after a manager has made the request for a meeting, and in no event, later than _____ days after the request for the meeting. A quorum for such a formal managers' meeting shall consist of _____ _____ managers, and if a quorum is not present, the meeting shall be adjourned to a new place and time with notice of the adjourned meeting given to all managers. An adjournment shall not be necessary, however, and a managers' meeting with less than a quorum may be held if all nonattending managers agreed in writing prior to the meeting to the holding of the meeting. All such written consents to the holding of a formal management meeting shall be kept and filed with the records of the meeting.

The proceedings of all formal managers' meetings shall be noted or summarized with written minutes of the meeting and a copy of the minutes shall be placed and kept in the records book of this LLC.

(6) Managers' Commitment to LLC: Managers shall devote their best efforts and energy working to achieve the business objectives and financial goals of this LLC. By agreeing to serve as a manager for the LLC, each manager shall agree not to work for another business, enterprise, or endeavor owned or operated by himself or herself or others, if such outside work or efforts would compete with the LLC's business goals, mission, products, or services or would diminish or impair the manager's ability to provide maximum effort and performance to managing the business of this LLC.

(7) Compensation of Managers: Managers of this LLC may be paid per-meeting or per diem amounts for attending management meetings, may be reimbursed actual expenses advanced by them to attend management meetings or attend to management business for the LLC, and may be compensated in other ways for performing their duties as managers. Managers may work in other capacities for this LLC and may be compensated separately for performing these additional services, whether as officers, staff, consultants, independent contractors, or in other capacities.

III. Membership Provisions

(1) Nonliability of Members: No member of this LLC shall be personally liable for the expenses, debts, obligations, or liabilities of the LLC, or for claims made against it.

(2) Reimbursement for Organizational Costs: Members shall be reimbursed by the LLC for organizational expenses paid by the members. The LLC shall be authorized to elect to deduct and amortize organizational expenses and start-up expenditures as permitted by the Internal Revenue Code and as may be advised by the LLC's tax adviser.

(3) Members' Percentage Interests: A member's percentage interest in this LLC shall be computed as a fraction, the numerator of which is the total of a member's capital account and the denominator of which is the total of all capital accounts of all members. This fraction shall be expressed in this agreement as a percentage, which shall be called each member's "percentage interest" in this LLC.

(4) Membership Voting: Except as otherwise may be required by the articles of organization, certificate of formation, or a similar organizational document, by other provisions of this operating agreement, or under the laws of this state, each member shall vote on any matter submitted to the membership for approval in proportion to the member's percentage interest in this LLC. Further, unless defined otherwise for a particular provision of this operating agreement, the phrase "majority of members" means the vote of members whose combined votes equal more than 50% of the votes of all members in this LLC, and a majority of members, so defined, may approve any item of business brought before the membership for a vote unless a different vote is required under this operating agreement or state law.

(5) Compensation: Members shall not be paid as members of the LLC for performing any duties associated with such membership. Members may be paid, however, for any services rendered in any other capacity for the LLC, whether as officers, employees, independent contractors, or otherwise.

(6) Members' Meetings: The LLC shall not provide for regular members' meetings. However, any member may call a meeting by communicating his or her wish to schedule a meeting to all other members. Such notification may be in person or in writing, or by telephone, facsimile machine, or other form of electronic communication reasonably expected to be received by a member, and the other members shall then agree, either personally, in writing, or by telephone, facsimile machine, or other form of electronic communication to the member calling the meeting, to meet at a mutually acceptable time and place. Notice of the business to be transacted at the meeting need not be given to members by the member calling the meeting, and any business may be discussed and conducted at the meeting.

If all members cannot attend a meeting, it shall be postponed to a date and time when all members can attend, unless all members who do not attend have agreed in writing to the holding of the meeting without them. If a meeting is postponed, and the postponed meeting cannot be held either because all members do not attend the postponed meeting or the nonattending members have not signed a written consent to allow the postponed meeting to be held without them, a second postponed meeting may be held at a date and time announced at the first postponed meeting. The date and time of the second postponed meeting shall also be communicated to any members not attending the first postponed meeting. The second postponed meeting may be held without the attendance of all members as long as a majority of the percentage interests of the membership of this LLC is in attendance at the second postponed meeting. Written notice of the decisions or approvals made at this second postponed meeting shall be mailed or delivered to each nonattending member promptly after the holding of the second postponed meeting.

Written minutes of the discussions and proposals presented at a members' meeting, and the votes taken and matters approved at such meeting, shall be taken by one of the members or a person designated at the meeting. A copy of the minutes of the meeting shall be placed in the LLC's records book after the meeting.

(7) Membership Certificates: This LLC shall be authorized to obtain and issue certificates representing or certifying membership interests in this LLC. Each certificate shall show the name of the LLC and the name of the member, and state that the person named is a member of the LLC and is entitled to all the rights granted members of the LLC under the articles of organization, certificate of formation, or a similar organizational document; this operating agreement; and provisions of law. Each membership certificate shall be consecutively numbered and signed by one or more officers of this LLC. The certificates shall include any additional information considered appropriate for inclusion by the members on membership certificates.

In addition to the above information, all membership certificates shall bear a prominent legend on their face or reverse side stating, summarizing, or referring to any transfer restrictions that apply to memberships in this LLC under the articles of organization, certificate of formation, or a similar organizational document, and/or this operating agreement, as well as the address where a member may obtain a copy of these restrictions upon request from this LLC.

The records book of this LLC shall contain a list of the names and addresses of all persons to whom certificates have been issued, show the date of issuance of each certificate, and record the date of all cancellations or transfers of membership certificates.

IV. Tax and Financial Provisions

(1) **Tax Classification of LLC:** The members of this LLC intend that this LLC be initially classified as a _____ for federal and, if applicable, state income tax purposes. It is understood that, subject to federal and state law requirements, all members may agree to change the tax treatment of this LLC by signing, or authorizing the signature of, IRS Form 8832, Entity Classification Election, and filing it with the IRS and, if applicable, the state tax department within the prescribed time limits.

(2) **Tax Year and Accounting Method:** The tax year of this LLC shall be _____ _____ . The LLC shall use the _____ method of accounting. Both the tax year and the accounting period of the LLC may be changed with the consent of all members or all managers if the LLC qualifies for such change, and may be effected by the filing of appropriate forms with the IRS and state tax authorities.

(3) **Tax Matters Partner:** If this LLC is required under Internal Revenue Code provisions or regulations, it shall designate from among its members or member-managers a "tax matters partner" in accordance with Internal Revenue Code Section 6231(a)(7) and corresponding regulations, who will fulfill this role by being the spokesperson for the LLC in dealings with the IRS as required under the Internal Revenue Code and Regulations, and who will report to the members and managers on the progress and outcome of these dealings.

(4) **Annual Income Tax Returns and Reports:** Within 60 days after the end of each tax year of the LLC, a copy of the LLC's state and federal income tax returns for the preceding tax year shall be mailed or otherwise provided to each member of the LLC, together with any additional information and forms necessary for each member to complete his or her individual state and federal income tax returns. If this LLC is classified as a partnership for income tax purposes, this additional information shall include a federal (and, if applicable, state) Schedule K-1 (Form 1065, Partner's Share of Income, Deductions, Credits) or equivalent income tax reporting form. This additional information shall also include a financial report, which shall include a balance sheet and profit and loss statement for the prior tax year of the LLC.

(5) **Bank Accounts:** The LLC shall designate one or more banks or other institutions for the deposit of the funds of the LLC, and shall establish savings, checking, investment, and other such accounts as are reasonable and necessary for its business and investments. One or more employees of the LLC shall be designated with the consent of all managers to deposit and withdraw funds of the LLC, and to direct the investment of funds from, into, and among such accounts. The funds of the LLC, however and wherever deposited or invested, shall not be commingled with the personal funds of any members or managers of the LLC.

(6) Title to Assets: All personal and real property of this LLC shall be held in the name of the LLC, not in the names of individual members or managers.

V. Capital Provisions

(1) Capital Contributions by Members: Members shall make the following contributions of cash, property, or services as shown next to each member's name below. Unless otherwise noted, cash and property described below shall be paid or delivered to the LLC on or by _____
_____. The fair market values of items of property or services as agreed between the LLC and the contributing member are also shown below. The percentage interest in the LLC that each member shall receive in return for his or her capital contribution is also indicated for each member.

Name	Contribution	Fair Market Value	Percentage Interest in LLC
_____	_____	$_____	_____
_____	_____	$_____	_____
_____	_____	$_____	_____
_____	_____	$_____	_____
_____	_____	$_____	_____
_____	_____	$_____	_____

(2) Additional Contributions by Members: The members may agree, from time to time by unanimous vote, to require the payment of additional capital contributions by the members, on or by a mutually agreeable date.

(3) Failure to Make Contributions: If a member fails to make a required capital contribution within the time agreed for a member's contribution, the remaining members may, by unanimous vote, agree to reschedule the time for payment of the capital contribution by the late-paying member, setting any additional repayment terms, such as a late payment penalty, rate of interest to be applied to the unpaid balance, or other monetary amount to be paid by the delinquent member, as the remaining members decide. Alternatively, the remaining members may, by unanimous vote, agree to cancel the membership of the delinquent member, provided any prior partial payments of capital made by the delinquent member are refunded by the LLC to the member promptly after the decision is made to terminate the membership of the delinquent member.

(4) No Interest on Capital Contributions: No interest shall be paid on funds or property contributed as capital to this LLC, or on funds reflected in the capital accounts of the members.

(5) Capital Account Bookkeeping: A capital account shall be set up and maintained on the books of the LLC for each member. It shall reflect each member's capital contribution to the LLC, increased by each member's share of profits in the LLC, decreased by each member's share of losses and expenses of the LLC, and adjusted as required in accordance with applicable provisions of the Internal Revenue Code and corresponding income tax regulations.

(6) Consent to Capital Contribution Withdrawals and Distributions: Members shall not be allowed to withdraw any part of their capital contributions or to receive distributions, whether in property or cash, except as otherwise allowed by this agreement and, in any case, only if such withdrawal is made with the written consent of all members.

(7) Allocations of Profits and Losses: No member shall be given priority or preference with respect to other members in obtaining a return of capital contributions, distributions or allocations of the income, gains, losses, deductions, credits, or other items of the LLC. The profits and losses of the LLC, and all items of its income, gain, loss, deduction, and credit shall be allocated to members according to each member's percentage interest in this LLC.

(8) Allocation and Distribution of Cash to Members: Cash from LLC business operations, as well as cash from a sale or other disposition of LLC capital assets, may be distributed from time to time to members in accordance with each member's percentage interest in the LLC, as may be decided by _____ of the _____ .

(9) Allocation of Noncash Distributions: If proceeds consist of property other than cash, the _____ shall decide the value of the property and allocate such value among the members in accordance with each member's percentage interest in the LLC. If such noncash proceeds are later reduced to cash, such cash may be distributed among the members as otherwise provided in this agreement.

(10) Allocation and Distribution of Liquidation Proceeds: Regardless of any other provision in this agreement, if there is a distribution in liquidation of this LLC, or when any member's interest is liquidated, all items of income and loss shall be allocated to the members' capital accounts, and all appropriate credits and deductions shall then be made to these capital accounts before any final distribution is made. A final distribution shall be made to members only to the extent of, and in proportion to, any positive balance in each member's capital account.

VI. Membership Withdrawal and Transfer Provisions

(1) Withdrawal of Members: A member may withdraw from this LLC by giving written notice to all other members at least _____ days before the date the withdrawal is to be effective.

(2) Restrictions on the Transfer of Membership: A member shall not transfer his or her membership in the LLC unless all nontransferring members in the LLC first agree to approve the admission of the transferee into this LLC. Further, no member may encumber a part or all of his or her membership in the LLC by mortgage, pledge, granting of a security interest, lien, or otherwise, unless the encumbrance has first been approved in writing by all other members of the LLC.

Notwithstanding the above provision, any member shall be allowed to assign an economic interest in his or her membership to another person without the approval of the other members. Such an assignment shall not include a transfer of the member's voting or management rights in this LLC, and the assignee shall not become a member of the LLC.

VII. Dissolution Provisions

(1) **Events That Trigger Dissolution of the LLC:** The following events shall trigger a dissolution of the LLC, except as provided:

(a) the death, incapacity, bankruptcy, retirement, resignation, or expulsion of a member, except that within _____ of the happening of any of these events, all remaining members of the LLC may vote to continue the legal existence of the LLC, in which case the LLC shall not dissolve;

(b) the expiration of the term of existence of the LLC if such term is specified in the articles of organization, certificate of formation, or a similar organizational document, or this operating agreement;

(c) the written agreement of all members to dissolve the LLC;

(d) entry of a decree of dissolution of the LLC under state law.

VIII. General Provisions

(1) **Officers:** The managers of this LLC may designate one or more officers, such as a president, vice president, secretary, and treasurer. Persons who fill these positions need not be members or managers of the LLC. Such positions may be compensated or noncompensated according to the nature and extent of the services rendered for the LLC as a part of the duties of each office. Ministerial services only as a part of any officer position will normally not be compensated, such as the performance of officer duties specified in this agreement, but any officer may be reimbursed by the LLC for out-of-pocket expenses paid by the officer in carrying out the duties of his or her office.

(2) **Records:** The LLC shall keep at its principal business address a copy of all proceedings of membership meetings, as well as books of account of the LLC's financial transactions. A list of the names and addresses of the current membership of the LLC also shall be maintained at this address, with notations on any transfers of members' interests to nonmembers or persons being admitted into membership in the LLC. A list of the current managers' names and addresses shall also be kept at this address.

Copies of the LLC's articles of organization, certificate of formation, or a similar organizational document, a signed copy of this operating agreement, and the LLC's tax returns for the preceding three tax years shall be kept at the principal business address of the LLC. A statement also shall be kept at this address containing any of the following information that is applicable to this LLC:

- the amount of cash or a description and value of property contributed or agreed to be contributed as capital to the LLC by each member;

- a schedule showing when any additional capital contributions are to be made by members to this LLC;

- a statement or schedule, if appropriate, showing the rights of members to receive distributions representing a return of part or all of members' capital contributions; and

- a description of, or date when, the legal existence of the LLC will terminate under provisions in the LLC's articles of organization, certificate of formation, or a similar organizational document, or this operating agreement.

If one or more of the above items is included or listed in this operating agreement, it will be sufficient to keep a copy of this agreement at the principal business address of the LLC without having to prepare and keep a separate record of such item or items at this address.

Any member or manager may inspect any and all records maintained by the LLC upon reasonable notice to the LLC. Copying of the LLC's records by members and managers is allowed, but copying costs shall be paid for by the requesting member or manager.

(3) All Necessary Acts: The members, managers, and officers of this LLC are authorized to perform all acts necessary to perfect the organization of this LLC and to carry out its business operations expeditiously and efficiently. The secretary of the LLC, or other officers, or one or more managers, or all members of the LLC, may certify to other businesses, financial institutions, and individuals as to the authority of one or more members, managers, or officers of this LLC to transact specific items of business on behalf of the LLC.

(4) Mediation and Arbitration of Disputes Among Members: In any dispute over the provisions of this operating agreement and in other disputes among the members, if the members cannot resolve the dispute to their mutual satisfaction, the matter shall be submitted to mediation. The terms and procedure for mediation shall be arranged by the parties to the dispute.

If good-faith mediation of a dispute proves impossible or if an agreed-upon mediation outcome cannot be obtained by the members who are parties to the dispute, the dispute may be submitted to arbitration in accordance with the rules of the American Arbitration Association. Any party may commence arbitration of the dispute by sending a written request for arbitration to all other parties to the dispute. The request shall state the nature of the dispute to be resolved by arbitration, and, if all parties to the dispute agree to arbitration, arbitration shall be commenced as soon as practical after such parties receive a copy of the written request.

All parties shall initially share the cost of arbitration, but the prevailing party or parties may be awarded attorney fees, costs, and other expenses of arbitration. All arbitration decisions shall be final, binding, and conclusive on all the parties to arbitration, and legal judgment may be entered based upon such decision in accordance with applicable law in any court having jurisdiction to do so.

(5) Entire Agreement: This operating agreement represents the entire agreement among the members of this LLC, and it shall not be amended, modified, or replaced except by a written instrument executed by all the parties to this agreement who are current members of this LLC as well as any and all additional parties who became members of this LLC after the adoption of this agreement. This agreement replaces and supersedes all prior written and oral agreements among any and all members of this LLC.

(6) **Severability:** If any provision of this agreement is determined by a court or arbitrator to be invalid, unenforceable, or otherwise ineffective, that provision shall be severed from the rest of this agreement, and the remaining provisions shall remain in effect and enforceable.

IX. Signatures of Members, Members' Spouses, and Managers

(1) **Execution of Agreement:** In witness whereof, the members of this LLC sign and adopt this agreement as the operating agreement of this LLC.

Date:_____

Signature: _____

Printed Name:_____ , Member

Date:_____

Signature: _____

Printed Name:_____ , Member

Date:_____

Signature: _____

Printed Name:_____ , Member

Date:_____

Signature: _____

Printed Name:_____ , Member

Date:_____

Signature: _____

Printed Name:_____ , Member

Date:_____

Signature: _____

Printed Name:_____ , Member

(2) Consent of Spouses: The undersigned are spouses of the members of this LLC who have signed this operating agreement in the preceding provision. These spouses have read this agreement and agree to be bound by its terms in any matter in which they have a financial interest, including restrictions on the transfer of memberships and the terms under which memberships in this LLC may be sold or otherwise transferred.

Date: _____

Signature: _____

Printed Name: _____

Spouse of: _____

Date: _____

Signature: _____

Printed Name: _____

Spouse of: _____

Date: _____

Signature: _____

Printed Name: _____

Spouse of: _____

Date: _____

Signature: _____

Printed Name: _____

Spouse of: _____

Date: _____

Signature: _____

Printed Name: _____

Spouse of: _____

Date: _____

Signature: _____

Printed Name: _____

Spouse of: _____

(3) Signatures of Managers: The undersigned managers of this limited liability company have read this agreement and agree to be bound by its terms in discharging their duties as managers.

Date: _____

Signature: _____

Printed Name: _____ , Manager

Date: _____

Signature: _____

Printed Name: _____ , Manager

Date: _____

Signature: _____

Printed Name: _____ , Manager

Date: _____

Signature: _____

Printed Name: _____ , Manager

Date: _____

Signature: _____

Printed Name: _____ , Manager

Minutes of Meeting of the

_____

of

_____

A meeting of the _____ of the above named limited liability company

was held on _____ , at _____ __.M.,

at _____

_____ , State of _____ ,

for the following purpose(s):

_____

_____

_____

_____ .

_____ acted as chairperson,

and _____ acted as secretary of the meeting.

The chairperson called the meeting to order.

The following _____ were present at the meeting:

_____

_____

_____

_____

_____

_____ .

The following persons were also present at the meeting, and any reports given by these persons are noted next to their names below:

Name and Title   Reports Presented, If Any

_____   _____

_____   _____

_____   _____

_____   _____

_____   _____

After discussion, on motion duly made and carried by the affirmative vote of

_____ of the _____,

the following resolution(s) was/were adopted:

_____

_____

_____

_____

_____

_____

_____

_____

_____

_____

_____

_____

_____

_____

_____ .

There being no further business to come before the meeting, it was adjourned on motion duly made and carried.

Date: _____

Signature(s): _____

_____

Title: _____

Certification of Authority

This LLC is managed by its _____ . The names and addresses
of each of its current _____ as of _____
are listed below. Each of these persons has managerial authority of the LLC and is empowered to transact
business on its behalf.

Name of _____   Address

_____   _____

                                            _____

_____   _____

                                            _____

_____   _____

                                            _____

_____   _____

                                            _____

_____   _____

                                            _____

Further, each of the following _____ is specifically authorized
to transact the following business on behalf of the LLC:

_____

_____

_____

Date: _____

Name of LLC: _____

by _____

Printed Name: _____

Title: _____

The tear-out forms in Appendix B are included on a CD-ROM in the back of the book. This CD-ROM, which can be used with Windows computers, installs files that you use with software programs that are already installed on your computer. It is not a standalone software program. Please read this appendix and the README.TXT file included on the CD-ROM for instructions on using the Forms CD.

Note to Mac users: This CD-ROM and its files should also work on Macintosh computers. Please note, however, that Nolo cannot provide technical support for non-Windows users.

How to View the README File

If you do not know how to view the file README.TXT, insert the Forms CD-ROM into your computer's CD-ROM drive and follow these instructions:

- **Windows 2000, XP, and Vista:** (1) On your PC's desktop, double click the My Computer icon; (2) double click the icon for the CD-ROM drive into which the Forms CD-ROM was inserted; (3) double click the file README.TXT.

- **Macintosh:** (1) On your Mac desktop, double click the icon for the CD-ROM that you inserted; (2) double click on the file README.TXT.

While the README file is open, print it out by using the Print command in the File menu.

Two different kinds of forms are on the CD-ROM:

- Word processing (RTF) forms that you can open, complete, print, and save with your word processing program (see "Using the Word Processing Files to Create Documents," below), and

- An Internal Revenue Service (IRS) Form (PDF) that can be viewed only with Adobe Acrobat Reader 4.0 or higher (see "Using IRS Forms," below). This form has "fill-in" text fields and can be completed using your computer.

See the end of this appendix for a list of forms, their file names, and their file formats.

Installing the Form Files Onto Your Computer

Before you can do anything with the files on the CD-ROM, you need to install them onto your hard disk. In accordance with U.S. copyright laws, remember that copies of the CD-ROM and its files are for your personal use only.

Insert the Forms CD and do the following:

Windows 2000, XP, and Vista Users

Follow the instructions that appear on the screen. (If nothing happens when you insert the Forms CD-ROM, then (1) double click the My Computer icon; (2) double click the icon for the CD-ROM drive into which the Forms CD-ROM was inserted; and (3) double click the file WELCOME.EXE.)

By default, all the files are installed to the \LLC Forms folder in the \Program Files folder of your computer. A folder called "LLC Forms" is added to the "Programs" folder of the Start menu.

Macintosh Users

Step 1: If the "LLC Forms CD" window is not open, open it by double clicking the "LLC Forms CD" icon.

Step 2: Select the "LLC Forms" folder icon.

Step 3: Drag and drop the folder icon onto the icon of your hard disk.

How to Use the CD-ROM

Using the Word Processing Files to Create Documents

This section concerns the files for forms that can be opened and edited with your word processing program.

All word processing forms come in rich text format. These files have the extension ".RTF." For example, the articles of organization form discussed in Chapter 4 is on the file articles.rtf. All forms, their file names, and their file formats are listed in at the end of this appendix.

RTF files can be read by most recent word processing programs including all versions of MS Word for Windows and Macintosh, WordPad for Windows, and recent versions of WordPerfect for Windows and Macintosh.

To use a form from the CD to create your documents you must: (1) open a file in your word processor or text editor; (2) edit the form by filling in the required information; (3) print it out; and (4) rename and save your revised file.

The following are general instructions. However, each word processor uses different commands to open, format, save, and print documents. Please read your word processor's manual for specific instructions on performing these tasks.

Do not call Nolo's technical support if you have questions on how to use your word processor or your computer.

Step 1: Opening a File

There are three ways to open the word processing files included on the CD-ROM after you have installed them onto your computer.

- Windows users can open a file by selecting its shortcut as follows: (1) Click the Windows Start button; (2) open the Programs folder; (3) open the LLC Forms subfolder; and (4) open the RTF subfolder; and (5) click on the shortcut to the form you want to work with.

- Both Windows and Macintosh users can open a file directly by double clicking on it. Use My Computer or Windows Explorer (Windows 2000, XP, and Vista) or the Finder (Macintosh) to go to the folder you installed or copied the CD-ROM's files to. Then, double click on the specific file you want to open.

- You can also open a file from within your word processor. To do this, you must first start your word processor. Then, go to the File menu and choose the Open command. This opens a dialog box where you will tell the program (1) the type of file you want to open (*.RTF); and (2) the location and name of the file (you will need to navigate through the directory tree to get to the folder on your hard disk where the CD's files have been installed).

Where Are the Files Installed?

Windows Users

- RTF files are installed by default to a folder named \LLC Forms in the \Program Files folder of your computer.

Macintosh Users

- RTF files are located in the "LLC Forms" folder.

Step 2: Editing Your Document

Fill in the appropriate information according to the instructions and sample agreements in the book. Underlines are used to indicate where you need to enter your information, frequently including instructions in brackets. Be sure to delete the underlines and instructions from your edited document. You will also want to make sure that any signature lines in your completed documents appear on a page with at least some text from the document itself.

Editing Forms That Have Optional or Alternative Text

Some of the forms have check boxes before text. The check boxes indicate:

- optional text, where you choose whether to include or exclude the given text, or
- alternative text, where you select one alternative to include and exclude the other alternatives.

If you are using the tear-out forms in Appendix B, you simply mark the appropriate box to make your choice.

If you are using the Forms CD, however, we recommend that instead of marking the check boxes, you do the following:

Optional text

If you don't want to include optional text, just delete it from your document.

If you do want to include optional text, just leave it in your document.

In either case, delete the check box itself as well as the italicized instructions that the text is optional.

Alternative text

First delete all the alternatives that you do not want to include.

Then delete the remaining check boxes, as well as the italicized instructions that you need to select one of the alternatives provided.

Step 3: Printing Out the Document

Use your word processor's or text editor's "Print" command to print out your document.

Step 4: Saving Your Document

After filling in the form, use the "Save As" command to save and rename the file. Because all the files are read-only, you will not be able to use the "Save" command. This is for your protection. *If you save the file without renaming it, the underlines that indicate where you need to enter your information will be lost, and you will not be able to create a new document with this file without recopying the original file from the CD-ROM.*

Using the IRS Form

An electronic copy of an IRS form is included on the CD-ROM in Adobe Acrobat PDF format. You must have the Adobe Reader installed on your computer to use this form. Adobe Reader is available for all types of Windows and Macintosh systems. If you don't already have this software, you can download it for free at www.adobe.com.

All forms, their file names, and their file formats are listed at the end of this appendix. Form 8832 was created by the IRS, not by Nolo.

To create your document, you must: (1) open the file; (2) fill in the text fields using either your mouse or the TAB key on your keyboard to navigate from field to field; and (3) print it out.

Saving a filled-in form: The IRS form is enabled with "document rights" that allow you to save your filled-in form to your hard disk. Version 5.1 or later of Adobe Reader is required. When you open this IRS form in Reader, you'll see a document rights message box if this feature is available. If you are using an earlier version of Adobe Reader, you will be prompted to download a newer version that will allow you to save. (You will not be able to save PDF forms that do not have document rights enabled, but you can still print out completed versions of these forms.)

Step 1: Opening the Form

PDF files, like the word processing files, can be opened one of three ways.

- Windows users can open a file by selecting its "shortcut" as follows: (1) Click the Windows "Start" button; (2) open the "Programs" folder; (3) open the "LLC Forms" subfolder; (4) click the shortcut to the form you want to work with.

- Both Windows and Macintosh users can open a file directly by double clicking on it. Use My Computer or Windows Explorer (Windows 2000, XP, or Vista) or the Finder (Macintosh) to go to the folder you created and copied the CD-ROM's files to. Then, double click the specific file you want to open.

- You can also open a PDF file from within Adobe Reader. To do this, you must first start Reader. Then, go to the File menu and choose the Open command. This opens a dialog box where you will tell the program the location and name of the file (you will need to navigate through the directory tree to get to the folder on your hard disk where the CD's files have been installed).

> ### Where Is the PDF File Installed?
>
> **Windows Users**
>
> - PDF files are installed by default to a folder named \LLC Forms in the \Program Files folder of your computer.
>
> **Macintosh Users**
>
> - PDF files are located in the "LLC Forms" folder.

Step 2: Filling in the Form

Use your mouse or the TAB key on your keyboard to navigate from field to field within this form.

If document rights are enabled, you can save your completed form to disk using Adobe Reader 5.1 or higher.

If document rights are not enabled, be sure to have all the information you will need to complete the form on hand, because you will not be able to save a copy of the filled-in form to disk. You can, however, print out a completed version.

Step 3: Printing the Form

Choose "Print" from the Acrobat Reader File menu. This will open the Print dialog box. In the Print Range section of the Print dialog box, select the appropriate print range, then click OK.

Files Included on the Forms CD

The following files are in Rich Text Format (RTF):

File Name	Form Title
articles.rtf	Articles of Organization
certify.rtf	Certification of Authority
contact.rtf	LLC Filing Office Contact Letter
filing.rtf	LLC Articles Filing Letter
minutes.rtf	Minutes of Meeting
opmanger.rtf	Management Operating Agreement
opmember.rtf	Operating Agreement for Member-Managed Limited Liability Company
reserve.rtf	Reservation of LLC Name Letter

The following is an Adobe Acrobat PDF file:

File Name	Form Title
f8832.pdf	IRS Form 8832: Entity Classification Election

Index

	PRICE	CODE
The Manager's Legal Handbook	$39.99	ELBA
Marketing Without Advertising...	$20.00	MWAD
Music Law (Book w/CD-ROM)	$39.99	ML
Negotiate the Best Lease for Your Business	$24.99	LESP
Nolo's Guide to Social Security Disability (Book w/CD-ROM)	$29.99	QSS
Nolo's Quick LLC	$29.99	LLCQ
The Performance Appraisal Handbook	$29.99	PERF
The Progressive Discipline Handbook (Book w/CD-ROM)	$34.99	SDHB
The Small Business Start-up Kit (Book w/CD-ROM)	$24.99	SMBU
The Small Business Start-up Kit for California (Book w/CD-ROM)	$24.99	OPEN
Starting & Running a Successful Newsletter or Magazine................................	$29.99	MAG
Tax Deductions for Professionals	$34.99	DEPO
Tax Savvy for Small Business	$36.99	SAVVY
Whoops! I'm in Business	$19.99	WHOO
Working for Yourself: Law & Taxes for Independent Contractors,		
Freelancers & Consultants	$39.99	WAGE
Working With Independent Contractors (Book w/CD-ROM)............................	$29.99	HICI
Your Crafts Business: A Legal Guide (Book w/CD-ROM)	$26.99	VART
Your Limited Liability Company: An Operating Manual (Book w/CD-ROM)	$49.99	LOP
Your Rights in the Workplace...	$29.99	YRW

CONSUMER

How to Win Your Personal Injury Claim..	$29.99	PICL
Nolo's Encyclopedia of Everyday Law...	$29.99	EVL
Nolo's Guide to California Law	$24.99	CLAW
Your Little Legal Companion (Hardcover)	$9.95	ANNI

ESTATE PLANNING & PROBATE

8 Ways to Avoid Probate	$19.99	PRAV
The Busy Family's Guide to Estate Planning (Book w/CD-ROM)....................	$24.99	FAM
Estate Planning Basics	$21.99	ESPN
The Executor's Guide: Settling a Loved One's Estate or Trust........................	$34.99	EXEC
How to Probate an Estate in California	$49.99	PAE
Make Your Own Living Trust (Book w/CD-ROM)..	$39.99	LITR
Nolo's Simple Will Book (Book w/CD-ROM)	$36.99	SWIL
Plan Your Estate	$44.99	NEST
Quick & Legal Will Book (Book w/CD-ROM)	$19.99	QUIC
Special Needs Trusts: Protect Your Child's Financial Future		
(Book w/CD-ROM)...	$34.99	SPNT

CATALOG

...more from Nolo

BUSINESS	PRICE	CODE
Business Buyout Agreements (Book w/CD-ROM)	$49.99	BSAG
The California Nonprofit Corporation Kit (Binder w/CD-ROM)	$69.99	CNP
California Workers' Comp	$34.99	WORK
The Complete Guide to Buying a Business (Book w/CD-ROM)	$24.99	BUYBU
The Complete Guide to Selling a Business (Book w/CD-ROM)	$24.99	SELBU
Consultant & Independent Contractor Agreements (Book w/CD-ROM)	$29.99	CICA
The Corporate Records Handbook (Book w/CD-ROM)	$69.99	CORMI
Create Your Own Employee Handbook (Book w/CD-ROM)	$49.99	EMHA
Dealing With Problem Employees	$44.99	PROBM
Deduct It! Lower Your Small Business Taxes	$34.99	DEDU
Effective Fundraising for Nonprofits	$24.99	EFFN
The Employer's Legal Handbook	$39.99	EMPL
The Essential Guide to Family and Medical Leave (Book w/CD-ROM)	$39.99	FMLA
The Essential Guide to Federal Employment Laws	$39.99	FEMP
The Essential Guide to Workplace Investigations (Book w/CD-ROM)	$39.99	NVST
Every Nonprofit's Guide to Publishing (Book w/CD-ROM)	$29.99	EPNO
Form a Partnership (Book w/CD-ROM)	$39.99	PART
Form Your Own Limited Liability Company (Book w/CD-ROM)	$44.99	LIAB
Home Business Tax Deductions: Keep What You Earn	$34.99	DEHB
How to Form a Nonprofit Corporation (Book w/CD-ROM)—National Edition	$49.99	NNP
How to Form a Nonprofit Corporation in California (Book w/CD-ROM)	$49.99	NON
How to Form Your Own California Corporation (Binder w/CD-ROM)	$59.99	CACI
How to Form Your Own California Corporation (Book w/CD-ROM)	$34.99	CCOR
How to Write a Business Plan (Book w/CD-ROM)	$34.99	SBS
Incorporate Your Business (Book w/CD-ROM)	$49.99	NIBS
Investors in Your Backyard (Book w/CD-ROM)	$24.99	FINBUS
The Job Description Handbook	$29.99	JOB
Legal Guide for Starting & Running a Small Business	$34.99	RUNS
Legal Forms for Starting & Running a Small Business (Book w/CD-ROM)	$29.99	RUNSF
LLC or Corporation?	$24.99	CHENT

Prices subject to change.

	PRICE	CODE
The Manager's Legal Handbook	$39.99	ELBA
Marketing Without Advertising	$20.00	MWAD
Music Law (Book w/CD-ROM)	$39.99	ML
Negotiate the Best Lease for Your Business	$24.99	LESP
Nolo's Guide to Social Security Disability (Book w/CD-ROM)	$29.99	QSS
Nolo's Quick LLC	$29.99	LLCQ
The Performance Appraisal Handbook	$29.99	PERF
The Progressive Discipline Handbook (Book w/CD-ROM)	$34.99	SDHB
The Small Business Start-up Kit (Book w/CD-ROM)	$24.99	SMBU
The Small Business Start-up Kit for California (Book w/CD-ROM)	$24.99	OPEN
Starting & Running a Successful Newsletter or Magazine	$29.99	MAG
Tax Deductions for Professionals	$34.99	DEPO
Tax Savvy for Small Business	$36.99	SAVVY
Whoops! I'm in Business	$19.99	WHOO
Working for Yourself: Law & Taxes for Independent Contractors, Freelancers & Consultants	$39.99	WAGE
Working With Independent Contractors (Book w/CD-ROM)	$29.99	HICI
Your Crafts Business: A Legal Guide (Book w/CD-ROM)	$26.99	VART
Your Limited Liability Company: An Operating Manual (Book w/CD-ROM)	$49.99	LOP
Your Rights in the Workplace	$29.99	YRW

CONSUMER

	PRICE	CODE
How to Win Your Personal Injury Claim	$29.99	PICL
Nolo's Encyclopedia of Everyday Law	$29.99	EVL
Nolo's Guide to California Law	$24.99	CLAW
Your Little Legal Companion (Hardcover)	$9.95	ANNI

ESTATE PLANNING & PROBATE

	PRICE	CODE
8 Ways to Avoid Probate	$19.99	PRAV
The Busy Family's Guide to Estate Planning (Book w/CD-ROM)	$24.99	FAM
Estate Planning Basics	$21.99	ESPN
The Executor's Guide: Settling a Loved One's Estate or Trust	$34.99	EXEC
How to Probate an Estate in California	$49.99	PAE
Make Your Own Living Trust (Book w/CD-ROM)	$39.99	LITR
Nolo's Simple Will Book (Book w/CD-ROM)	$36.99	SWIL
Plan Your Estate	$44.99	NEST
Quick & Legal Will Book (Book w/CD-ROM)	$19.99	QUIC
Special Needs Trusts: Protect Your Child's Financial Future (Book w/CD-ROM)	$34.99	SPNT

	PRICE	CODE
The Inventor's Notebook	$24.99	INOT
Nolo's Patents for Beginners	$24.99	QPAT
Patent, Copyright & Trademark	$39.99	PCTM
Patent It Yourself	$49.99	PAT
Patent Pending in 24 Hours	$34.99	PEND
Patenting Art & Entertainment: New Strategies for Protecting Creative Ideas	$39.99	PATAE
Profit from Your Idea (Book w/CD-ROM)	$34.99	LICE
The Public Domain	$34.99	PUBL
Trademark: Legal Care for Your Business and Product Name	$39.99	TRD
Web and Software Development: A Legal Guide (Book w/ CD-ROM)	$44.99	SFT
What Every Inventor Needs to Know About Business & Taxes		
(Book w/CD-ROM)	$21.99	ILAX

RESEARCH & REFERENCE
Legal Research: How to Find & Understand the Law	$39.99	LRES

SENIORS
Long-Term Care: How to Plan & Pay for It	$19.99	ELD
Social Security, Medicare & Goverment Pensions...	$29.99	SOA

SOFTWARE
Call or check our website at www.nolo.com for special discounts on Software!
Incorporator Pro..	89.99	STNC1
LLC Maker—Windows..	$89.95	LLP1
Patent Pending Now!..	$199.99	PP1
PatentEase—Windows	$349.00	PEAS
Personal RecordKeeper 5.0 CD—Windows	$59.95	RKD5
Quicken Legal Business Pro 2008—Windows...	$109.99	SBQB8
Quicken WillMaker Plus 2008—Windows..	$79.99	WQP8

Special Upgrade Offer

Save 35% on the latest edition of your Nolo book

Because laws and legal procedures change often, we update our books regularly. To help keep you up-to-date, we are extending this special upgrade offer. Cut out and mail the title portion of the cover of your old Nolo book and we'll give you 35% off the retail price of the New Edition of that book when you purchase directly from Nolo. This offer is to individuals only.

ORDER 24 HOURS A DAY @ www.nolo.com
Call 800-728-3555 • Mail or fax the order form in this book

Order Form

Name

Address

City

State, Zip

Daytime Phone

E-mail

Our "No-Hassle" Guarantee

Return anything you buy directly from Nolo for any reason and we'll cheerfully refund your purchase price. No ifs, ands or buts.

☐ Check here if you do not wish to receive mailings from other companies

Item Code	Quantity	Item	Unit Price	Total Price

Method of payment

☐ Check ☐ VISA

☐ American Express

☐ MasterCard

☐ Discover Card

Subtotal	
Add your local sales tax (California only)	
Shipping: RUSH $12, Basic $9 (See below)	
"I bought 3, ship it to me FREE!"(Ground shipping only)	
TOTAL	

Account Number

Expiration Date

Signature

Shipping and Handling

Rush Delivery—Only $12

We'll ship any order to any street address in the U.S. by UPS 2nd Day Air* for only $12!

* Order by noon Pacific Time and get your order in 2 business days. Orders placed after noon Pacific Time will arrive in 3 business days. P.O. boxes and S.F. Bay Area use basic shipping. Alaska and Hawaii use 2nd Day Air or Priority Mail.

Basic Shipping—$9

Use for P.O. Boxes, Northern California and Ground Service.

Allow 1-2 weeks for delivery.

U.S. addresses only.

For faster service, use your credit card and our toll-free numbers

Call our customer service group Monday thru Friday 7am to 7pm PST

Phone
1-800-728-3555

Fax
1-800-645-0895

Mail
Nolo
950 Parker St.
Berkeley, CA 94710

NOLO

Order 24 hours a day @ www.nolo.com

Get the Latest in the Law

1 **Nolo's Legal Updater**
We'll send you an email whenever a new edition of your book is published!
Sign up at **www.nolo.com/legalupdater**.

2 **Updates at Nolo.com**
Check **www.nolo.com/update** to find recent changes in the law that
affect the current edition of your book.

3 **Nolo Customer Service**
To make sure that this edition of the book is the most recent one, call us at
800-728-3555 and ask one of our friendly customer service representatives
(7:00 am to 6:00 pm PST, weekdays only). Or find out at **www.nolo.com**.

4 **Complete the Registration & Comment Card ...**
... and we'll do the work for you! Just indicate your preferences below:

- -

Registration & Comment Card

NAME _____ DATE _____

ADDRESS _____

CITY _____ STATE _____ ZIP _____

PHONE _____ EMAIL _____

COMMENTS _____

WAS THIS BOOK EASY TO USE?   (VERY EASY)   5   4   3   2   1   (VERY DIFFICULT)

☐ Yes, you can quote me in future Nolo promotional materials. *Please include phone number above.*

☐ Yes, send me **Nolo's Legal Updater** via email when a new edition of this book is available.

Yes, I want to sign up for the following email newsletters:

    ☐ **NoloBriefs** (monthly)
    ☐ **Nolo's Special Offer** (monthly)
    ☐ **Nolo's BizBriefs** (monthly)
    ☐ **Every Landlord's Quarterly** (four times a year)

☐ Yes, you can give my contact info to carefully selected
partners whose products may be of interest to me.

NOLO

LIAB 5.0

Nolo
950 Parker Street
Berkeley, CA 94710-9867
www.nolo.com

YOUR LEGAL COMPANION